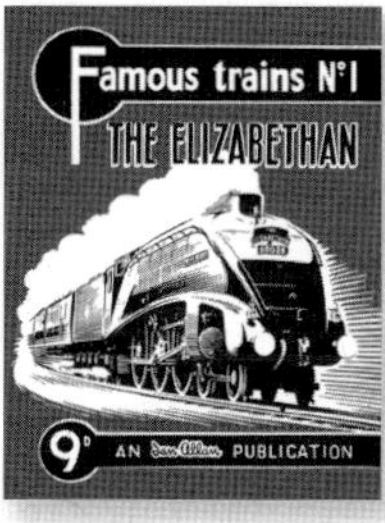
Famous trains Nº1
THE ELIZABETHAN
9D
AN Ian Allan PUBLICATION

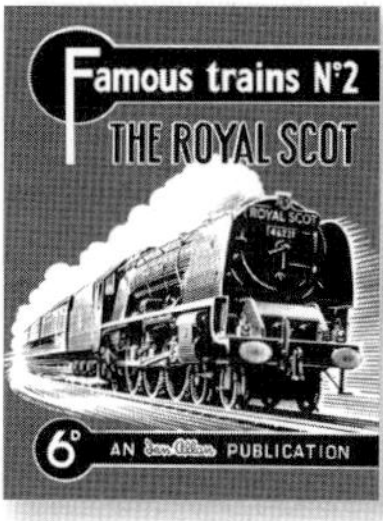
Famous trains Nº2
THE ROYAL SCOT
ROYAL SCOT
6D
AN Ian Allan PUBLICATION

Famous trains Nº3
THE CORNISH
RIVIERA EXPRESS
6D
AN Ian Allan PUBLICATION

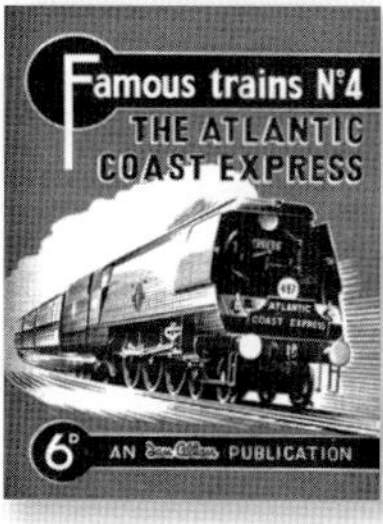
Famous trains Nº4
THE ATLANTIC
COAST EXPRESS
ATLANTIC COAST EXPRESS
6D
AN Ian Allan PUBLICATION

Famous trains Nº5
THE SOUTH
WALES PULLMAN
164
6D
AN Ian Allan PUBLICATION

Famous trains Nº6
THE QUEEN OF SCOTS
9D
AN Ian Allan PUBLICATION

Famous trains Nº7
THE ROYAL WESSEX AND
THE BOURNEMOUTH BELLE
THE BOURNEMOUTH BELLE
9D
AN Ian Allan PUBLICATION

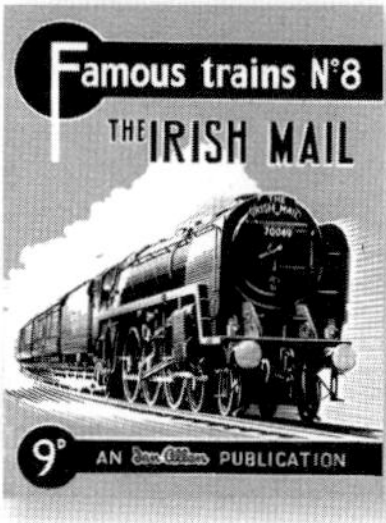
Famous trains Nº8
THE IRISH MAIL
THE IRISH MAIL
70046
9D
AN Ian Allan PUBLICATION

First published 1955-1956
Reprinted 2024

ISBN 9781800353206

Printed in Malta by Gutenberg Press

FSC www.fsc.org MIX Supporting responsible forestry FSC® C022612

Published by Crécy Publishing Ltd
1a Ringway Trading Est, Shadowmoss Rd
Manchester M22 5LH

Visit the Crécy Publishing website at www.crecy.co.uk

Contents

Introduction 5

No.1 The Elizabethan 7

No.2 The Royal Scot 35

No.3 The Cornish Riviera Express 63

No.4 The Atlantic Coast Express 91

No.5 The South Wales Pullman 121

No.6 The Queen of Scots 151

No.7 The Royal Wessex and Bournemouth Belle 181

No.8 The Irish Mail 209

Introduction

Almost from the start of the railway age, there were named expresses running on Britain's main lines. They added glamour and romance to the services whilst a certain degree of kudos attached to the locomotives and crews that operated them. The early decades of the 20th century, as competition between the various railway companies increased, so too did the number of named services; thus; for example, to the West Country there were the 'Atlantic Coast Express' and the 'Cornish Riviera Express'.

With the outbreak of the Second World War in September 1939, the country's priorities were not on the operation of prestigious express services but on running a war economy. As a result, most of these trains lost their names for the duration of the hostilities and they were only gradually restored in the post-war years.

With nationalisation in 1948, the railways came under common ownership for the first time; the competition now was not between the individual railway companies – although that did not stop interregional rivalry between the newly established BR regions – but increasingly from the threat of road transport. There was a need to emphasise again the glamour and speed that the railways could offer in an age when the private motorcar was growing in popularity and increasing numbers were also opting to use comfortable coaches to make their trips to the traditional seaside resorts. The 1950s represented perhaps the last decade the named trains were the pinnacle of railway travel with BR reviving a number of the old services and, indeed, launching a number of new ones such as the 'Elizabethan'.

In the mid-1950s Ian Allan Ltd took the decision to capitalise upon the popularity of these named trains by publishing a series of eight volumes during 1955 and 1956 that examined the operation of eight of these classic services. In part a history of the expresses covered, the bulk of each of the volumes was a description of the route that the services operated over, providing the readers with a 'from the carriage window' guide. Some 70 years on, the bulk of the main lines described still form the core of the railway network and it is fascinating to see how much has changed over these intervening years.

The author of the series was Geoffrey Freeman Allen. The son of the noted railway writer Cecil J. Allen, who was one of the formative figures in the early years of Ian Allan Ltd as a publishing company, GFA as he was known to colleagues first joined the business as a 26-year-old in 1948 as a writer for *Trains Illustrated*. He took over the editorship of the magazine in 1950 and, over the next decade, saw the publication become one of the most influential in the business and overseeing its transition to *Modern Railways* in 1962. He continued with that role along with an increasing involvement with the management of the company for a number of years. After leaving Ian Allan Ltd he became the editor of *Jane's World Railways* and a prolific freelance author of railway books. He died in 1995.

famous trains — I

The

ELIZABETHAN

KING'S CROSS—EDINBURGH (WAVERLEY)

(Eastern, North Eastern and Scottish Regions)

by

G. FREEMAN ALLAN

Ian Allan Ltd

[A. R. Carpenter

CLIMBING OUT OF KING'S CROSS—The northbound "Elizabethan", headed by Class "A4" 4-6-2 No. 60017 *Silver Fox*, emerges from Copenhagen Tunnel.

2

The World's Longest Daily Non-stop Run

THE record books show that the " Elizabethan " was introduced in 1953, but in fact it owes much of its fame to a world-renowned train whose history goes back to 1862. It was in June of that year that the " Flying Scotsman " began its daily trip between London (King's Cross) and Edinburgh (Waverley), which it has maintained without interruption ever since. At first the " Flying Scotsman " made several stops en route and by 1887 it was still needing all of 9 hours to complete the journey.

The traditional rivalry between East and West Coast railway routes to Scotland soon brought that schedule down with a run, for the next year, 1888, witnessed a breathless "Race to Edinburgh", That summer the companies on both sides of the country slashed the schedules of their Anglo-Scottish day trains almost from week to week, so that by the end of August the " Flying Scotsman " was rolling into Edinburgh in just under $7\frac{1}{2}$ hours from London. Racing ceased for a few years, but in 1895 the ashes of the earlier contest were fanned to new heat, this time with Aberdeen as the destination. Soon there was much more excitement than sense in the struggle, for the trains had been bared to featherweight loads and were reaching Aberdeen at most inconveniently early hours of the morning. Peace was therefore agreed between the rivals who undertook never to accelerate their respective day trains between London and Glasgow and Edinburgh beyond $8\frac{1}{4}$ hours.

Rivalry was not dead, however, and since schedule improvement was forbidden, the novelty of a non-stop run was the only other new attraction which could be devised. In May, 1928, all intermediate stops were cut out of the summer schedule of the " Flying Scotsman " between King's Cross and Edinburgh, which thus set up a world's record for the longest daily non-stop journey, one of 392.9 miles. Every summer until the outbreak of war in 1939 this non-stop running was the rule, but by 1932 the old schedule agreement had been tacitly buried, and the running time had been cut back to 7 hours when the war put an end to such exploits. Non-stop running between King's Cross and Edinburgh was resumed in the summer of 1949—but not by the " Flying Scotsman". An additional London-Edinburgh day train was put on. It was named the " Capitals Limited ", but renamed " Elizabethan" in 1953 in honour of the Queen's Coronation.

The Route of the "Elizabethan"

NOTE: The figures in brackets after station names indicate mileage from Kings Cross.

THE journey begins with hard work for the engine, 12¾ miles of climbing the Northern Heights of London to the summit beyond Potters Bar station. A particularly testing start is the steep 1 in 107 bank through the two tunnels, Gas Works (528 yds. long) and Copenhagen (594 yds. long) just outside King's Cross. The slope eases through Finsbury Park, once thronged morning and evening by City-goers, but not quite so busy now that the L.T. tube trains serve Barnet and Cockfosters and the Alexandria Palace branch is closed. At Hornsey, the big Ferme Park goods yard sprawls on both sides of the track, with a freight engine shed on the right, and the television mast of Alexandra Palace overlooking Wood Green comes into sight on the left. The gradient is a steady 1 in 200 up as we thread the 705 yd. Wood Green and 605 yd. Barnet Tunnels and, beyond New Barnet, the terminus of some suburban trains, enter Hadley Wood. In 1471 the deciding battle of the Wars of the Roses was fought on the slopes to the left. Four tracks converge into a troublesome bottleneck of two, now at last being widened to four, to pass through Hadley South (384 yds.), North (232 yds.) and Potters Bar (1,214 yds.) Tunnels.

Beyond Potters Bar station is the summit, and four tracks are resumed. As the engine increases speed down a gradient of 1 in 200/350, the masts of the B.B.C.'s Brookmans Park transmitter come into view on the right. On the other side of Welwyn Garden City station the line is carried 100 ft. high above the Mimram

[R. E. Vincent

WELWYN VIADUCT, which carries the railway high above the Mimram River. Class " B17 " 4-6-0 No. 61657 *Doncaster Rovers* crosses with a King's Cross-Cambridge train.

5

valley on a superb stone viaduct.

We have been climbing again at 1 in 200 since Hatfield to a summit at Woolmer Green signalbox, just the other side of the two tunnels beyond Welwyn North Station. Now there begins a long and almost unbroken descent of nearly 20 miles to the Ouse valley beyond Sandy, and after the Hertford line has rejoined us on the right at Stevenage, the slope sharpens to 1 in 200 down through the busy junction of Hitchin. By Three Counties the " Elizabethan's " speed will be up in the 80's—possibly the 90's. If you want to check, look on the left-hand side of the train for the little white mileposts by the trackside. They are spaced at quarter-mile intervals; every fourth one shows the mileage from King's Cross (at York and Newcastle they begin again at " 0 ", and at Berwick they switch to the right-hand side of the train and thereafter show mileage from Edinburgh), while the remainder show " ¼ ", " ½ " and " ¾ ". If you count the number of seconds the train takes to cover any quarter-mile and divide that number into 900, you will have your speed in m.p.h.; thus, a quarter-mile covered in 15 seconds means a speed of 60 m.p.h. The other little posts to the left of the track, with hands raised or lowered like those of a clock, indicate a change of gradient to the figure printed on them.

The gradient flattens a little beyond Three Counties, for we are reaching the Ouse, which joins us on the left-hand side at Tempsford—and anyway speed must be kept down to 70 m.p.h. round the sweeping curves on which the railway keeps company with the river through Offord & Buckden.

PETERBOROUGH NORTH — An East Coast Route express passes behind Class "A3" 4-6-2 No. 60055 *Woolwinder.* [R. E. Vincent

Apart from a climb of nearly 3 miles at 1 in 200 from Huntingdon to Leys summit, and 4 miles down at the same slope the other side, there is little to remark until, at Yaxley & Farcet, the massive chimneys of the extensive Fletton brickworks herald the approach to Peterborough. The "Elizabethan" slows as it crosses the Nene river on a fine girder bridge, for the North station is nastily curved and speed must be limited to 20 m.p.h. as we pass through it. Peterborough cathedral, seen to the right, was nearly two centuries building; hence the choir, tower and nave, built between 1117 and 1193, are of Norman style, while the grand West front seen from the train, put up between 1200 and 1250, is in the Early English style. Beyond the North station on the right lie the big New England goods yard and engine shed.

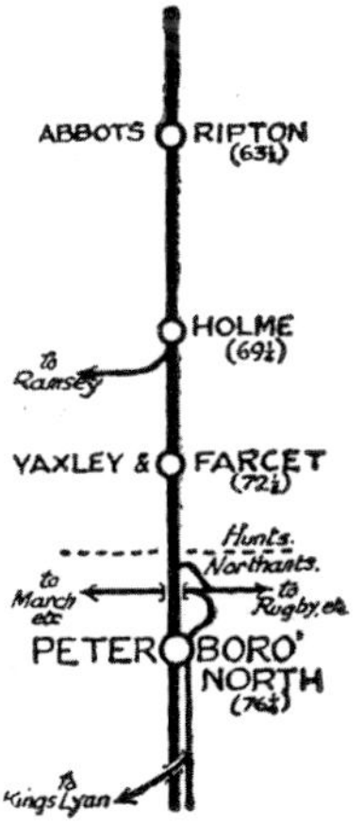

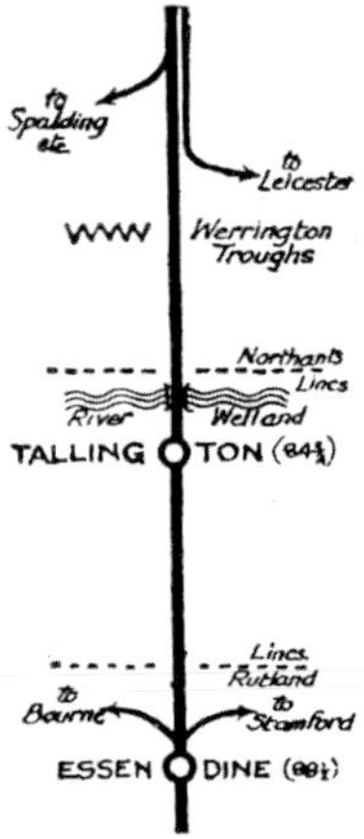

At Werrington, just over 3 miles from Peterborough, our engine takes on water for the second time since it left London (its first pick-up was at Langley, between Knebworth and Stevenage). Even the big eight-wheel tenders of a Class "A4" Pacific hold only 5,000 gallons, whereas its boiler consumes water at the rate of 40-50 gallons a mile. To avoid frequent stops for water, therefore, narrow water-troughs are laid between the running rails, from which the engine "drinks on the run". As his engine approaches the troughs, the fireman lowers a sharp-bladed scoop beneath the tender that cuts into the water, forcing it up at high velocity into the tank within the tender.

At Tallington we begin the long climb to Stoke summit, 345 ft. above sea level and the highest point reached by the

WERRINGTON WATER TROUGHS—Class "A2/3" 4-6-2 No. 60513 *Dante* picks up water from the gleaming troughs laid between the running rails. [*P. H Wells*

8

The LUXURIOUS BUFFET CAR OF THE " ELIZABETHAN "

[British Railways

" Elizabethan " south of the Border. Stoke Bank is over 15 miles long and gradually steepens from 1 in 440 to 1 in 178. In the opposite direction it forms the finest railway racing ground in Britain. There is at least one record of the southbound " Elizabethan " touching 100 m.p.h. down Stoke bank, while speeds in the 90's are quite common. It was on this descent that most of the pre-war L.N.E.R. speed records were achieved, ranging from 100 m.p.h. by the engine *Flying Scotsman* in 1934 to the climax of 126 m.p.h. by *Mallard* in July, 1938, a world's rail speed record still unbeaten by steam. Just beyond Stoke summit we plunge into the 880 yd. Stoke Tunnel and begin the descent to the Trent valley with 5 miles of 1 in 200 down.

Grantham is a thriving manufacturing town which developed by leaps and bounds

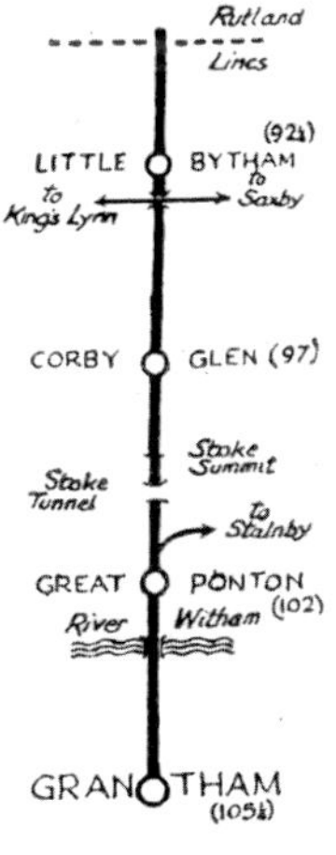

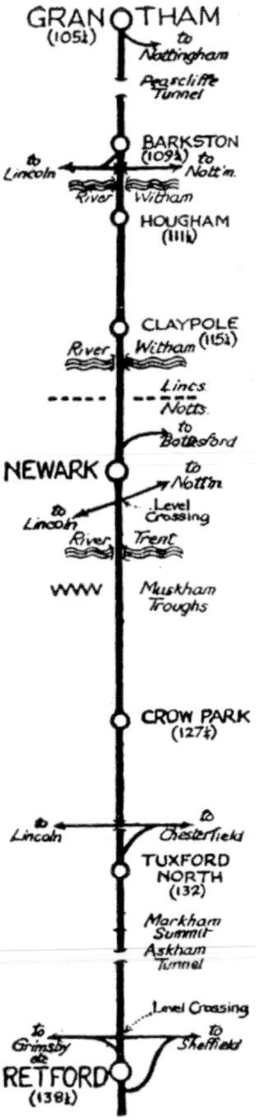

in the last war; the lofty spire of St. Wulfram parish church is 280 ft. high. On the railway side it is well served, for most of the expresses between London, Newcastle and Scotland stop here to change engines; the locomotive shed is on the left, alongside the station. The slope flattens through the station, but steepens again to 1 in 200 through the 987 yd. Peascliffe Tunnel, easing to level by the time the railway crosses the Trent beyond Newark.

Newark Parish church is another fine example of the Perpendicular style, with a 223 ft. spire. Just north of the station is a rarity in this country, a flat crossing of two railways; this one is even more interesting because the line which we cross at right-angles was built by the former Midland Railway from Nottingham to Newark before the East Coast route, a precedence which gave the Midland signalman control over the crossing and allowed him to stop the most important East Coast expresses to give a Midland train passage—indeed, the crossing is still regulated from the L.M. signalbox. Just over a mile further on, our engine takes water again, from Muskham troughs.

At Crow Park the line begins a climb of 1 in 300, then 1 in 200, to Tuxford; on a clear day there are glimpses in the right distance of Lincoln Cathedral on this section. Then, from the short Askham Tunnel (57 yds.), there is a descent at 1 in 200 and 1 in 178 to the manufacturing town of Retford, approached over another flat railway crossing, for which it is now proposed to substitute a bridge.

At Scrooby we traverse more water-troughs at the foot of a three-mile ascent to

RETFORD LEVEL CROSSING—Class "B1" 4-6-0 No. 61162 crosses the route of the "Elizabethan" on an express from the Midlands to the East Coast. [*M. N. Clay*

the Nottinghamshire-Yorkshire boundary. Now we have reached the tangle of junctions and yards at the approaches to Doncaster, the busiest railway centre we have passed since London. From the right we are joined by an important route feeding heavy passenger and freight traffic from East Anglia to the north into our main line. while above us there crosses a much-used goods line for traffic between the Midlands and the ports of Hull and Goole, which can thereby avoid busy Doncaster station. On the right are big goods yards and Doncaster engine shed. Goods traffic from the Sheffield area to Hull also avoids the station by another by-pass which bridges our line north of the station to join the main line from Manchester and Merseyside to Hull.

Alongside the station on the left is the famous Doncaster works, where the engine

11

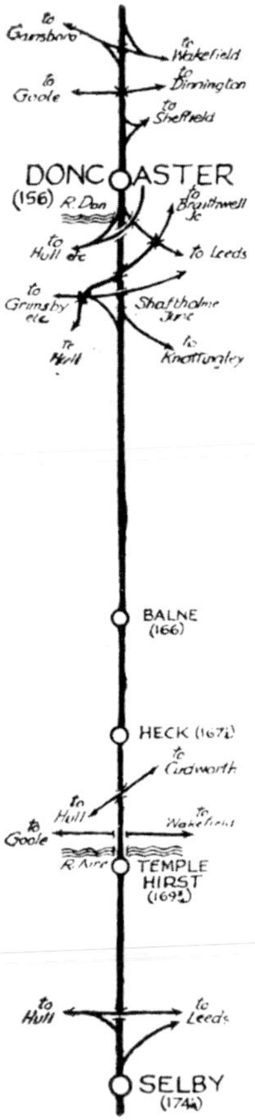

hauling our train and most of the East Coast Route's biggest locomotives were built, not to mention innumerable carriages and wagons; established in 1853, the works is still building and repairing engines and rolling stock and now covers 93 acres. The signalling at Doncaster Central station is of an ultra-modern pattern, which we shall discuss in more detail when we reach York. Since the last war, six old-type signalboxes have been replaced by two all-electric boxes and the old semaphore signals by colour lights. Doncaster racecourse, home of the St. Leger, is a mile south-east of the town and is not visible from the train. The large town itself is the centre of the South Yorkshire coalfield, of which we are now beginning to see evidence from the train.

At Shaftholme Junction we pass from the Eastern into the North-Eastern Region. This border perpetuates history, for the junction was also the meeting-place of the old Great Northern and North Eastern Railways. The N.E.R. line from this point to York, by the way, was the last link of the present London-Edinburgh route to be laid down. From 1850 the first East Coast route London-York trains ran via Peterborough, Boston, Lincoln and Retford to Shaftholme, there diverging left to Knottingley; in 1852 the direct Grantham-Newark line came into being, avoiding Lincoln, and in January 1871 the Shaftholme-Selby-York line was opened.

We slow to 40 m.p.h. through Selby, as this limit is enforced over the interesting swing bridge just north of the station; one span of this bridge pivots so that it can be swung at right-angles to the railway to allow passage to water-borne traffic on the Ouse river. The town's fine Abbey Church of St. Mary and St. Germain, though severely damaged by fire in 1906, is still rich in traces of its Norman origin as the church of a wealthy Benedictine monastery. Tradition has it that King Henry I was born in Selby.

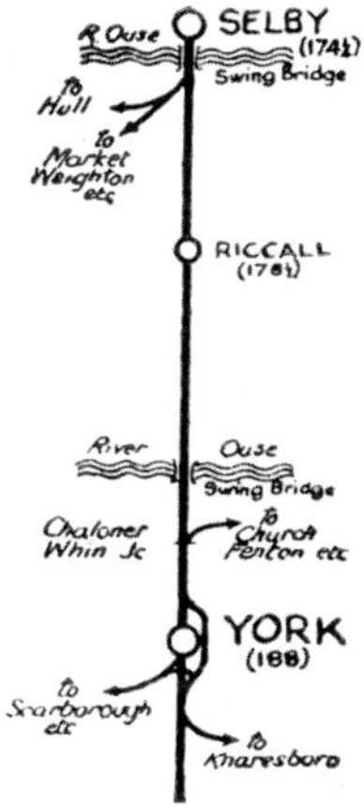

The Ouse swings back beneath us at Naburn, and again the railway is carried over it by a swingbridge requiring another slack to 40 m.p.h. By now the stately towers of York Minster can be discerned ahead, within sight of its Archbishop's Palace at Bishopthorpe, the little village on the right beyond Naburn. Two miles past Naburn is Chaloner's Whin Junction, where the original Doncaster-York route joins us on the left; nowadays it funnels into the East Coast Route expresses from Leeds, the Midlands, Bristol and even further West.

By now the first lunch is under way in the comfortable restaurant cars. As you make your way to your meal, pause for a glance through the hatch into that marvellously compact kitchen, where the chef can produce up to 200 meals simultaneously, despite his strictly limited space. The cooking is by anthracite, but dynamos running off the car's axles supply electricity for water-boiling, coffee-making, refrigeration and other jobs.

As we approached Chaloner's Whin Junction we came under control of one of the most amazing signalling installations in the world. From this point onward through the maze of tracks approaching and running through the great York station, to a spot 1½ miles beyond it, all lines and train movements are governed and signalled from one room on the station. The most astounding thing about this ultra-modern signalbox, which has taken over the work of eight separate signalboxes of the old type, is that the men who operate it are cut off from the sight of a train! Such are the marvels of modern science that they can rely entirely on electrical interlocking apparatus to prevent them clearing conflicting routes and bringing about collisions. In front of them is a vast diagram

14

of the station layout, on which little bulbs (there are over 5,000 of them) light up as a train moves from section to section, so that the operators always have in front of them a complete picture of the way tracks are occupied, while other apparatus, known as a "train describer", flashes details of each train from one screen to another down the length of the diagram as it moves through the station. There is no heaving on levers as in the old manual type of signalbox; at York the signalman sits at a keyboard of thumb switches, some of which will set up a complicated route through a whole series of points—simultaneously proving electrically that it is safe to do so—at a single flick. The most amazing of these switches is one that, by itself, will clear a path at the south end of the station through no fewer than 21 pairs of points, test and lock 130 other possible switches which, if moved, would conflict with it —and all within 9 seconds. In all, 827 different combinations of routes can be switched from this panel: small wonder that it incorporates 3,000 electrical relays and over 400 miles of wire.

YORK OLD AND NEW

Top left: York Minster and, in the foreground, Bootham Bar. *[Crown Copyright*

Centre left: The amazing York signal cabin.

Bottom left: The complicated maze of tracks at the approach to York from the south. *[British Railways*

The big 16-platform station of York, with its great arched roof and adjacent railway hotel, was the noble headquarters of the former North Eastern Railway. Damage it sustained from a direct hit during the German air raid of April 29, 1942 (when a streamlined Pacific at the shed north of the station and to the left of the main line was destroyed) has been repaired. Just outside the station is Britain's Railway Museum, open to the public, which houses many historic old locomotives. The wonderful old walled city itself, and the great Gothic Minster need a full book to do them justice, but we must speed further north.

Would the ladies of the party care to freshen up? They will find a cosy retiring room towards the rear of the train, a luxury inherited from the old non-stop "Flying Scotsman". Incidentally, a gentlemen's hairdressing saloon, a feature of the pre-war "Flying Scotsman", was unique on British trains.

RACING NORTH OF YORK—The northbound "Elizabethan", headed by Class "A4" 4-6-2 No. 60011 *Empire of India*, speeds through colour-light signalled territory near Pilmoor. [*J. W. Hague*

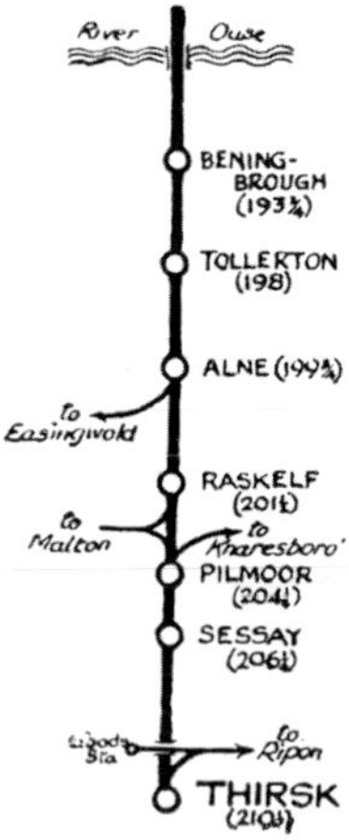

Between Beningbrough and Tollerton you will see flash by a sign indicating the half-way point between London and Edinburgh, and hereabouts there will be some unusual activity at the front of the train. To fire and drive our engine continuously for nearly 400 miles would be a strain too great for any engine crew—the fireman, for example, would have to move 6 to 8 tons of coal from the tender to the engine firebox. A narrow passageway, 18 in. wide and 5 ft. high, runs down the side of the engine tender and is connected by a vestibule with the leading coach of the train. Just before Tollerton, an Edinburgh engine crew which has been riding in the train from London makes it way through this corridor on to the footplate, whereupon the London crew which has driven us thus far retires to the train for the rest of the way to Edinburgh. Look out on the right near Tollerton for the two-acre White Horse cut on the Hambleton Hills by a local man in 1857.

The 44½ miles from York to Darlington were the racing ground of the old North Eastern Railway; curves are gentle and gradients easy, for there is dead level all the way from York to beyond Alne, and thereafter stretches of faintly rising gradient are interspersed with more level track. To-day some of the fastest British running is done here and speeds up to 90 m.p.h. are common in the southbound direction. Modern signalling with colour lights is installed throughout, and at Thirsk and Northallerton we are sped on our way by two more ultra-modern all-electric signal-boxes. The rolling Cleveland Hills can be seen on the right as we take water from Danby Wiske troughs.

ANCIENT MODERN—The Old Stockton & Darlington engine, *Locomotion No. 1*, on its pedestal at Darlington. [*R. E. Vincent*

DURHAM CATHDERAL dominates the Wear. *[Crown Copyright*

The " Elizabethan " takes the avoiding lines outside Darlington Bank Top station, so you will not glimpse the historic *Locomotion No.* 1, George Stephenson's celebrated engine built in 1825 for the Stockton & Darlington Railway, the world's first to use steam traction; with another early S. & D. engine it stands proudly on a pedestal on one of the station platforms. You will make contact with the route these old engines used, however, for a mile north of Darlington our main line strikes its third flat crossing, this time with the track of the old Stockton & Darlington Railway itself, now used only for goods traffic. It is fitting that this birthplace town of railways should still maintain a locomotive works, which lies north of Bank Top station on the left. Many other engineering firms have their plant at Darlington, which is especially renowned for its bridge-building.

From the S. & D. crossing north of Darlington for the next 10 miles past the picturesque village of Aycliffe, with its 12th Century church, the line climbs gradually across the broad moorland to Bradbury, a summit 292 ft. above sea level. We are in colliery country again, and between Ferryhill and Newcastle we shall cross numerous private pit wagon ways, in addition to tracks of British Railways. Beyond Ferryhill the railway descends again to cross the fine Croxdale Viaduct over the Wear river, and now the towers of Durham Cathderal are visible ahead on the right. But a superb view of this stately Norman edifice is to come as the "Elizabethan" slows over another lofty viaduct at the approach to Durham station. To the left of the Cathedral is a castle erected by William the Conqueror in 1072.

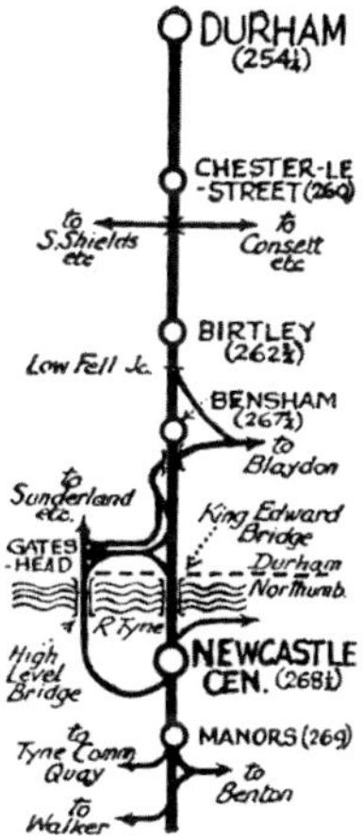

CROXDALE VIADUCT—A Class "V2" 2-6-2 crosses with a southbound fast freight.

[*A. M. Bowman*

19

THE KING EDWARD BRIDGE over the Tyne at Newcastle; the cathedral peeps over the parapet at the extreme right. A Class "A1" Pacific is crossing the river with the southbound "Flying Scotsman"

[British Railways

Some 3 miles north of Durham speed will creep up to the 80's as the " Elizabethan " comes to 2½ miles of 1 in 150 down through Plawsworth; on the right here is Lumley Castle, seat of the Earl of Scarborough. The descent continues, though not quite so steeply, through Chester-le-Street and Birtley, a section where one notices on a hill in the right distance what appears to be a Grecian temple; it is the Penshaw Monument, erected to the memory of the first Earl of Durham in the middle of the last century, and is in fact a copy of the Temple of Theseus in Greece, 100 ft. long, 52 ft. wide and 70 ft. high. At Low Fell the line begins to climb again to cross high over the Tyne at Newcastle, which is now coming into sight ahead.

About ½-mile beyond Bensham we take the left-hand side of a triangle, curving away from Gateshead engine shed (on the right) on to the King Edward VII bridge over the Tyne, opened by that monarch in 1906; to the right downstream is the much older High Level bridge, built by Robert Stephenson in 1850, which carries another railway 112 ft. high above the water (a road runs beneath the railway), and beyond that, first a low swing bridge, and then the graceful arch of the Tyne Road Bridge, opened by King George V in 1928.

As we run into Newcastle Central Station, notice the massive signal gantry at the west end with its forest of signal arms, one of the biggest in the country; it is soon to be demolished, for work is already under way to provide the 15-platform station with all-electric signalling of the type installed at York. From the other end of the station a busy service of electric trains runs to Tynemouth, Whitley Bay and South Shields. Another notable railway feature at this end of Central station is the great series of crossings by which tracks curving away to cross the High Level Bridge diverge right from the East Coast main line, with the Norman castle erected by Henry II in 1172 standing in the " V " of the junction. So heavily used are these crossings that they are specially cast in very hard alloy steel to stand up to the constant battering they take from passing trains. On the left-hand side, as we pull away from Newcastle, you will notice the 193½ ft. lantern tower of Newcastle cathedral, under which John Knox once occupied the pulpit. Newcastle is 8 miles from the sea, but the largest ships can sail up to its quays and yards; in the latter no less a craft than the grand old Cunarder and Blue Riband-holder *Mauretania* was built.

We have the company of Tyneside electric trains on parallel tracks as far as Heaton, where the railway-minded should keep their eyes peeled to the right for Heaton locomotive shed. They should also keep a look-out at Killingworth for an old ivy-covered house near the line on the right; this was once the home of George Stephenson. We have been climbing more or less continuously since we left Newcastle and we reach the summit at Cramlington; thereafter gradients undulate all the way to Alnmouth. At Morpeth we come within sight of the North Sea, a pleasant prospect for the unfortunate inmates of the Northumberland County Lunatic Asylum, which nestles in the trees on a hill to the left overlooking Pegswood. The ruins of Warkworth Castle are visible on the right before Warkworth; this was once the seat of the Percy family, celebrated in the lore of the Border Country. Beyond Alnmouth Junction, where the sea cuts inland close to the railway, the line is carried over the Aln river on a fine stone viaduct.

Out of Alnmouth the engine faces 4 miles of 1 in 170 up Longhoughton bank to Little Mill, but soon after gets a breather on 2½ miles of 1 in 150 down gradient through Christon Bank. Beyond Chathill there are glimpses of the Cheviot Hills to the left if the weather is clear. The engine's last chance of refreshment before Edinburgh comes at Lucker water troughs On the coast is Bamburgh Castle, built by King Ida as long ago as 541. Soon the sea is sweeping up towards the railway again in Budle Bay, and from Smeafield the lighthouses of Farne Island, 2 miles out to sea, are visible; it was from the outer

THE CORRIDOR TENDER of a Class "A4" Pacific. This shows the gangway which is connected to the train.

[British Railways

lighthouse, Longstone, that Grace Darling and her father made their celebrated rescue. Another historic island is Lindisfarne, or Holy Island, standing offshore from Beal; one can walk across to it in a causeway at low tide. Here one of earliest Christian missions to Britain was founded by St. Aidan in the 7th Century.

At Goswick there begins a long climb of some 22 miles up to the flanks of the Lammermuir Hills at Gransthouse, broken by two level or slightly downhill sections through Tweedmouth and Ayton. Just beyond Tweedmouth there is a good view ahead of the stately Royal Border Bridge. over which we shall cross the Tweed into Berwick. This 28-arch viaduct, built by

THE ROYAL BORDER BRIDGE, BERWICK—Class " A4 " 4-6-2 No. 60011 *Empire of India* crosses the Tweed with the northbound " Flying Scotsman ". [*E. R. Wethersett*

Robert Stephenson in 1847-50, was opened by Queen Victoria; it is 2,160 ft. long and 126½ ft. high above the water. Downstream to the right is the graceful ferro-concrete Royal Tweed Bridge, carrying the Great North Road, and opened by the Prince of Wales in 1928, and beyond that the ancient stone bridge which it replaced.

As one might expect from its situation astride the Anglo-Scottish border—the actual boundary is three miles north of the station, and is marked by an attractive lineside sign—the history of Berwick has been eventful. Since it was first sacked by William the Conqueror it has suffered burning and plundering in succession and changed hands many times. For many years it was considered to be in neither country, but formed a "buffer state" of its own. The railway station stands on the site of the old Castle, but a portion of its fortifications still reach down to the water's edge.

Beyond Berwick the railway hugs the rocky coastline and there are some magnificent prospects to the right as the engine attacks the 4 miles of 1 in 190 up to Burnmouth. Then the engine enjoys a respite of level and downhill through Ayton, until it is faced with the final 7½ miles up, mostly at 1 in 200, to Grantshouse and the summit, after which the train threads the 267 yds. Penmanshiel Tunnel. We are now gathering speed fast, for the climb to Penmanshiel from the Edinburgh side is very much steeper and more sudden, the last 4½ miles being graded at 1 in 96—the steepest slope we have encountered since we left London. The line levels out at Innerwick, but the descent is resumed, though not so steeply,

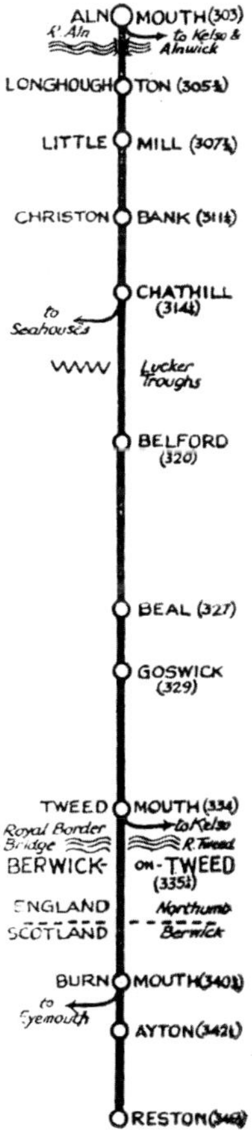

through the historic town of Dunbar.

Amid the trees on the right at the approach to Dunbar is Broxmouth House, where Oliver Cromwell set up his headquarters for the battle he fought here with the Scottish Covenanters in 1650 in the plain between the coast and the 650 ft. Doon Hill. On a hill above the harbour are the ruins of a castle which once sheltered Mary, Queen of Scots.

Between Dunbar and Drem there are frequent glimpses out to sea of the once volcanic Bass Rock, 3 miles offshore, where Cromwell consigned many of his Scotch Covenanter captives to prison. Further up the coast the conical outline of North Berwick Law, 614 ft. high, stands guard above the famous golfing town, while inland, on the other side of the line, is the 724 ft. Traprain Law, formed by the neck of an extinct volcano.

At Longniddry Junction the sea drives up close to the railway again, and if it is a clear day, you will see the line of the Fifeshire hills on the other shore of the Firth of Forth. Garleton Hill, some two miles to the left of the railway, is topped by the Hopetoun Monument, erected in 1824 in memory of the Earl who took over command of British troops at the Battle of Corunna, in Spain, after the death of Sir John Moore. The famous Battle of Prestonpans in 1745 was fought in the country between the railway south of that station and the coast; there is visible evidence of it in a monument to the left of the line, erected to a colonel who was killed in the struggle. Pinkie House, where Bonnie Prince Charlie slept after the battle, can be seen on the right just before Inveresk.

THE "ELIZABETHAN" IN EDINBURGH—Class "A4" 4-6-2 No. 60017 *Silver Fox* waits to start the southbound train on its mile-a-minute non-stop trip of 392.9 miles from Waverley station to Kings Cross in 6½ hours. [*Eric Treacy*

Our journey is nearing its end. Beyond the Braid Hills on the left, the unmistakeable outline of Arthur's Seat, that 822 ft. high mass of volcanic rock overlooking Edinburgh, is coming into sight. Soon after passing the popular seaside resort of Portobello, the railway enthusiasts will be keeping a look-out for St. Margaret's engine shed. Then the engine is climbing the last steep 1½ miles of 1 in 78 through Calton Tunnel and beneath the walls of the city gaol into the great Waverley station.

The "Elizabethan's" Locomotive

THE engine of the "Elizabethan" is a 4-6-2, or Pacific type, of Class "A4", a design first introduced by the former L.N.E.R. in 1935 to work the pre-war streamlined trains of that system—the "Silver Jubilee", the "Coronation" and the "West Riding Limited". The designer of the type was the late Sir Nigel Gresley, after whom one of the engines is named.

CLASS "A4" 4-6-2 DIMENSIONS

Weights:
Locomotive—102 tons 19 cwt.
Tender—64 tons 19 cwt.
Boiler Pressure: 250 lb. per sq. in.

Cylinders (3):
18½ in. diameter × 26 in. stroke
Driving Wheel Diameter: 6 ft. 8 in.
Tractive Effort: 35,455 lb.

CLASS "A4" NUMBERS AND NAMES

60001	Sir Ronald Matthews	60018	Sparrow Hawk
60002	Sir Murrough Wilson	60019	Bittern
60003*	Andrew K. McCosh	60020	Guillemot
60004*	William Whitelaw	60021	Wild Swan
60005	Sir Charles Newton	60022*	Mallard
60006	Sir Ralph Wedgwood	60023	Golden Eagle
60007*	Sir Nigel Gresley	60024*	Kingfisher
60008*	Dwight D. Eisenhower	60025*	Falcon
60009*	Union of South Africa	60026	Miles Beevor
60010*	Dominion of Canada	60027*	Merlin
60011*	Empire of India	60028*	Walter K. Whigham
60012*	Commonwealth of Australia	60029*	Woodcock
60013*	Dominion of New Zealand	60030*	Golden Fleece
60014*	Silver Link	60031*	Golden Plover
60015*	Quicksilver	60032*	Gannet
60016	Silver King	60033*	Seagull
60017*	Silver Fox	60034*	Lord Faringdon

*Fitted with corridor tender for working the "Elizabethan."

The eventual intention is to electrify the East Coast main line between London and York, and probably Newcastle as well, but before that the principal main line duties, including the haulage of the "Elizabethan", will be undertaken by 23 "Deltic" type 3,300 h.p. diesel-electrics of English Electric manufacture.

famous trains — 2

The
ROYAL SCOT

EUSTON—GLASGOW (CENTRAL)

(London Midland and Scottish Regions)

by

G. FREEMAN ALLEN

Ian Allan Ltd

CLIMBING OUT OF EUSTON—Pacific No. 46251 *City of Nottingham* ascends Camden bank with the northbound "Royal Scot". [*R. J. Blenkinsop*

Introduction

ALTHOUGH the title of " Royal Scot " was not bestowed on it until 1927, the train which leaves Euston and Glasgow at 10 a.m. is one of the oldest established trains in Britain. With only a few short breaks in its history, it has pulled out of London every day since June, 1862. The " Royal Scot " has travelled abroad, too. In 1933 an engine of the " Royal Scot " 4-6-0 class and a set of coaches representative of the train were shipped across the Atlantic to tour the U.S.A. and Canada, where they covered more than 11,000 miles. To mark the occasion, 4-6-0 No. 46100 *Royal Scot* was presented with a handsome bell by its American hosts, which the engine carried proudly on its bufferbeam until it was rebuilt a few years ago; the bell is now in York Railway Museum, but No. 46100's nameplate still incorporates a plaque commemorating its Transatlantic exploits. The " Royal Scot " 4-6-0s no longer haul the train whose name they share, for since 1933 larger 4-6-2 engines have been available.

Today the " Royal Scot " in winter is one of the very few trains in Britain to enjoy the luxury of two different sets of restaurant cars in the same train. One is included in the main train for Glasgow, but there is another in the three-coach section for Perth, at the rear; these three Perth coaches travel no farther than Crewe, where they are transferred to the 11.25 a.m. Birmingham-Glasgow as far as Carlisle, but thereafter they make their own way on to Perth. Between Euston and Crewe, therefore, the " Royal Scot " in winter is usually a heavy 16-coach train of over 500 tons' weight behind the engine. In summer Perth passengers are put aboard a following train, and the timetable shows the " Royal Scot " to make no public stop between Euston and Glasgow. In fact, however, a stop has to be made just north of Carlisle to change engine crews (and engine during the winter service); the run has been made non-stop, when the L.M.S. stole a march on the L.N.E.R. in May, 1928 by running the train right through to Glasgow behind " Royal Scot " No. 46113 *Cameronian* only a few days before a much-publicised non-stop " Flying Scotsman " service between London and Edinburgh was due to begin. In normal circumstances, however, 400 miles' driving without respite is too much of a strain on an engine crew.

NOTE: The figures in brackets after station names indicate mileage from Euston.

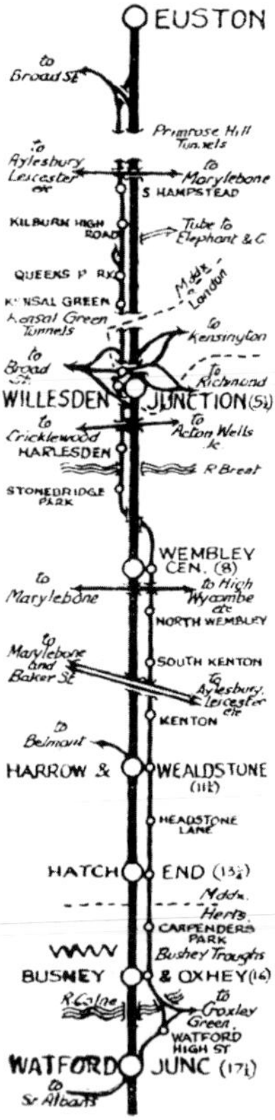

The Route of the "Royal Scot"

THE first mile out of Euston is an unpleasant start to a long journey for the engine, as it consists of a stiff climb, some of it graded at 1 in 70-77, up to Camden, where there is a big engine-shed on the left. A maze of complex burrowing junctions marks the approach to the 1,182 yd. Primrose Hill Tunnel, through which the engine has a chance to gather speed on level track. Another 320 yd. tunnel at Kensal Green precedes Willesden Junction, where we are joined from the left by a useful route, much used by freight all the year round and holiday expresses in summer, which avoids the centre of London and provides direct connection with the Southern Region. Willesden engine shed is on the left near the station and on the right big marshalling yards extend all the way to Wembley; beyond them you will catch a glimpse of the most modern carriage servicing depot in the country, where the " Royal Scot " is serviced.

Famous Wembley Stadium, home of the F.A. Cup Final, is a landmark on the right as we approach Wembley Central, whence a long rise at 1 in 339 extends to Carpenders Park. Before Kenton there is a fine view of Harrow-on-the-Hill on the left, rising abruptly from the surrounding plain; the taller of the two spires is the parish church, the smaller the chapel of the famous public school, whose buildings cluster round it. The big Commercial Travellers' Schools adjoin the lineside on the right just before Hatch End station. Water troughs are

WATFORD TUNNELMOUTH — "Royal Scot" Class 4-6-0 No. 46168 *The Girl Guide* emerges with a Blackpool-Euston express. [*S. Creer*

laid in the cutting before Bushey.

Watford Junction is the terminus of the L.M. electric trains from Euston and Broad Street and the L.T. Bakerloo tube trains. Just north of the station on the right, beyond the bridge, is the old Watford station, with a flight of steps built specially for the convenience of Queen Adelaide when she was travelling to and from nearby Cassiobury Park. To avoid desecrating this latter estate and Grove, onetime seats of the Earls of Essex and Clarendon, the old London & Birmingham railway was forced to construct the 1 mile 57 yd. Watford Tunnel. Beyond this tunnel, the Grand Union Canal joins us on the left as we climb the pleasant Gade valley, mainly at 1 in 335, to Tring, in the Chiltern Hills. Just before Berkhamsted, keep watch on the right-hand side for the few

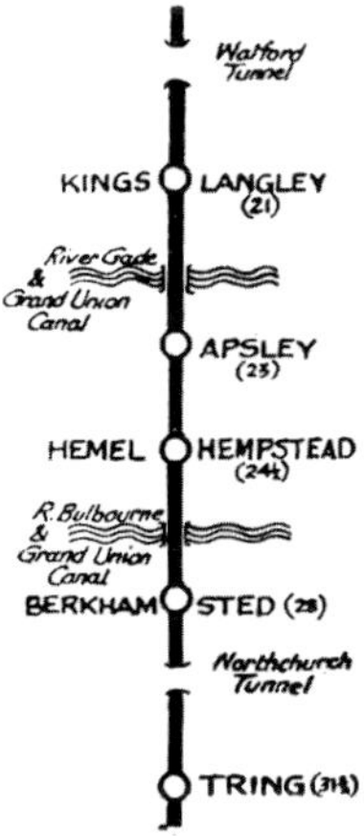

5

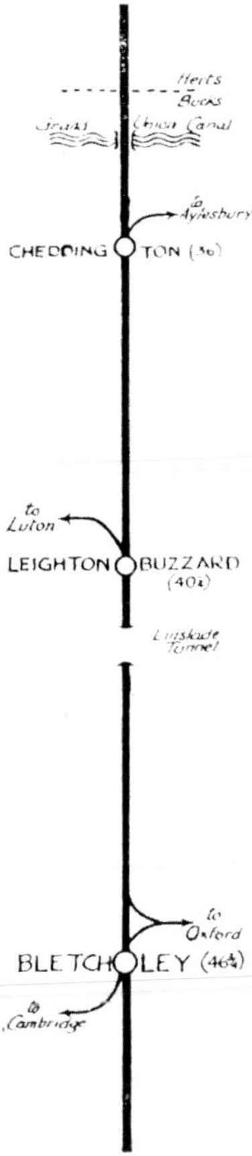

remaining traces of Berkhamsted Castle, where William the Conqueror was offered the crown of England and Geoffrey Chaucer once resided. The high ground on the right is mainly occupied by the historic Ashridge estate; the monument at its northernmost end was erected in honour of the third Duke of Bridgewater, great British advocate of canals in the late 18th Century.

Beyond Tring station the railway enters a deep cutting and begins an easy descent to Bletchley. Emerging from the cutting, the 762 ft. Ivinghoe Beacon, often the venue of gliding events, is conspicuous on the right; on the left, look out in clear weather for an obelisk crowning a hill-top, for it overlooks Chequers, the Prime Minister's country home. By the time we dive into the short Linslade Tunnel, beyond Leighton Buzzard, we shall probably have accelerated on the downgrade to 75 m.p.h. or more. If you want to check, keep a watch on the quarter mile posts as they speed past your window on the left; every fourth one shows the mileage from London as far as a point just north of Warrington, where they recommence at "0", as they do again at Preston, Lancaster and Carlisle, while the intervening posts show $\frac{1}{4}$, $\frac{1}{2}$ and $\frac{3}{4}$. If you time the number of seconds the train takes between any two of these quarter-mile posts and divide the result into 900, you will have the speed in miles per hour; e.g., a quarter-mile covered in 12 seconds equals 75 m.p.h. By the way, the other little trackside posts on the left, with two arms inclined at varying angles like the hands of a clock, indicate a change of gradient; e.g., a post with the arms at " twenty to four ", with the minute hand marked " 400 " and the hour hand " 200 ", indicates a change of incline from a rise of 1 ft. up in every 400 ft. along to 1 ft. down in every 200 ft. along.

There is a glimpse of an allegedly haunted house on the left just before Wolverton, the small church-like building with a Gothic window adjoining a farm-house. Known as Bradwell Priory, it is all that remains of 12th Century Benedictine priory once presented by Henry VIII to Cardinal Wolsey.

The big factory to the left of Wolverton station is the extensive carriage and wagon works of the L.M.R., where all manner of rolling stock from goods vans to the luxurious Royal Train have been manufactured; the latter is stored there when not in use. Originally the main line cut right through the middle of the factory.

Just before Castlethorpe, where the line begins a climb of 6 miles at 1 in 326-410, our big Pacific engine takes its second " drink " since we left London. Its tender holds only 4,000 gallons, whereas it will consume some 40-50 gallons per mile in the course of its 299 miles' run to Carlisle in winter (in summer an engine from Polmadie shed, Glasgow, heads the train throughout between London and Glasgow), so that it must take on fresh supplies en route. This is done at full speed. At suitably spaced intervals narrow troughs of water are laid between the running rails. As the engine approaches these troughs, the fireman lowers a sharp-bladed scoop beneath the tender which cuts into the water, forcing a stream of it up into the tank within the engine tender.

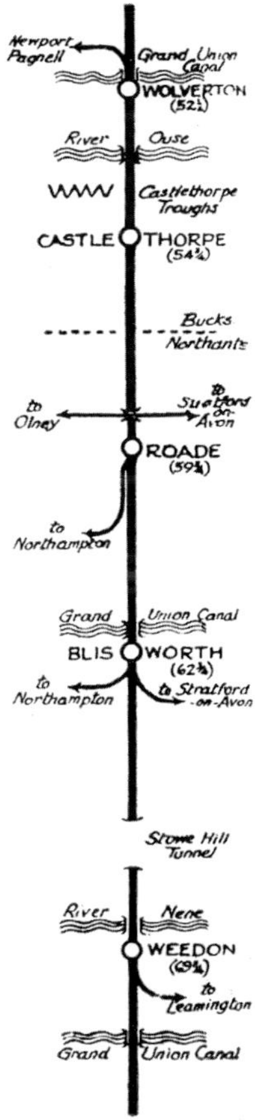

PACIFIC ON TEST—"Britannia" Class 4-6-2 No. 70005 *John Milton* undergoes trials on the Rugby Testing Plant. [*British Railways*

THE APPROACH TO RUGBY—With the tall aerials of the Hillmorton G.P.O. radio station in the background, "Royal Scot" Class 4-6-0 No. 46149 *The Middlesex Regiment* makes its way through the complicated junctions south of Rugby on a Euston-Manchester express. [*H. Weston*

After we have threaded the 492 yd. Stowe Hill Tunnel, the Army's big Ordnance Depot is conspicuous on the left at the approach to Weedon, where roughly level track since Blisworth terminates before the 6-mile ascent to Kilsby Tunnel, mainly at 1 in 350. In the distance you will soon see on the left the tall masts of the B.B.C.'s short-wave transmitter for overseas broadcasts at Daventry. Then, beyond Welton, we dive into the 1 mile 666 yd. Kilsby Tunnel through a limestone mass which is an interesting watershed; from its southern flank flows water which, via the Nene river, runs into the North Sea, while streams from its other side join the Avon, which enters the Severn and thus the Bristol Channel. Kilsby Tunnel, built by George Stephenson, has had a chequered history; the workings were flooded during its construction, and ever since drainage of the tunnel has been a perpetual problem.

The twelve masts of the Hillmorton G.P.O. radio station on the right, one of the world's most powerful transmitters, herald the complicated junctions beyond the 3½-mile downhill approach to Rugby. On the other side of the long girder bridge carrying the former Great Central Marylebone-Leicester main line over us at right-angles, look out on the right for the big building labelled " British Railways Testing Station ". Inside it a big locomotive can be mounted on rollers and worked up to the highest speeds while it is still stationary; the engine is coupled to testing instruments, and, by varying the resistance the rollers offer to the engine's driving wheels, the engineers can simulate all types of load and gradient.

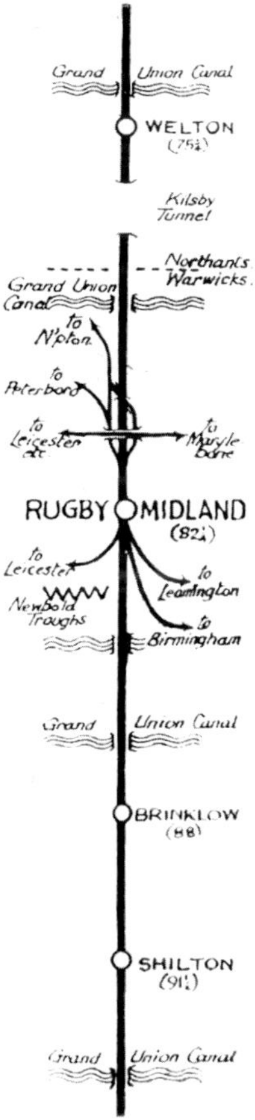

LICHFIELD CATHEDRAL—Though one of the smallest cathedrals in England, it is one of the most lovely with its slender spires, known as the Ladies of the Vale. Built between 1200 and 1340, it is entirely in Early English and decorated styles. The beautiful windows contain much 16th century Flemish stained glass.

[*Crown Copyrigh*

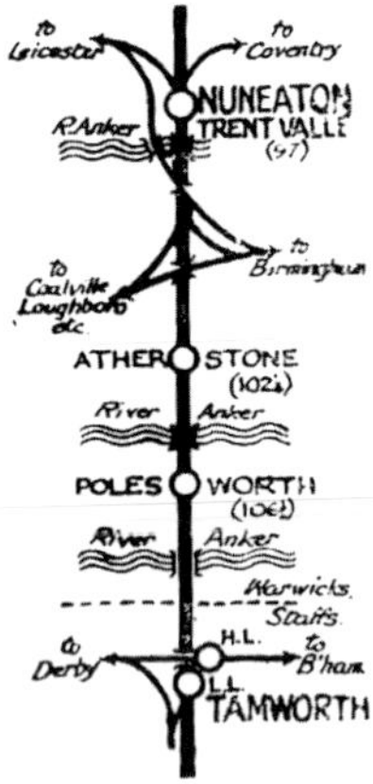

The celebrated Rugby School is invisible from the railway, except for the short spire of its octagonal chapel tower, which will be noticed above the town on the hill to the left as we leave the station. Soon we cross more water troughs and begin an undulating section of track to Bulkington, after which there is a noticeable descent through Nuneaton, the centre of a thriving colliery area. Incidentally, if the day is clear, there may be glimpse of the spires of Coventry beyond the second bridge over the line after Brinklow. From Atherstone, there is again a long and gradual descent through Tamworth, an interchange station of special importance to the G.P.O.; every night the special mail trains between

Euston and Glasgow stop at Tamworth to exchange bags with trains running between York, Lincoln and Bristol on the former Midland Railway main line, which crosses over us here.

Some 3½ miles from Tamworth the engine has another chance to take water, at Hademore; then, on the left of the line, we shall be looking out for the three graceful spires of Lichfield Cathedral, severely damaged and desecrated in other ways by Cromwell's men in the Civil war, but since restored. Between Rugeley and Stafford the wooded ridge of Cannock Chase is visible to the left; despite its modern development as a coalfield, deer still roam its woodlands. Beyond Colwich one should keep a look-out for the richly decorated parapet, surmounted by heraldic beasts, of a bridge which carries the railway over the drive to Shugborough Hall, seat of the Earl of Lichfield; soon after we enter the 776 yd. Shugborough Tunnel.

Speed is slackened over the sweeping Queensville curve at the approach to Stafford, amongst other things the birthplace of Isaak Walton; the famous angler's timbered cottage, with one of his favourite streams running close by, adjoins the line on the right-hand site just beyond Great Bridgeford station. Here the railway begins a long climb of 12 miles at 1 in 400-600 to Whitmore troughs. From Whitmore there is a steeper descent, including 3 miles of 1 in 177, to Crewe, which is one of the racing grounds of the West Coast Route; it was down this bank that Pacific No. 46220 *Coronation* was whipped up to 114 m.p.h. on the trial trip of the pre-war "Coronation Scot" streamliner in June, 1937.

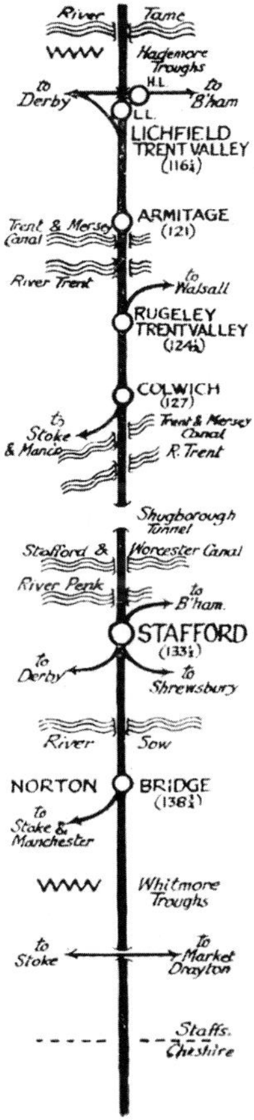

PACIFIC UNDRESSED—The boiler of a big Stanier Pacific, of the type which hauls the " Royal Scot ", is lifted on to its frames in Crewe works. [*British Railways*

THE " ROYAL SCOT " photographed south of Hartford, Cheshire, behind Pacific No. 46227 *Duchess of Devonshire.* [*T. Lewis*

At the height of the summer season, between 400 and 500 trains will be dealt with on a Saturday in Crewe's 16 platforms. It is small wonder, then, that Crewe's two engine sheds house some 250 locomotives. Crewe South is mainly for freight locomotives; the big express engines are allocated to Crewe North, which you will see on the left, beyond the cutting hiding the avoiding lines that keep through goods trains out of the busy station, as we thread our way through the junctions north of Crewe. In the "V" of our junction with the Chester line, you will see on the left a corner of the great Crewe locomotive works, where our own engine was built and where all the British Railways standard Pacifics have been constructed so far.

Our route now follows a generally level path through the Cheshire saltfield—indeed, the headquarters of Britain's largest salt-manufacturing concern is the big works on the left at Winsford. We are now traversing one of the busiest sections of main line in the country. Since Stafford it has been carrying traffic between the Midlands and North-west and Scotland, while at Crewe we were joined by the trunk route from Shrewsbury and the West Country; true, we bid farewell to Manchester traffic at Crewe, but trains for Liverpool do not branch off until we reach Weaver Junction, north of Acton Bridge. At Weaver there is a fine example of that boon to speedy railway operation, the flying junction. Instead of crossing our path on the level, the up line from Liverpool is carried across us on a bridge, so that trains from Liverpool can join the up West Coast main line without baulking down main line trains to

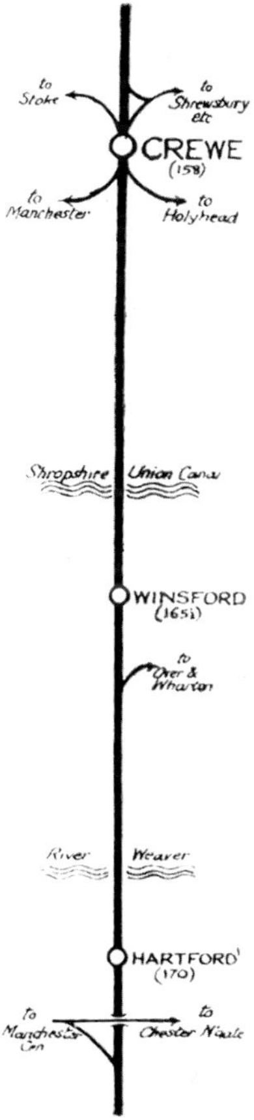

Preston and Carlisle.

Just before Weaver Junction, we cross the Weaver river on Dutton Viaduct; then it is worth looking out on the right for the entrance to the $\frac{3}{4}$-mile long Preston-on-the-Hill tunnel, one of five threaded by the Grand Trunk Canal, which will cross us by an aqueduct north of what was once Preston Brook station. Further water-troughs are at Moore, and then there is a hump approached from both sides on 1 in 135 gradients to carry the railway high over the Manchester Ship Canal on Acton Grange Viaduct. To the left you may notice the Norman Halton Castle on its hill and beyond, if the weather is clear, the Runcorn Transporter and railway bridges and the chimneys of Widnes. On the other side of the track, the conspicuous 281 ft. spire of Warrington church is a sign that we are entering Lancashire. Warrington is also on the fringe of the great Lancashire coalfield, whose pits soon begin to scar the country on the left. Just after Winwick Junction, railway enthusiasts will notice on the left the big Vulcan Engineering works, birthplace of many British and overseas locomotives. Soon afterward the historic Liverpool & Manchester Railway, scene of George Stephenson's triumph with his *Rocket* in the Rainhill Trials of 1830 crosses over the West Coast Route, now engaged in a sharp little climb up to Golborne. Wigan is next seen ahead on the right. This busy industrial town, home of cotton and engineering and the centre of a coalfield, claims to be Lancashire's oldest borough, with a charter dating from 1246; its tallest chimneys are those of the Wigan Iron & Coal Co.

THE KITCHEN CAR of the " Royal Scot ". [*British Railways*

Soon after we leave Wigan there is a sharp climb of nearly 2 miles at 1 in 104 up to Boar's Head Junction. Then it eases a little, but there is a stretch of 1 in 119 before the summit is reached south of Coppull. On the right the beacon hill of Rivington Pike, crowned by a tower, stands out, the westernmost of the hills of Rossendale Forest. In earlier days some high speeds might have been recorded on the descent from Coppull to Preston, but in modern times subsidence as a result of mine working has necessitated frequent speed restrictions to the north of Warrington; at Boar's Head the subsidence was so severe that the windows of the station waiting room (now closed) sank to the level of the platform! A bridge over the Ribble river brings us into Preston; well-known as a big industrial town, Preston is also a port, for the Ribble is tidal there.

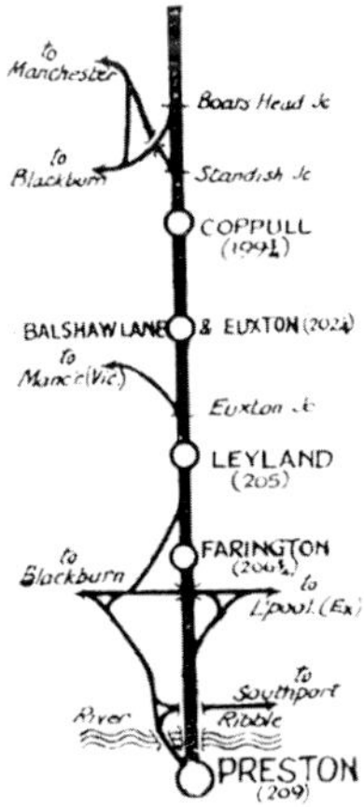

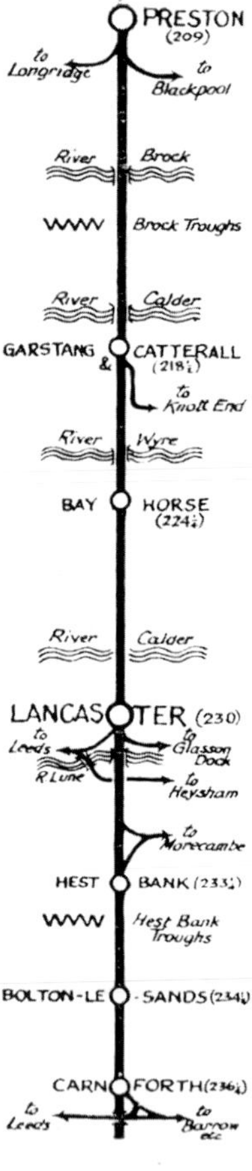

Preston is on the fringe of industrial Lancashire. Beyond it the line traces an almost level path through the green lowland between the Ribble and Wyre rivers, known as the Fylde. On the right it is bordered by the wild fells of Bleasdale and Bowland Forest, which come into sight as we emerge from the cutting north of Preston. As we cross the Conder river north of Bay Horse there should be a glimpse in the left distance of the celebrated Blackpool Tower, while to the right there is a prospect up Wyresdale to the hills of the Forest of Bowland; ahead Clougha Fell looms threateningly over the ancient town of Lancaster, which the railway approaches on a sudden steep descent of 1 in 88.

The impressive castle on the hill (to be seen on the right) was built mainly by John of Gaunt, third Duke of Lancaster, whose son, Henry Bolingbroke, usurped the throne of Richard II and became Henry IV. You will probably see in the station one of the green electric trains which shuttle between Lancaster, Morecambe and Heysham. This service is of interest since it was recently modernised to take its current at the national industrial frequency, instead of at a reduced voltage, as is the case with other electrified lines in Britain; the importance of this innovation, which is still experimental, is that it reduces considerably the amount of equipment needed, and hence the cost, of railway electrification. The curious mausoleum-like domed building on the hill overlooking the railway on the right as you leave Lancaster is a monument raised to his family in 1907 by Lord Ashton, proprietor of a linoleum factory in the town.

LANCASTER CASTLE dominates the scene from its hill as Pacific No. 46256 *Sir William Stanier, F.R.S.* pulls out of Lancaster station with the southbound " Mid-day Scot ". [*Eric Treacy*

The railway runs down to the coastline at Hest Bank and in clear weather a magnificent prospect of the Lakeland mountains opens up across the waters of Morecambe Bay, with the valleys of Coniston and Windermere discernible. On the other side of the line there is a view up the Greeta valley to the massive Ingleborough, 2,373 ft. high, soon after passing Carnforth. Now the railway has started the first of its great ascents of the Westmorland-Cumbrian fells. It begins with 2¼ miles of 1 in 134 up from Carnforth; then comes a respite, but at Milnthorpe a climb commences which does not end until we reach Grayrigg, over 13 miles away, and which is graded mostly between 1 in 106 and 1 in 175. After the fourth overbridge north of Oxenholme do not miss the fine panorama to the left of the Lakeland Hills, all between

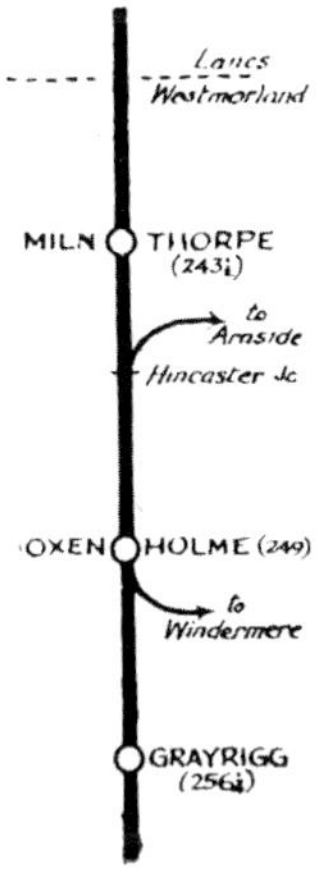

A PACIFIC DRINKS—No. 46249 *City of Sheffield* takes water from Dillicar troughs as it threads the beautiful Lune valley wth the northbound " Mid-day Scot " [*E. D. Bruton*

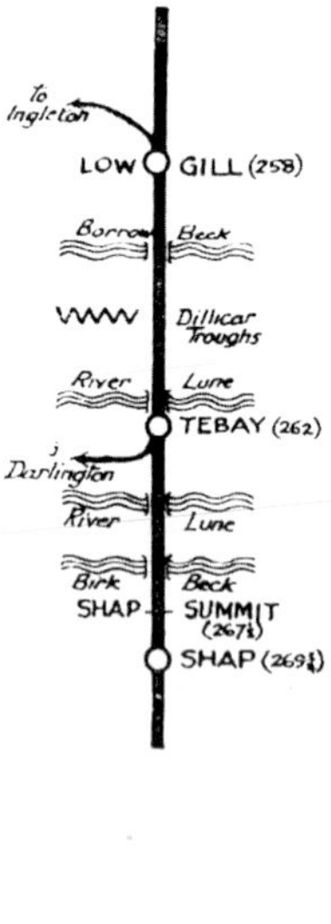

2,000 and 3,000 ft. high, and ranging from Coniston Old Man on the left to the Langdale Pikes on the right.

From Grayrigg to Dillicar watertroughs, just before Tebay, the engine can take a breather as the line resumes an almost level course through beautiful valley of the Lune, now a racing torrent unlike the smooth stream it was when we bridged it at Lancaster. Then, refreshed at the troughs, our Pacific has to tackle one of the steepest main line inclines in Britain; for, after 1½ miles at 1 in 145 through Tebay station, the gradient steepens to a wicked 1 in 75 for the last 4 miles to Shap summit, 916 ft. above sea level in the wild fells. Many trains stop at Tebay for a push up the bank by one of the 2-6-4 tanks stationed at Tebay to provide rear-end assistance of this kind, but normally our Pacific will battle its way up the hill unaided, despite its 400 odd tons of train behind the tender.

From Shap summit there is a glorious run of almost unbroken downhill running for just over 32 miles to Carlisle, but there is a speed restriction round the sharp curve through Penrith to prohibit continuous fast running all the way. From Shap station the jagged outline of Kidsty Pike, the 2,560 ft. peak at the head of Haweswater, is conspicuous on the left. Soon the " Royal Scot " is racing down a tempting 7 miles of 1 in 125. Once a cutting and a short tunnel have been threaded, there is suddenly a splendid view to the right across the broad Eden valley to the hump of the Pennines' highest peak, the 2,930 ft. Crossfell, which crowns the long range of hills in the distance; these hills are the source of the Tees and Tyne rivers. On the other side of the line, two other Lakeland giants come into view as we approach Penrith, the 3,118 ft. Helvellyn at the head of Ullswater to the left, and the 2,847 ft. Blencathra, or Saddleback, which hides the equally well-known Skiddaw from our view; these mountains are all grouped round Keswick. Penrith is one of those Anglo-Scottish border area towns rich in history of a violent kind; it is overlooked by the tower-crowned Penrith Beacon hill, a landmark for many miles of our route further north.

Our long descent is briefly levelled out through Penrith, but beyond Plumpton it is resumed and continues all the way to Carlisle at from 1 in 114 to 1 in 228. Soon the outskirts of the city come into view on the right, the castle and cathedral tower vying with a tall 305 ft. factory chimney for dominance of the city.

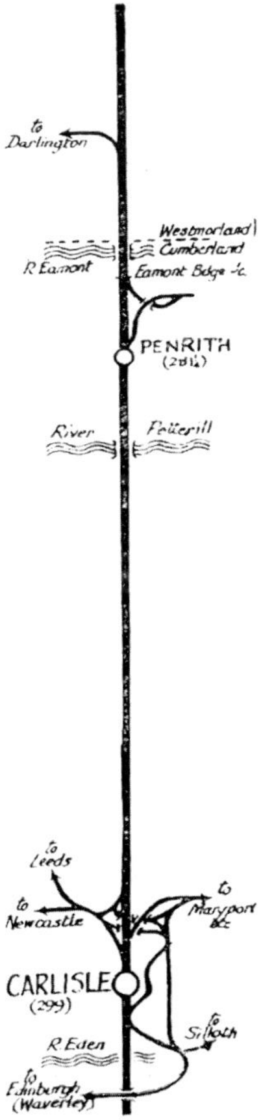

Carlisle has always been and still is one of the most important British railway junctions, for it is the gateway to two different routes to Glasgow and another to Edinburgh. Up to the 1923 railway grouping, it was certainly one of the most colourful; there was the glorious blue of the Caledonian engines, the crimson of the Midland, the bright green of the North Eastern, the more sober green of the Glasgow & South Western and the dark yellow of the North British, all meeting with the less vivid liveries of other companies beneath the roof of the great Citadel station. It is the only place at which the "Royal Scot" halts in winter and summer alike. In winter the train pauses in the station to change engines and crews, as well as deal with passenger traffic, but in summer the stop is made outside one of the city's motive power depots to change crews only; the southbound train halts at Upperby, just south of the maze of burrowing junctions at the approach to the Citadel station from London, and the northbound train at Kingmoor shed, on the Glasgow side of the river Eden north of the station (the city has a third major engine depot, known as Canal, which serves the former L.N.E.R. line to Edinburgh and Newcastle). It is here, too, that the Perth portion of the "Royal Scot" in winter parts company with the 11.25 Birmingham-Glasgow and proceeds northward as a train in its own right.

Carlisle as a town has existed since Saxon times and was for long a frontier town of the Roman empire. As might be imagined, its history is one of blood and strife. It was completely destroyed by the Danes, but was re-established at the end of the 11th Century by William Rufus, who built its moated castle, though only its keep now remains much as he left it. Historic Carlisle unfolds before us as we leave the station. The mediaeval city wall appears on the right, with the Deanery, house of the prior who once governed the city's great Augustinian monastery, perched on it; beyond the Deanery can be seen the tower of the beautiful Norman cathedral, whose 58 ft. high decorated East window is probably the finest extant. At the second overbridge north of the station the City wall ends and the Castle wall begins, some of it built with great blocks of masonry from the Roman Hadrian's wall. The tower in the wall marks the point where Cromwell's soldiers broke through in 1646 after cannonading a breach in the wall from the hill on the other side of the track (now surmounted by Carlisle Infirmary), and destroyed much of the nave of the Cathedral.

LEAVING CARLISLE—Pacific No. 46200 *Princess Royal* draws out of the Citadel station with a Glasgow-Birmingham express. The main line from Leeds climbs up into the station between the train and the goods yard on the right. [*Eric Treacy*

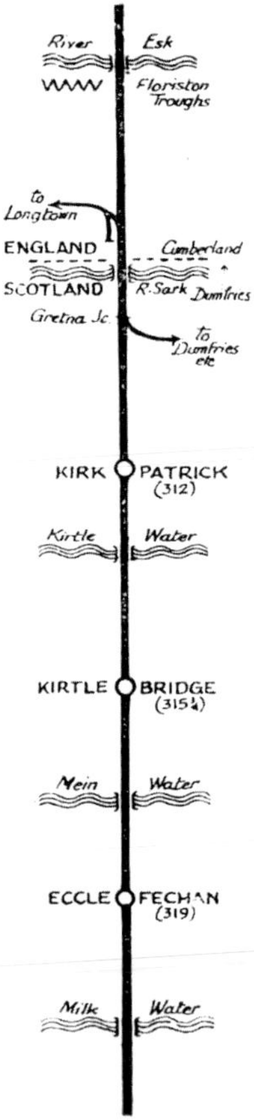

Immediately we have crossed the first river north of the city, the Caldew, look out for a small stone pillar on the right; this is on the site of the great Hadrian's wall, the Roman rampart which stretched from the Solway to the Tyne. The obelisk to be seen on the right after Rockcliffe is to the memory of Sir John Malcolm, a Knight of Eskdale, and stands on White Hill above Langholm. At Floriston water troughs the line strikes uphill for $7\frac{1}{2}$ miles at 1 in 193-200 through Gretna, the traditional Mecca of eloping couples: the coming of the railway to Gretna in 1847 doubled the matrimonial business there—indeed, until an Act of 1856 restricted the town's quick marriage trade, the station's platforms were usually lined by priests touting for custom as each train arrived! Between Gretna and Kirkpatrick there is a superb prospect of Solway Firth to the left in clear weather, with Skiddaw, above faraway Keswick, dominating the Cumbrian shore.

By now, if it is summer and our Pacific is working right through from London to Glasgow, much of the 10 tons of coal which filled the engine tender when we started will have been exhausted, and the engine crew will probably be setting an ingenious device known as the "coal-pusher" to work. This saves the fireman having to lunge right into the back of the tender for coal on the last stage of the journey. A steam-operated piston operates a sheet of metal shaped like a plough, which shoves the coal forward from the rear of the tender to the front. If you ever see a "Duchess" Pacific (the latest British Railways standard "Britannia" Pacifics have the device as well) speeding past you and notice a jet of

COAL-PUSHER AT WORK—A plume of steam from the rear of the tender of Pacific No. 46237 *City of Bristol* indicates that the crew are using their coal-pusher. [B. Sackville

steam trailing from the top of the tender, it is a sign that the " coal-pusher " is in action.

The line is climbing again at 1 in 200 through Ecclefechan, birthplace of Thomas Carlyle, and beyond the town there is another view of Solway Firth and Skiddaw on the left. On the right the eye is struck by the conspicuous Burnswark Hill, which still exhibits traces of Celtic and Roman fortifications. Hereabouts the engine can take its last " breather " on 5 miles of 1 in 528 down before it begins the grim ascent of Beattock bank. By Dinwoodie we can see the Lowther Hills closing in on us from the left, with Queensberry Hill, the 2,284 ft. high peak which is the highest of the range, prominent on the left beyond Dinwoodie station.

The ascent to Beattock summit, possibly the most gruelling climb on any British

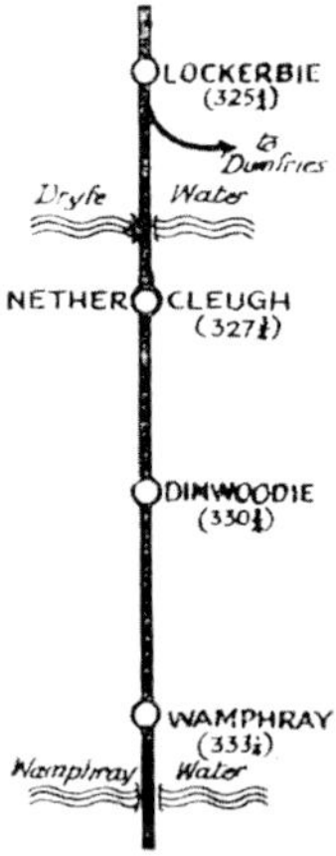

23

THE BATTLE OF BEATTOCK—Pacific No. 46255 *City of Hereford* climbs the formidable Beattock bank with th northbound "Royal Scot". [*W. J. V. Anderson*

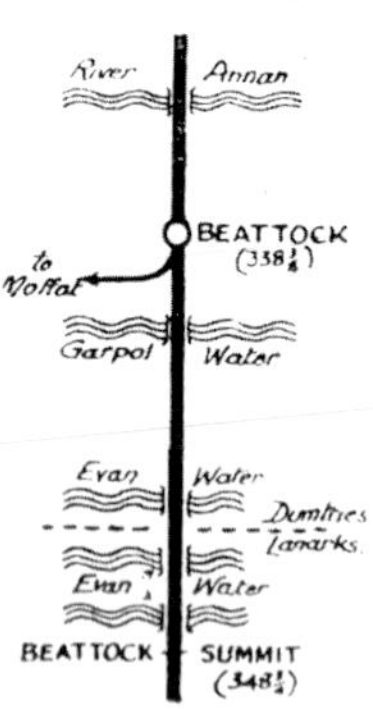

main line, begins a mile beyond Wamphray at 1 in 202. At Beattock station many trains stop to take on rear-end assistance from a banking engine to the summit, for the next 10 miles are graded all the way at between 1 in 74 and 1 in 88. Our Pacific, however, normally charges the steep slope unaided. Indeed, there is on record a magnificent test trip by No. 46234 *Duchess of Abercorn*, in February 1939, when she lifted a 20-coach train of over 600 tons up both Shap and Beattock banks unaided—and in both directions, with a pause of only 2 hours at Glasgow before returning south. In the northbound direction No. 46234 took swift advantage of the " breather " down to Nethercleugh, reaching 80 m.p.h. to get a good run at the hill; as a result, despite her huge load, she was able to climb the arduous 10 miles in no more than 16½ min. and pass the summit at a minimum of 30 m.p.h. Yes, there's plenty of stamina in a West Coast Route Pacific.

The lonely signalbox and the nearby Little Clyde Farm in the wild, heather-covered hills of the summit are 1,043 ft. above sea level. The farm is so named because the little brook which the railway crosses hard by it is the stream which swells into the mighty river on which Glasgow stands, and which later will carry the largest ocean liners down to the sea. Indeed, it is the Clyde valley we shall follow now all the way to Glasgow, with the river in the closest attendance to the railway as far as Carstairs. At first the descent from Beattock is 1 in 99 for 2 miles, but then it becomes gentler than south of the summit, for there is a long upland before the Lowther Hills drop away towards Glasgow. Rich veins of lead—and even a small quantity of gold—were once mined in this area. Beyond Abington the hills begin to fall away, and on the left we get a view of the Upper Clyde valley, broken by the conspicuous outline of Tinto Hill, from whose summit there is a remarkable view of 16 counties. At Lamington the line sweeps briefly uphill again to Symington.

Two miles beyond Cleghorn the railway goes " over the top " for the long descent to the suburbs of Glasgow, a bank of over 15 miles in length and graded for the most part between 1 in 100 and 1 in 200. At Carluke the panorama of Lower Clydesdale opens out before us and soon the pitheads

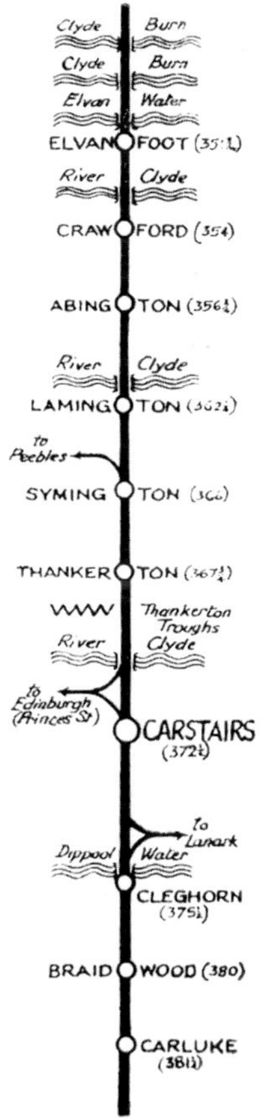

25

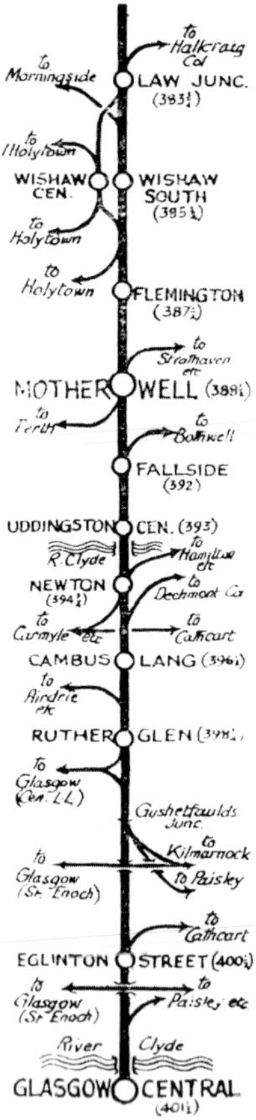

of the big coalfield come into view as we near the big marshalling yards of Law Junction, a clearing house for Anglo-Scottish freight trains; here traffic from England is sorted into trains for different Scottish destinations, while in the reverse direction goods from all parts of Scotland is formed into bulk loads for the big English traffic centres. By Wishaw we have reached the industrial suburbs of Glasgow and factories line the railway on both sides. Football enthusiasts will have their eyes peeled for the famous Hampden Park stadium, home of international soccer matches, which we pass on the left beyond Rutherglen. Then we are crossing the great bridge over the Clyde and rolling to a stop in Central station.

The West Coast Pacifics

THE first Pacifics designed by Sir William Stanier for the former L.M.S. were introduced in 1933. These were the "Princess Royals", four-cylinder engines with 6 ft. 6 in. driving wheels. To one of these, No. 46201 *Princess Elizabeth*, stands the credit of a remarkable run from Euston to Glasgow and back, carried out in November, 1936 as a prelude to the introduction of the stream-lined "Coronation Scot" train. With a 7-coach load, No. 46201 covered the 401½ miles to Glasgow in 6 min. under 6 hours; then, on the following day, sped back to London with a load one coach heavier in 5¾ hours. On this amazing run, mile after mile in both directions were reeled off at between 80 and 90 m.p.h., with a top speed of 95 m.p.h. in both directions.

CLOSE-UP of " Princess Royal " Class 4-6-2 No. 46210 *Lady Patricia.*
[J. E. Wilkinson

To haul the " Coronation Scot ", five improved Pacifics, fully streamlined and with larger 6 ft. 9 in. driving wheels—the largest on any British engine running to-day—were put on the road. Despite the performance of No. 46201, the streamliner was allowed $6\frac{1}{2}$ hours for its Euston-Glasgow journeys, but even so the new Pacifics were called upon for some very smart running. Some of the high-speed and haulage feats of the " Duchesses ", " Princess

" PRINCESS CORONATION " Class 4-6-2 No. 46235 *City of Birmingham.* [B. Sackville

27

Coronations " or " Cities "—as the first five and their later sisters are variously known—have already been described. Nos. 46220-9 and 46235-48 were all built with streamlined casing, but this was removed after the last war to make it easier for running shed staffs to maintain them; except at very high speeds, streamlining has little effect on the performance of an engine, and the difficulties it makes for those who have to overhaul the engine's " works " are worth more consideration than any publicity value it may have. In 1939 No. 46229 *Duchess of Hamilton*, then streamlined for working the pre-war " Coronation Scot ", was exhibited with a brand-new " Coronation Scot " train at New York, U.S.A.

" PRINCESS CORONATION " CLASS 4-6-2—DIMENSIONS

Weights: Locomotive	105 tons 5 cwt.
Tender	56 tons 7 cwt.
Pressure:	250 lb.
Cylinders (4):	16½" diameter × 28" stroke.
Driving Wheel Diameter:	6 ft. 9 in.
Tractive Effort:	40,000 lb.

" PRINCESS CORONATION " NUMBERS AND NAMES

46220 Coronation
46221 Queen Elizabeth
46222 Queen Mary
46223 Princess Alice
46224 Princess Alexandra
46225 Duchess of Gloucester
46226 Duchess of Norfolk
46227 Duchess of Devonshire
46228 Duchess of Rutland
46229 Duchess of Hamilton
46230 Duchess of Buccleuch
46231 Duchess of Atholl
46232 Duchess of Montrose
46233 Duchess of Sutherland
46234 Duchess of Abercorn
46235 City of Birmingham
46236 City of Bradford
46237 City of Bristol
46238 City of Carlisle
46239 City of Chester
46240 City of Coventry
46241 City of Edinburgh
46242 City of Glasgow
46243 City of Lancaster
46244 King George VI
46245 City of London
46246 City of Manchester
46247 City of Liverpool
46248 City of Leeds
46249 City of Sheffield
46250 City of Lichfield
46251 City of Nottingham
46252 City of Leicester
46253 City of St. Albans
46254 City of Stoke-on-Trent
46255 City of Hereford
46256 Sir William A. Stanier, F.R.S.
46257 City of Salford

famous trains — 3

The

CORNISH RIVIERA EXPRESS

PADDINGTON — PLYMOUTH, NEWQUAY, ST. IVES AND PENZANCE

(Western Region)

by

G. FREEMAN ALLEN

Ian Allan Ltd

[J. F. Russell-Smith

CLIMBING WELLINGTON BANK—The westbound "Cornish Riviera Express" hauled by "King" Class 4-6-0 No. 6025 *King Henry III*.

2

Introduction

ALTHOUGH the " Cornish Riviera Express " is a train with a great tradition, it was not the first titled train to run between Paddington and Plymouth. Few but the older readers of this booklet will recall its illustrious predecessor, the " Flying Dutchman ", which was the principal train from Paddington to Cornwall from 1862 to 1904 and which, in the latter years of the 19th Century, was claimed to be the fastest train in the world. The time-honoured departure hour of the " Flying Dutchman " from London was 11.45 a.m.; it reached Plymouth in $6\frac{1}{4}$ hours.

In July, 1904, the " Cornish Riviera Express " appeared on the scene and put the " Flying Dutchman " into the shade, setting up a new world's record to boot. For two years the new train left London at 10 a.m., but in 1906 its departure time from London was altered to 10.30 a.m. and has so remained ever since. Plymouth was reached in 4 hr. 27 min., far faster than by the " Dutchman ", even though the latter was simultaneously speeded up to reach Plymouth in $5\frac{1}{2}$ hours.

The new " Cornish Riviera Express " ran non-stop to Plymouth. This was at the time the longest daily journey in the world made without stopping, but in later years it has been excelled in this country by runs between Euston and Carlisle (299 miles) and Kings Cross and Edinburgh (393 miles). In 1904 the " Cornish Riviera " covered 245.7 miles on its trip from London to Plymouth, for it travelled via Bath and through the outskirts of Bristol. Two years later the construction of 24 miles of track from Castle Cary to Cogload Junction, near Taunton, completed the direct Great Western route to Plymouth and cut Bath and Bristol out of the " Cornish Riviera's " itinerary, reducing the London-Plymouth mileage to 225.7 miles. Finally, in 1933, avoiding lines were completed to iron out two kinks in the line through Westbury and Frome and the direct Paddington-Plymouth mileage was reduced to the present figure of $225\frac{1}{2}$.

For the summer of 1955 the London-Plymouth time of the " Cornish Riviera " has been cut back to the pre-war 4 hours, an exacting task for its " King " locomotive in view of the arduous climbing west of Newton Abbot. It means that the $173\frac{1}{2}$ miles to Exeter must be reeled off at an average of better than a mile a minute, despite a load that may be up to 15 bogies of 500 tons.

NOTE: The figures in brackets after station names indicate mileages from Paddington.

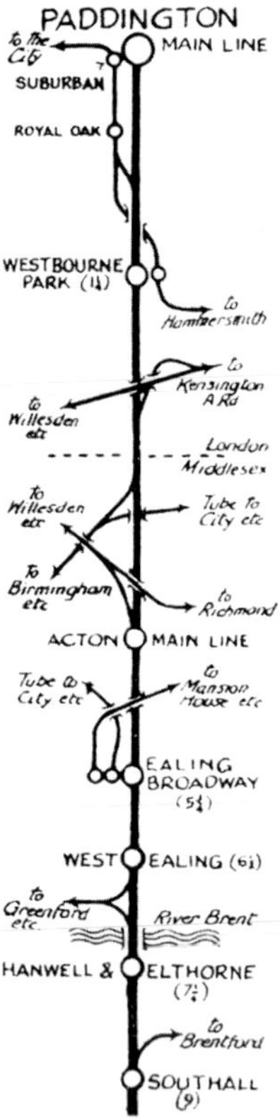

The Route of the "Cornish Riviera Express"

OUR journey begins beneath the great arch of Paddington station, designed by Brunel after the style of Paxton's Crystal Palace for the 1851 Exhibition and erected in 1854. The first few miles of the trip are not exactly attractive, as we thread a path through the gaunt terraces and tenements of West London and past the extensive carriage sidings of Old Oak, where our train was cleaned and prepared for its journey. Just before Westbourne Park the electric line of London Transport from the City to Hammersmith crosses beneath us. Near Old Oak sidings and also on the right is the big Old Oak Common locomotive depot, which services the motive power for trains out of Paddington. A "flying junction" allows engines and carriage stock to cross from the down side to Old Oak over our heads, thus avoiding interference with the main line. Acton is also the location of a great freight yard, connected by cross-London railways with the other main lines out of the capital to North, East and South; a heavy transfer goods traffic is worked over these orbital lines, and you will possibly notice engines of the London Midland, Eastern and Southern Regions in the Acton goods yards.

The Western exit from London is one of the most encouraging of any from the capital so far as the driver is concerned, for the line is either dead level or very faintly against the engine all the way to Reading; this is part of the old London-Bristol main line of Brunel, who spared no

4

expense to avoid undue gradients. Thus we shall be gathering speed swiftly as we cross the Brent river and Uxbridge Road—the continuation of London's celebrated shopping centre, Oxford Street—on the lofty Wharncliffe Viaduct, near Hanwell. Rightwards there is a distant view of Harrow-on-the-Hill, crowned by its parish church spire, beneath the shadow of which is the famous public school that educated Byron, Sir Winston Churchill and many another famous man. Beyond Hanwell on the left is the great A.E.C. motor works, where many of London's buses—and the Western Region's diesel railcars—amongst other vehicles, have been manufactured.

Southall is another busy goods centre, with yards served by their own engine shed (on the left), for we are in the midst of the extensive industrial areas of West London and passing factories labelled with the names of many famous products; one of the biggest is the E.M.I. plant, home of His Master's Voice and Columbia gramophone records, which adjoins the line on the right just beyond Hayes station.

Beyond Langley there will be a view on the left-hand horizon of Windsor Castle, and we shall have frequent glimpses of it as far as Maidenhead; Windsor is about 2 miles from our route at Slough, a busy junction and industrial centre with its own locomotive depot (on the left beyond the station), which is the terminus of many suburban services from London. On the other side of Slough there is a distant view of Burnham Beeches, the last relics of an ancient forest. The Thames is approaching us from the left and just before Maidenhead we cross the wide river on a graceful bridge, from Buckinghamshire into Berkshire.

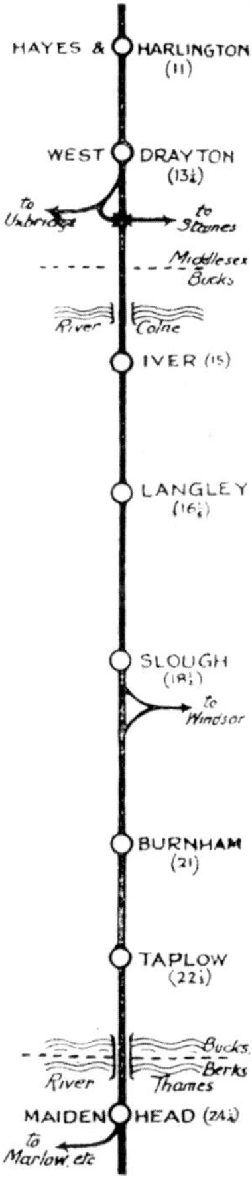

A.T.C. IN ACTION—W.R. 2-6-0 No. 5380 at Southall passes over an A.T.C. ramp and whistles, for the neighbouring distant signal is on and a horn has sounded in the engine's cab. [*P. Ransome-Wallis*

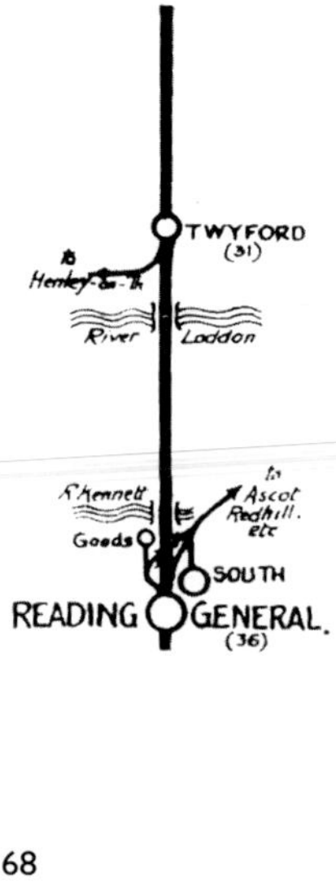

The Thames valley is prone to mist, but even in thick fog Western expresses are able to keep moving at a good pace quite safely, thanks to Automatic Train Control, or A.T.C. for short. At each " distant signal ", the warning signal which tells a driver whether he must be prepared to halt at the next "stop" signal, a ramp is laid between the running rails. A contact beneath the locomotive buffer beam strikes the ramp as the engine passes over it; if the distant signal is showing a caution aspect the ramp is dead, a loud horn blasts in the engine cab and automatically the brakes are partially applied as a warning to the driver, but if the signal is showing clear, the ramp is electrified, sounds a cheerful bell on the footplate to reassure the driver, and the train can proceed in security.

Southern electric trains are soon running

parallel with us on the left, past Huntley & Palmer's big biscuit works, into their own station at Reading, while we slow slightly through the bigger Western station for the curve beyond it, which will carry us away leftward from Brunel's original Bristol main line on to the newer "Berkshire & Hampshire" route to the West Country. There is a good view on the right of the Reading locomotive depot in the "V" of this junction. After a short stretch of downhill beyond Reading the railway begins a long climb up the valley of the Kennet River which lasts for 31 miles. Except for the last three miles, however, the slope is very gentle.

Incidentally, if you want to check your speed, keep watch on the right-hand, or "up" side, for the mileposts. These are spaced at intervals of a quarter-mile, and each shows a mileage figure, or a mileage figure and below it "1", "2" or "3", indicating an additional "$\frac{1}{4}$", "$\frac{1}{2}$" or "$\frac{3}{4}$" mile. If you count the number of seconds the train takes to cover a quarter-mile between any two of these posts and divide the answer into 900, the result will be your speed in miles per hour, e.g., a quarter-mile covered in 15 seconds equals 60 m.p.h. As far as Westbury these points indicate the mileage from Paddington by the direct route we have travelled; from Westbury, however, the mileage shown is from Paddington via Swindon and Trowbridge, and from Taunton onwards from Paddington via Bristol (Temple Meads). The reason for these variations, of course, is the fact that sections of the present route to the West Country were constructed at widely spaced intervals, as was mentioned in the introduction to this booklet.

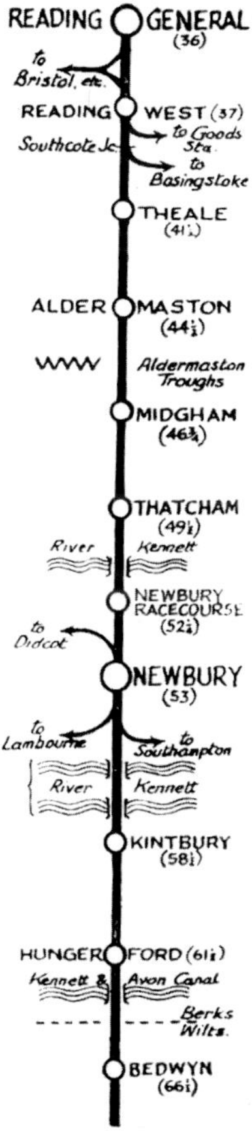

Inside the slip-guard's compartment. The light-painted handle is his hand-brake control, while the lever underneath the window controls the coupling hook. [British Railways

A slip-coach at the rear of a Western Region express. Notice the additional white-ringed tail lamp denoting the fact that the last vehicle is a slip-coach. [G. F. Heiron

8

A large racecourse on the left heralds our approach to the old town of Newbury, a borough at least as early as the 12th Century. Hungerford is another picturesque old market town, and there is an excellent view of its main street on the left as soon as you have passed the station. On the same side of us the Kennet river becomes the Kennet & Avon canal, built to provide a through waterway from London to Bristol, and several locks are visible from the train. More interesting still is the tunnel into which the canal dives to pass underneath us at Savernake station ; you can see the entrance on the left. The $3\frac{1}{2}$ miles from Bedwyn to Savernake are the culmination of the long climb from Reading, which ends somewhat steeply at gradients varying from 1 in 106 to 1 in 175.

The descent from Savernake is nearly as lengthy as the ascent and equally gentle for the most part. We are now threading the Vale of Pewsey with Salisbury Plain rolling away to the left and Marlborough downs on the right. At three places these chalk escarpments have been shaved of grass in the design of gigantic white horses. The first will be noticed on the left at Pewsey and was cut as recently as 1937 in honour of King George VI's Coronation. There is another, somewhat older, on the other side of the line at Woodborough, adorning Milk Hill; this one is 165 ft. long and 180 ft. high and was cut in 1812. The oldest of them all, however, is the Westbury Horse, on the left-hand side, of which the best view is obtained by looking backward as the train passes it. Tradition has it that the Westbury Horse was traced to commemorate a victory of the Saxon King Alfred over the Danes in A.D. 878.

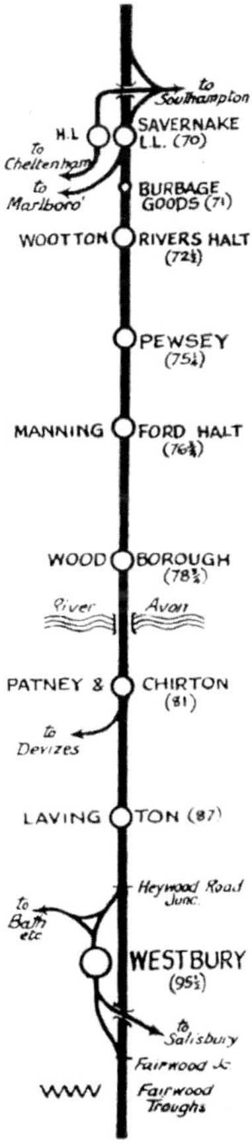

THE WESTBURY HORSE is cut in chalk on the hill in the extreme right background. "Castle" Class 4-6-0 No. 5071 *Spitfire* heads a Devon-bound express on the Westbury avoiding line.

[*R. J. Doran*

10

The "Cornish Riviera" sheds some of its load at Westbury (except on summer Saturdays), even though it does not stop there. It manages this by "slipping" a coach or two. This was a device much in British railway favour in earlier days, but now the Western Region alone persists with a few examples of it; the object is to serve as many stations as possible along a train's route without stopping and restarting the main train. The front coach of a "slip" portion includes a special guard's compartment and coupling arrangements. About half-a-mile from the destination of the "slip" the slip guard operates controls to release his section from the main train; a special hinged drawhook opens to release the coupling of the adjacent coach, the last vehicle on the main train, and the continuous brake pipes snap apart. The latter event would normally bring both main train and "slip" to a standstill automatically, but the pipes of the train's last coach and the slip coach are provided with valves which promptly seal each one off to maintain the brake pressure. The slip is now entirely under the slip guard's control, and using his own brake handle he brings it smoothly to rest at the required point.

At one time the "Riviera" used to slip a Minehead portion at Taunton and another at Exeter, but to-day only the Weymouth "slip" still operates; it is cut off at Heywood Road Junction and worked into Westbury by a shunting engine for attachment there to a Weymouth train, since the "Riviera" by-passes Westbury via the 1933 avoiding line.

Two miles beyond Westbury our engine will take a drink for the second time since it left London. The tender of a "King"

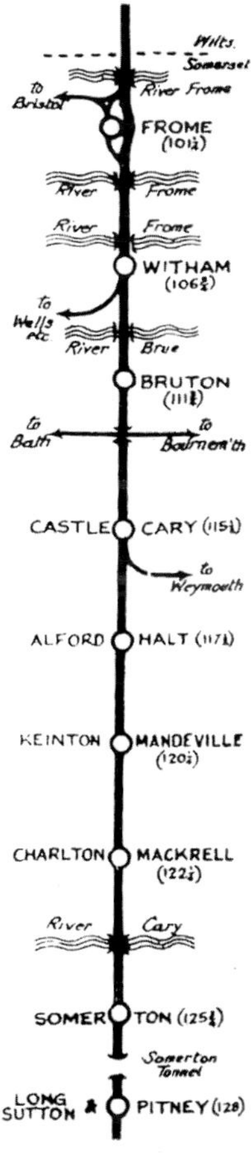

ON ALDERMASTON TROUGHS—" County " Class 4-6-0 No. 1010 *County of Caernarvon* takes a drink on its way west with the 11 a.m. Paddington-Plymouth express. [*C. G. Pearson*

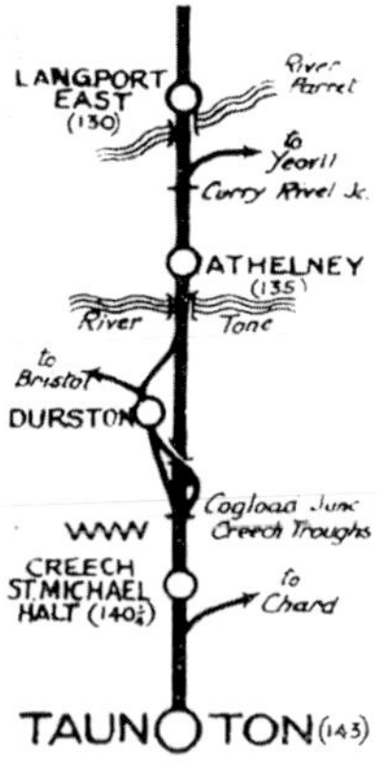

class locomotive holds only 4,000 gallons, whereas its boiler has been consuming water at the rate of 40-50 gallons per mile. To save having to stop especially for more water, water troughs are spaced out at suitable intervals along the route; the first was at Aldermaston, between Reading and Newbury, and there will be others near Taunton and beyond Exeter. As his train approaches the troughs, the fireman lowers a sharp-bladed scoop beneath the tender that cuts into the water, forcing it up at high velocity into the tender. Fine judgment is necessary to withdraw the scoop before the tender is overfull, or an overflow will burst out of the opening at the top of the tender, spattering unwary passengers in the first one or two coaches of the train who have their windows open.

From Frome the railway climbs up to the top of a limestone ridge and then strikes the steep descent of Brewham bank beyond Witham; there are pitches varying from 1 in 81 to 1 in 98, and speed may well be in the 80-85 m.p.h. range by the time we rush through Castle Cary, where the slope flattens. To the right there is a distant view of the pinnacle of Glastonbury Tor before we plunge into Somerton Tunnel and resume our descent to Athelney Marshes.

The line is now fringed on the right by the plain of Sedgemoor (where the last battle on English soil was fought in 1685), backed by the Polden Hills. As we race across Athelney marsh one recalls the apocryphal legend of King Alfred and the cakes, an improbable incident which is supposed to have occurred when the Saxon monarch was holding out in the area in his long struggle against the Danes.

At Cogload Junction the old Bristol route of the "Cornish Riviera" makes a flying junction with the present line. Then, after taking water from Creech troughs, we pass through Taunton, Somerset's county town, with a full history going back to Saxon times.

As we leave the long ridge of the Quantock Hills, which has been visible on the right for some distance before Taunton, we begin at Norton Fitzwarren our attack on another range, the Blackdowns, which bestride our path. You can see the hills ahead, with the conspicuous Wellington Monument on a ridge overlooking the town.

The bank gradually increases in severity, culminating in three miles of 1 in 80-90 before the train enters Whiteball Tunnel. It was down this incline, in the reverse

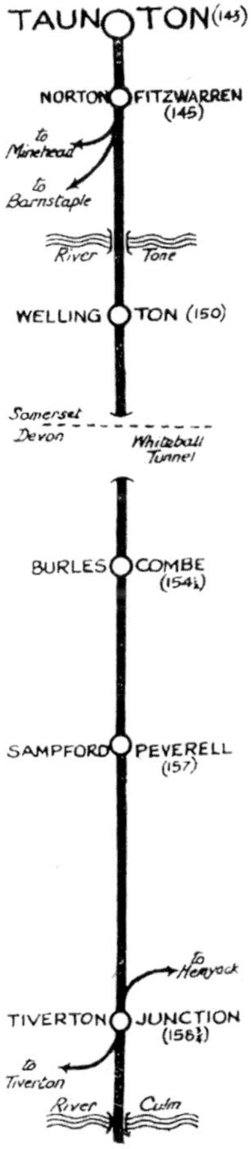

EMERGING FROM WHITEBALL TUNNEL, 4-6-0 No. 6021 *King Richard II* begins the long descent to Exeter with the westbound "Cornish Riviera Express." [*J. G. Hubback*

direction, that the first 100 m.p.h. was reputedly achieved in 1904, by a Great Western 4-4-0 with a lightweight Ocean Mails flier from Plymouth to London in 1904; the engine concerned, *City of Truro*, is now preserved in York Railway Museum.

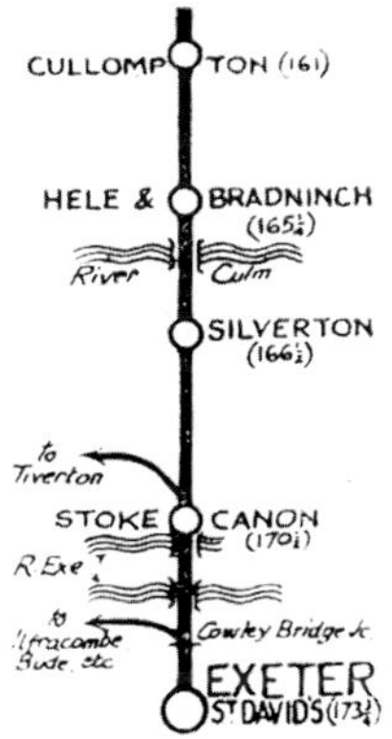

From Whiteball it is downhill through the Culm valley for the next 20 odd miles to Exeter, first for two miles at 1 in 115, and then on gradually more easy gradients. In Whiteball tunnel we crossed the border from Somerset into Devon; you will notice visible evidence of this in the Cullompton church spire, whose red Devon stone is in contrast to the grey of similar buildings in Somerset. At Stoke Canon the Exe river, sweeping down from distant Exmoor, joins the Culm for the last few miles through a beautiful wooded valley into Exeter.

St. David's station at Exeter is one of the small number in Britain at which you have to be careful that the train you are catching is going in the right direction. In addition to W.R. trains, it offers hospitality to Southern trains between London and Plymouth and the North Devon coast. The latter trace nearly a semi-circle down a very steep bank (1 in 37) from their own Central station to St. David's, so that S.R. trains *from* London arrive in St. David's facing the direction we have come, and actually retrace just over a mile of our route before diverging leftward at Cowley Bridge Junction; similarly any Southern train standing in the station and facing westward as we pass through is headed *for* London. You can clearly see the steepness of the Southern line up to Central station as it climbs away leftward beyond St. David's.

The best view of the ancient city, on its hill—or *Rougemont*, the name taken by its castle—is not to be seen until we have passed St. Thomas station, when a glance rearward to the left finds the sturdy towers of the Norman cathedral dominating the skyline. The West Front of this building, which was erected between 1280 and 1369, is one of the most ornate in the country and is covered with statuary. Little remains of the neighbouring Rougemont Castle, which was built by William the Conqueror.

EXETER CATHEDRAL—The superbly decorated West Front. [*British Railways*

ALONG THE DAWLISH SEAWALL—Freight 2-8-0 No. 3803 heads for Exeter with a goods from the West Country. [*H. Gordon Tidey*

16

On a fine day, the run westwards from Exeter is a delight. Once the clutter of terraces and industry round the old port of Exeter is left behind, the train glides through rich pastureland rolling down from Great Haldon, the ridge on the right, to the Exe river and its attendant canal, up which small coastal ships still sail to Exeter. Then, just short of Exminster, the river suddenly broadens into an estuary, speckled with all manner of birds from swans to herons. As you run over Exminster watertroughs and round the promontory at Powderham, there is a glimpse of Powderham Castle nestling in the trees on the right, while on the left the wide sea is coming into view beyond Exmouth, across the estuary.

Beyond Starcross the rolling Channel fills the view from the carriage window, for the railway appropriates a sea-wall position which it occupies for most of the way to Teignmouth; in fact, the sea wall and the fine railside walk along it from Dawlish Warren to Dawlish and from Parson's Tunnel to Teignmouth belong to the railway. After Teignmouth, the railway turns inland up the bank of the Teign estuary, and one can discern on the skyline ahead the granite " fangs " of Hay Tor, 1,491 ft. above sea level, an intimation of the railway's approach to Dartmoor and the hard work ahead of the engine, which is soon drifting past the extensive Hackney marshalling yards and into Newton Abbot.

Although the timetable does not indicate a stop at Newton Abbot, the " Cornish Riviera " does in fact make one away from the platforms and alongside the Newton Abbot locomotive works (on the left), to take on a pilot engine for help up the steep South Devon banks to come.

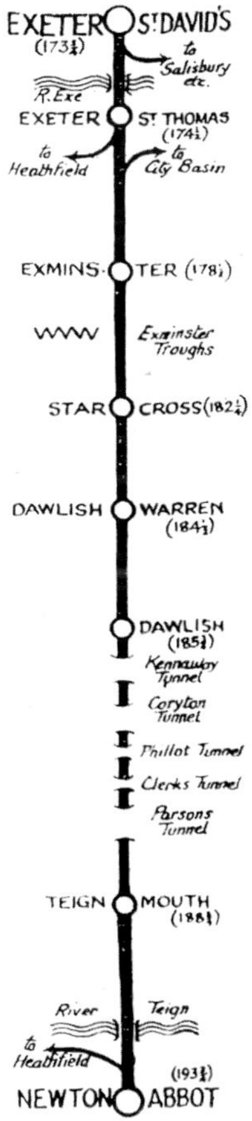

17

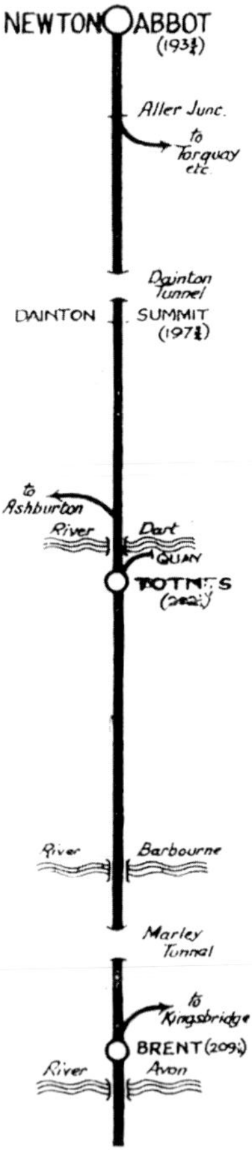

We steam out of Newton Abbot, past the locomotive shed on the left, to attack one of the most severe inclines on British Railways. It begins at Aller Junction. The ruling gradient for the next 2½ miles, as the line winds upwards, is 1 in 46 and 1 in 36 at its steepest pitch near the summit. Even a mighty " King " is not allowed to attempt more than 360 tons—about 10 or 11 coaches—up this and the following incline unaided, so that almost all trains are double-headed or banked between Newton Abbot and the summit. On summer Saturdays this is one of the few places you can regularly see a train double-headed by two " Kings ". On those days the " Cornish Riviera " proper does not stop at Plymouth, but changes engines at Newton Abbot and then runs non-stop to Truro on its way to St. Ives; the " King " with which it parts company at Newton Abbot is then attached in front of the " King " hauling the following 10.35 a.m. from Paddington and pilots the latter through from Newton Abbot to Plymouth.

Near the top of Dainton bank is a quarry, in which the exhausts of our pounding engines reverberate fiercely, until they are suddenly stilled by the 272-yard Dainton Tunnel, at the other end of which is the summit. The descent from the top to Totnes, one of the oldest boroughs in England, nestling in the hollow of the Dart Valley, is equally precipitous.

Then, straight from the platform end of Totnes station the line is launched on the 9 miles of Rattery bank, which is mostly steeper than 1 in 60 for the first 2½ miles and 1 in 46 at its worst. The drivers' eyes will be searching for the welcome tall spire of Tigley church, where the gradient eases

DAINTON BANK—" Grange " Class 4-6-0 No. 6874 *Haughton Grange* pilots " King " Class 4-6-0 No. 6022 *King Edward III* up the steep climb from Newton Abbot with a Paddington-Plymouth express. [*M. E. Ware*

19

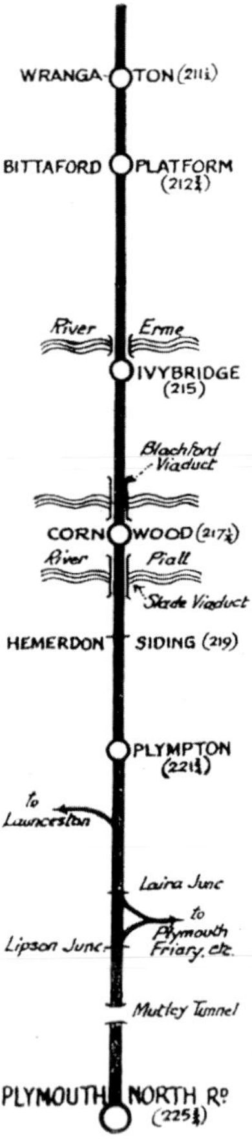

to the 1 in 90s and better, and the shapes of Brent and Dean Moor, outliers of Dartmoor, rise ahead above the intervening hills. By Rattery signalbox the line has climbed 351 ft. in just over 4½ miles from Totnes and the bleaker southern slopes of the moors have been reached. Just beyond this box the line enters the 869 yards Marley Tunnel.

At Wrangaton we reach a summit 442 ft. above the level of Totnes and a glorious descent to the outskirts of Plymouth begins; high speeds are barred, however, owing to the sharp curvature of the railway, To the left there is a broad rolling view over a series of ridges, while to the right the line is skirting the edge of Butterdon Hill, whose slopes are rich with the relics—pillars, hut circles and barrows—of Bronze Age man that abound on Dartmoor. Now massive stone viaducts march across the glens that have been cut by streams flowing down from the moors, where once Brunel's timber spans linked slender stone piers with graceful tracery. All five of these viaducts—Glaze, Bittaford, Ivybridge, Blachford and Slade—were replaced by masonry structures in 1893, though at Ivybridge at least traces of Brunel's bridge may still be seen. Particularly impressive is the view up the Yealm valley to the grim Penn and Stall Moors and the 1,546 ft. summit of Shell Top as the train curves over Blachford viaduct into Cornwood.

At Hemerdon signalbox the line suddenly sweeps downhill. through a wooded avenue where falling leaves in autumn can make the track a greasy nightmare for eastbound trains grinding up the 1 in 42 bank. Beyond Plympton the yards of Tavistock Junction come into sight before the railway crosses the Plym river and enters the rather drab suburbs of Plymouth, passing Laira locomotive depot on the left.

Our powerful "King" is not allowed to work beyond Plymouth, as it is too heavy for some of the bridges to come, and it will be replaced there by a "Castle" 4-6-0 or possibly a "Britannia" Pacific for the remainder of our journey westward. This begins somewhat drearily through the suburbs of Plymouth and Devonport, but after a sharp descent through Keyham, the railway climbs steeply up to cross the Tamar Estuary to Saltash by one of the most celebrated and graceful bridges in Britain, Brunel's Royal Albert Bridge. The railway is single-track across it, and if you lean out of the window as the "Cornish Riviera" approaches it you will see the driver collect from a signalbox the token, or "tablet", of which he must be in possession before he can enter the single-line section; possession of this token reassures him, in addition to the normal protection of semaphore signals and other safety apparatus, that he alone has the authority to be on the single line, and that there is no danger of a train from the opposite direction meeting us head-on 110 ft. above the water. This is the height of the rails above the estuary over the 2,220 ft. long bridge, from which there is a superb view of naval craft riding at anchor, and away to the moors above Tavistock.

Throughout much of Cornwall the railway traverses high ground and crosses the intervening valleys and gullies by a succession of lofty viaducts. Originally they were built completely of timber or of timber spans on stone pillars; in some of the latter cases the old pillars remain, but they are now surmounted by steelwork.

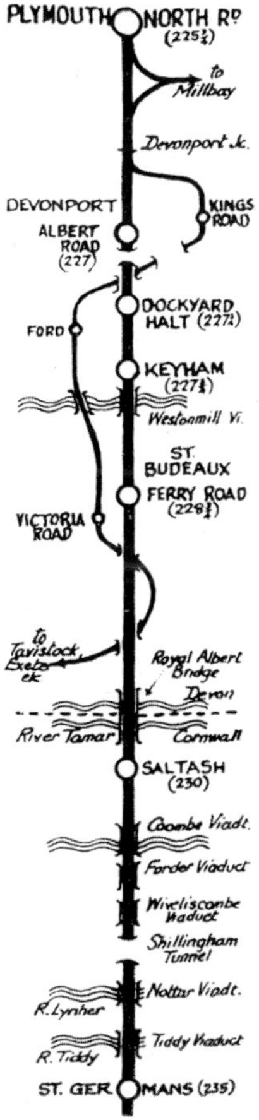

THE ROYAL ALBERT BRIDGE, SALTASH—A striking view of this magnificent structure from a coach of the up "Cornish Riviera Express" heading for Plymouth. [*N. R. Kemp*

The line through Cornwall is fiercely graded and at St. Germans we begin the long climb up to Doublebois, mostly on gradients steeper than 1 in 100 and in places as steep as 1 in 59. There is a short level " breather " at the approach to Menheniot, and then a sudden downhill plunge through Liskeard to the lengthy Moorswater viaduct. From the right-hand side of the carriage you can clearly see alongside the present structure the piers of the old timber viaduct which used to span the valley here; far below, too, you can see the branch line to Looe, which has curved right round in sharp descent from Liskeard station. Then the uphill grind is resumed to the fringe of Bodmin Moor, the heights of which can be seen in the right distance.

From Doublebois the railway sweeps steeply downhill through the richly wooded Glynn valley in company with the river Fowey to Lostwithiel; again the gradients are steeper than 1 in 100, but the curvature of the line precludes any really fast running. The second viaduct beyond Doublebois, St. Pinnock, is a fine example of a case where the pillars of the original viaduct, which were linked by timber spans, have been adapted to carry more modern steel spans. This is the highest vaiduct in Cornwall, lifting the railway 153 ft. above the ground.

Beyond Lostwithiel the railway surmounts a steeply-inclined hump crowned by Treverrin Tunnel, then comes to an unexpected hive of railway activity at Par. This is the junction for the fascinating branch which curves away to the right beyond the station and clambers up the Luxulyan Valley at 1 in 40 to the moors above Newquay. From these moors come many wagonloads of china clay, to be

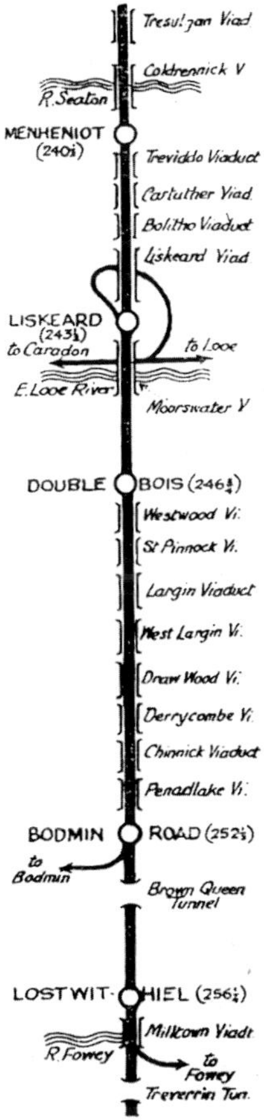

BY RAIL THROUGH THE CORNISH VALLEYS—A Penzance-Plymouth train climbs the Glynn Valley from Bodmin Road eastward, headed by "Castle" Class 4-6-0 No. 4087 *Cardigan Castle.* [*B. A. Butt*

24

hauled down the goods line extending south to Fowey. To deal with this traffic, more of which comes from pits we shall soon be seeing for ourselves, and the heavy summer passenger traffic on the Newquay branch, there is a sizeable engine shed on the right beyond Par, known as St. Blazey.

A long climb, again mainly 1 in 60-65, follows Par as the railway mounts up to the cliffs overlooking the 4-mile wide St. Austell bay, guarded at each end by Gribben Head and Black Head. Then, as the railway turns inland near St. Austell we catch our first glimpse of the curious white cones of the clay pit tips.

China clay was discovered in Cornwall in the 18th Century, and has since taken the place of copper and tin as Cornwall's chief mining product; in many parts of the county you will notice the derelict chimneys that mark the site of the once prosperous metal mines—perhaps you noticed some curious tower-like structures on the hills above Lostwithiel, on the left, which are the relics of abandoned copper workings. To-day china clay is transported all over the country and has many uses, notably in the manufacture of paper, pottery and calico.

The high ground on the right beyond St. Austell is Burngullow Common, 663 ft. high. Burngullow station, whence a goods line runs away rightward to the china clay pits inland, is a summit beyond which the railway sweeps downhill again to a viaduct over the Fal river and into a path between the Trevan and Tremouth woods. Then the work is uphill again at Grampound Road, and down one of Cornwall's steepest banks—nearly two miles of continuous 1 in 67—to Probus & Ladock.

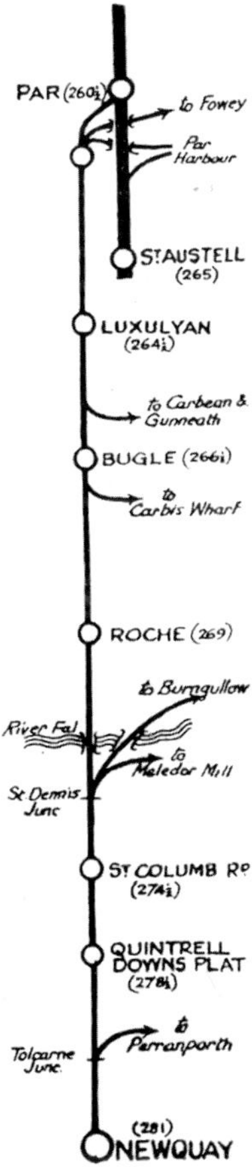

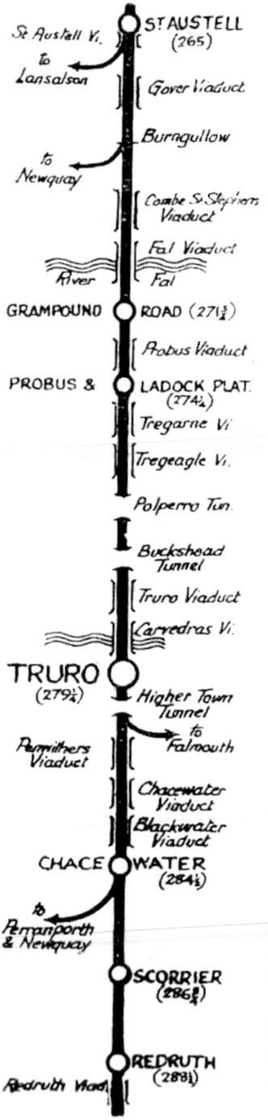

The long viaduct at Truro offers a splendid view of the city's cathedral on the left. This is a modern structure as cathedrals go, dating from the 19th Century. As the engine attacks the three-mile bank at 1 in 90 out of Truro there is a beautiful view down the river.

Redruth, the centre of Cornwall's once flourishing tin industry, is of special interest to the rail travellers who pass through it, for here worked one of the earliest pioneers of the steam locomotive. It was in the streets of this town that, legend has it, a parson was once scared out of his wits by a fearful contraption, snorting fiercely and emitting a shower of sparks, which advanced upon him as he took a late stroll one night in 1786. It was not the devil incarnate, as the reverend gentleman feared, but a small steam-driven carriage, the invention of a pumping engineer named William Murdoch. Unfortunately, Murdoch's employers thought he was wasting their time and forbade him to tinker any more with such a ridiculous project, but his friend Richard Trevithick was able to develop Murdoch's ideas and, in 1804, produced the first railway engine in the world.

Beyond Redruth, the 1,100 ft. high Carn Brea dominates the landscape to the left. Carn Brea was a fortified stronghold in pre-Roman times, and many stone Age relics have been found there. Soon we reach the north coast of Cornwall at Hayle, a picturesque town at the head of St. Ives Bay, and in the distance the delightful seaside resort of the bay's name can be seen.

The luxuriant palm trees on the platforms of St. Erth add point to the title of our train. From here runs a single-line branch down the western shore of the bay to St.

Ives, where the " Cornish Riviera " terminates just above the town's golden sands on a summer Saturday. On other days the express turns back across the peninsula to the south coast and Penzance. As you approach Marazion you can see across the marshes the 231 ft. high cone of St. Michael's Mount. This curious outpost of slate and granite 400 yards from the shore, can be reached on dry land by a narrow causeway at low tide. Soon the " Riviera " slows to its last halt in the terminus of Penzance.

TRURO CATHEDRAL [Crown Copyright

27

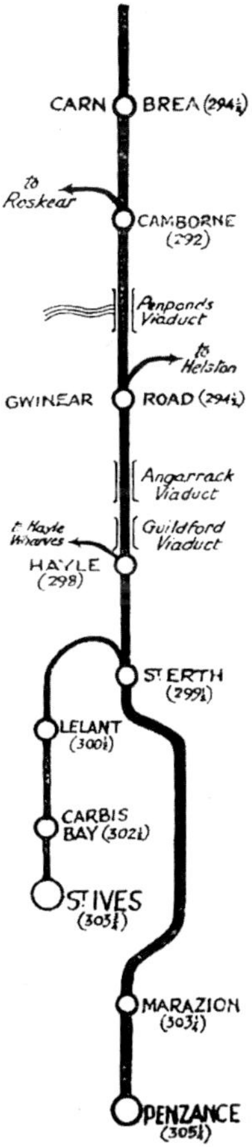

CLOSE-UP of " King " Class 4-6-0 No. 6000 *King George V*. [*G. R. Wheeler*

FROM Paddington to Plymouth our train will be hauled by a " King " Class 4-6-0 of a type introduced in 1927. No. 6000, the pioneer engine, carries a bell on its front bufferbeam presented by the Baltimore & Ohio Railroad after No. 6000 had visited the U.S.A. for the American railroad's centenary celebrations in the autumn of 1927.

" KING " CLASS 4-6-0 DIMENSIONS

Weights: *Locomotive*—89 tons 0 cwt. *Tender*—46 tons 14 cwt.
Boiler Pressure: 250 lb. per sq. in.
Cylinders(4): 16¼in. diameter × 28in. stroke.
Driving Wheel Diameter: 6 ft. 6 in. *Tractive Effort:* 40,285 lb.

" KING " CLASS 4-6-0 NUMBERS AND NAMES

6000	King George V	6010	King Charles I	6020	King Henry IV
6001	King Edward VII	6011	King James I	6021	King Richard II
6002	King William IV	6012	King Edward VI	6022	King Edward III
6003	King George IV	6013	King Henry VIII	6023	King Edward II
6004	King George III	6014	King Henry VII	6024	King Edward I
6005	King George II	6015	King Richard III	6025	King Henry III
6006	King George I	6016	King Edward V	6026	King John
6007	King William III	6017	King Edward IV	6027	King Richard I
6008	King James II	6018	King Henry VI	6028	King George VI
6009	King Charles II	6019	King Henry V	6029	King Edward VIII

famous trains — 4

The

ATLANTIC COAST EXPRESS

WATERLOO—ILFRACOMBE, PADSTOW & PLYMOUTH

(Southern Region)

by

G. FREEMAN ALLEN

Ian Allan Ltd

ON THE FRINGE OF DARTMOOR—" West Country " Pacific No. 34031 *Torrington* and a Waterloo-Plymouth express ride high above the West Okement river valley, crossing Meldon Viaduct on the last 1 in 77 stretch of their long climb up from Exeter. [*M. E. Ware*

Introduction

FROM the days of the former London & South Western Railway a train has left Waterloo for the holiday resorts of South Devon and North Cornwall at about 11 a.m., but the title of "Atlantic Coast Express" was not bestowed upon it until 1927. To-day it has several claims to distinction.

Firstly, the "Atlantic Coast Express"—or "ACE", as it is popularly known by its initials—includes through coaches for more different destinations than any other British express. At the front of the train are three coaches for Ilfracombe; then come four coaches, one each for Torrington, Padstow, Bude and Plymouth; the restaurant cars are next, and they are detached at Exeter; then come two more coaches, one for Exmouth and one for Sidmouth; and finally, one for stations from Salisbury to Seaton. This adds up to a remarkable total of nine different portions on one train! On summer Saturdays, however, the "ACE" runs as two separate trains, one for Ilfracombe and Torrington and one for Bude and Padstow; Sidmouth, Exmouth, Seaton and Lyme Regis are served by other trains.

Secondly, the "ACE" is one of the few trains in Britain that are already running faster than before the last war, for since the summer of 1952 it has been the first Southern train to be timed over a section of its journey at an average of better than 60 m.p.h. from start to stop; this it achieves by covering the 83.7 miles to Salisbury in 83 minutes. Schedules of this sort are by no means easy to achieve on the Southern Region. In the London area the train has to thread its way through the busiest suburban service in the country, while west of Salisbury the line is a series of fiercely graded switchbacks almost all the way to Exeter, so that the "ACE's" time of 185 minutes for the 171.7 miles from London to Exeter, including slowing for two stops and 8 minutes spent standing at them, is an excellent achievement.

The "ACE's" other feature worth comment is that it is one of the few British expresses which have been hauled by a diesel-electric, instead of a steam locomotive. Under the British Railways modernisation plan, diesel haulage will be extended to all traffic, passenger and freight, between Waterloo and the West Country, but it is likely to be a year or so before the last of the Pacific engines listed at the end of this booklet leave the route on which they achieved such great successes.

The Route of the " ACE"

THE start from Waterloo is the most interesting of any from London termini. The railway runs for most of the way to Clapham Junction on an embankment or over bridges among the city's rooftops, and parallel with the Thames as far as Vauxhall. Thus, as the "ACE" winds out of the station over the sharp curves at the approach to Waterloo, there is a wonderful view to the right of the Houses of Parliament, Big Ben and Westminster Abbey across the river; on the Waterloo bank the big red-tiled roof of County Hall, headquarters of the London County Council, is conspicuous and, a short distance further on, you will notice the tree-hedged Lambeth Palace, home of the Archbishop of Canterbury. At the approach to Vauxhall, the long facade and dome of the Tate Gallery can be glimpsed on the other side of the Thames, but on the other side of Vauxhall the right-hand view is taken up by the big Nine Elms goods station.

NOTE: The figures in brackets after station names indicate mileages from Waterloo.

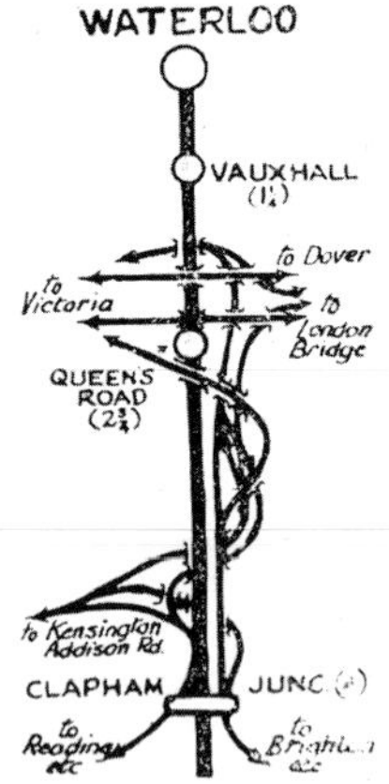

Railway enthusiasts will be looking left, however, for a sight of Nine Elms locomotive depot and then, just after the Victoria-Kent Coast main line has bridged us, for Stewarts Lane locomotive depot on a level below us. On the other side of the line the majestic chimneys of Battersea Power station, a great modern edifice designed by Lutyens, lazily disgorge white smoke.

Now we are among the maze of junctions and carriage sidings at the approach to Clapham Junction, where the Victoria-South Coast line sweeps down from the left to run parallel with us through the busiest station in the world. Over 2,000 trains pass through its platforms every weekday, and at the morning or evening rush-hour there is not a moment when you can stand on its platforms and not see a train approaching, leaving or standing at the station.

The big factory-like building close to the

lineside on the right as we approach Wimbledon is the Durnsford Road power station, supplier of current to the electric lines into and out of Waterloo; electric trains are stored in the car sheds just beyond it. Wimbledon is the terminus of District line trains of London Transport, which occupy platforms on the right of the station. If you are travelling in summer, the riot of colour in Carter's seed-testing beds will catch your eye on the left after Raynes Park. Here and at all the branch line junctions on this route as far as Hampton Court Junction, beyond Surbiton, you will see one reason why the Southern can run its expresses so smartly out of London, despite the intense surbuban service. In every case interference with main line traffic is avoided by carrying the branch line over by a flying junction or burrowing it under the main line to join the up or down slow line from Waterloo, according to whether the branch is coming in from the left or right of us, instead of laying it right across the main lines on the flat. Naturally, flying or burrowing junctions are a more expensive way of doing things than ordinary flat junctions, but in the long run they pay tremendous dividends in keeping heavy traffic moving efficiently, as the Southern, which has made extensive use of them in the London area, knows to its profit.

Beyond Malden the chimneys of the modern Kingston Power station can be seen on the horizon to the right. On the other side of the track, you will notice Sandown Park racecourse beyond Esher; this is one of the well-known trio of racecourses in this area, the other two being Hurst Park and Kempton Park.

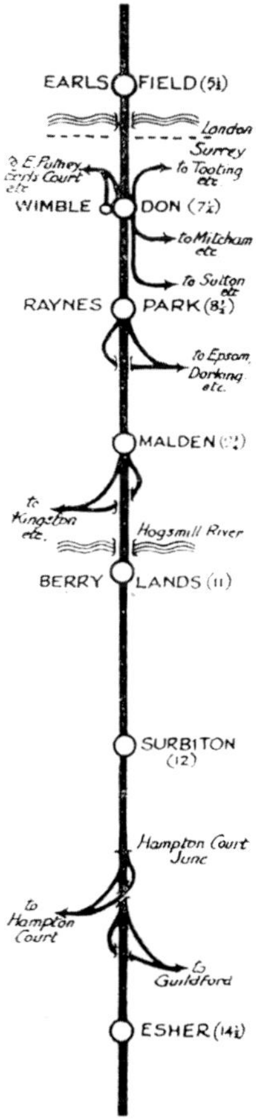

Above: WATERLOO STATION—A "West Country" Pacific sets out with an express for Devon and Cornwall. [*British Railways*

Left: PASSING WIMBLEDON—A Waterloo-West of England express headed by "Merchant Navy" Pacific No. 35016 *Elders Fyffes*. The chimneys in the background are those of Durnsford Road power station. [*R. H. Tunstall*

As the railway emerges from a long cutting at Weybridge, you will see on the left the remains of the famous Brooklands racing track, where in days gone by many a Southern express was paced by cars on the straight which paralleled the railway. Now the centre of the circuit is taken over by the Vickers-Armstrong aircraft works, and perhaps there will be a glimpse of a four-jet Valiant bomber amongst the Viscount and Viking airliners which are usually dispersed round the airfield. Hitherto the exit from Waterloo has been more or less level, but at West Byfleet there begins a long climb of some $10\frac{1}{2}$ miles at from 1 in 314 to 1 in 387 to a summit beyond Brookwood at milepost 31.

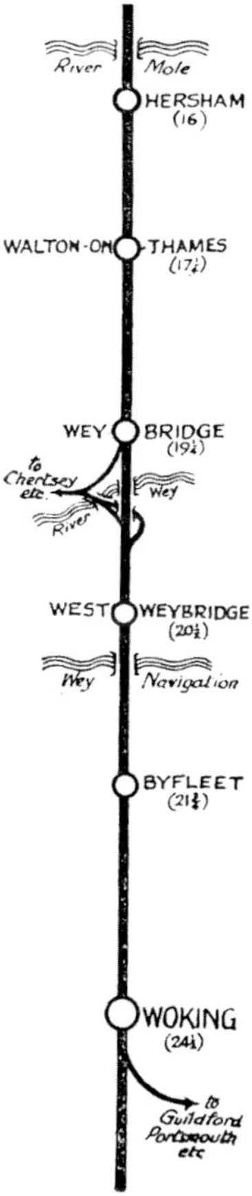

Incidentally, if you want at any time to check the distance you have travelled from Waterloo, it is continuously shown on these mileposts, which are spaced out at quarter-mile intervals by the trackside on the left; one, two or three dots or bars after the figure shown on the milepost indicates an additional $\frac{1}{4}$, $\frac{1}{2}$ or $\frac{3}{4}$ mile, though in some places the fractions are printed as such. You can use these mileposts to check the speed of your train. If you time the number of seconds you take to cover the quarter-mile between any two of these posts and divide the result into 900, the answer will be your speed in miles per hour, e.g. a quarter-mile covered in 12 seconds equals 75 m.p.h. Don't confuse the mileposts with the numbers shown on metal discs on the bridges you pass over or under, by the way; the latter are purely the reference numbers by which the bridges are known to railwaymen. The other little trackside posts, on the left, with two arms inclined at varying angles like the

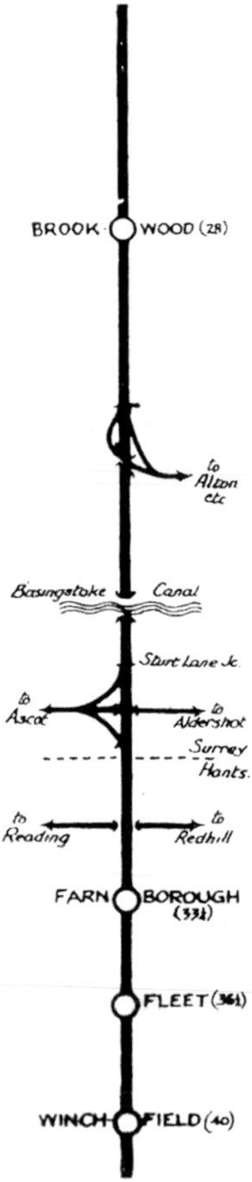

hands of a clock, indicate a change of gradient; e.g., a post with the arms at "twenty to four", with the minute hand marked "400" and the "hour hand" 200, indicates a change of incline from a rise of 1 ft. up in every 400 ft. along to 1 ft. down in every 200 ft. along.

Apart from its interest as a busy railway junction, a novel feature of Woking is the mosque you will notice on the left. The famous Necropolis lines the left side of the track before Brookwood; in days gone by special funeral trains were run to this cemetery from Waterloo. We are in Army territory now, with Pirbright Common on the left, the Bisley rifle ranges beyond the trees to our right and the line to nearby Aldershot diverging by another flying junction; just beyond this junction you will see the Basingstoke Canal on the right, and soon it crosses the railway on an aqueduct.

An interesting feature of the $23\frac{1}{2}$ miles from Woking to Basingstoke is that they are controlled by one of the earliest fully automatic signalling installations in Britain; hence the fact the signals are semaphores, whereas modern automatic installations use powerful colour lights of the type that signalled our way out from Waterloo to Hampton Court Junction, beyond Surbiton. Except at junctions, where obviously a signalman must be retained to route the trains on to their respective lines, the trains protect themselves. The basis of the system is that the two rails of each track act as outward and return leads from a source of weak electric current to the signalling apparatus and back, each track being insulated into sections controlled by a signal. When a train enters a section, it forms a short circuit for the current which, instead of reaching the signal, hops across to the opposite line straight away. This change in the current flow sets the signal to danger. It will stay at danger until the train has cleared the section, which will be long enough to leave a safe headway between it and any following train, whereupon the signal will clear again. This "track circuiting", as it is called, is the basis, not only of automatic signalling, but also of the safety devices in modern signalboxes, where it is used to lock apparatus and prevent signalmen accepting trains into sections already occupied.

From milepost 31 to a point 2 miles from Basingstoke the track is level or slightly against the engine. Perhaps by now you feel like some morning coffee? A feature of the "ACE", as of many Southern expresses, is its Tavern Car, half of which

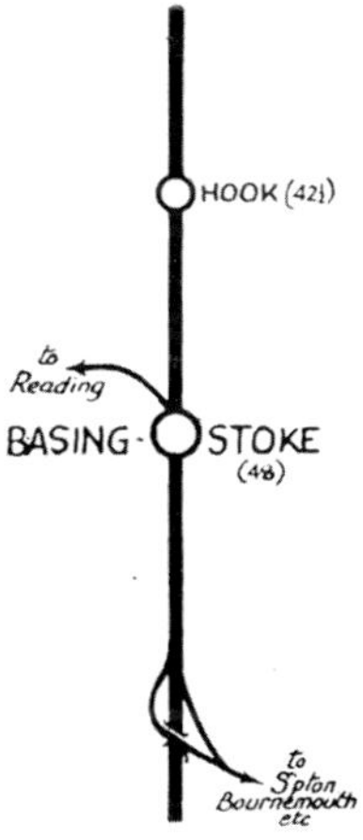

ALL SIGNALS OFF does not necessarily mean that four trains are due, for Pacific No. 34061 *73 Squadron* is speeding westward through automatically signalled territory near Hook. The signals have cleared as soon as the last trains on their respective lines have cleared the sections they protect.
[*M. W. Earley*

is given over to kitchen accommodation for the adjoining restaurant car, the remainder to a very fair reproduction of an old English inn on wheels, with imitation timbering on the walls and ceiling, leaded window-lights, tiled floor and jolly lanterns.

The market town of Basingstoke is an important junction, where we are joined by the cross-country route from the Western Region at Reading, which contributes a considerable amount of traffic from the Midlands—some of it hauled by W.R. engines—for Portsmouth and Southampton to the Southern. Basingstoke engine shed, by the way, is on the right just beyond the station. Some three miles further on is the last flying junction for many miles, at Worting, where the Southampton-Weymouth main line takes its leave of us to the

A SOUTHERN TAVERN CAR—The interior. [British Railways

left. Just before Basingstoke the gradient steepened a little to 1 in 249, a slope which, broken by a short stretch of level, takes us up to a summit 400 ft. above sea level just beyond Oakley. On this high ground the river Test, which flows into the head of Southampton Water, rises to the left of the railway. A gentle descent ensues to Hurstbourne Viaduct, which stands astride a celebrated centre for watercress and then, after a short up grade to milepost 62½, a steeper slope of 1 in 176 down for 3 miles takes us along the fringe of Harewood Forest (on the left) to Andover.

Beyond Andover we are in military territory again, for the rolling country to the right is the great Salisbury Plain. Since Andover we have been climbing once more, with a respite of only a mile downhill, and the last 3 miles up through Grateley to a summit at milepost 73¼ are graded at 1 in 165 up. On this ascent the 501 ft. high Quarley Hill, with its clear traces of the earthworks of Roman military encampments, is conspicuous on the right. From the summit we enjoy an unbroken descent to Salisbury, steepening to 1 in 140 through Porton, and here we shall probably reach speeds in the 80 m.p.h. range for the first time since we left London. As the main road from London comes in from the left at the approach to the city there will be a glimpse ahead of the superb 404 ft. high spire of the cathedral, the highest in England. Then brakes are applied to restrict speed over the sharp curve through the junction at the entrance to Fisherton Tunnel, 443 yds. long, from which we emerge to enjoy the fine view of the cathedral on the left as we approach Salisbury station.

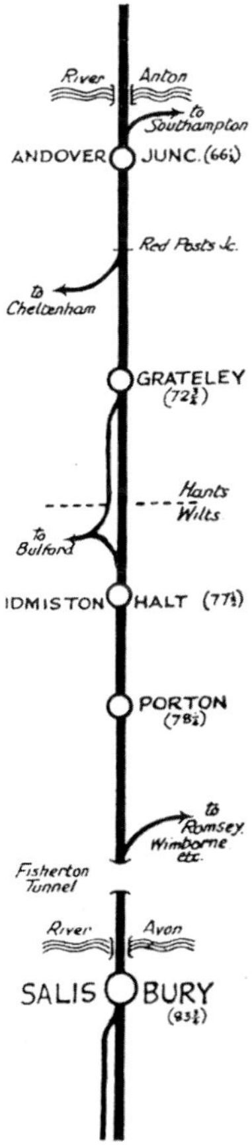

[*The Times*

SALISBURY CATHEDRAL from the air. A plume of steam to the left of the spire pin-points the railway station; the main line to Exeter skirts the high ground in the top left-hand corner of the picture on its way westward.

12

[R. E. Toop

THE SHAPE OF THINGS TO COME—Diesel-electric No. 10202 near Milborne Port with a down West of England express. Under the British Railways Modernisation Plan all traffic on this main line is to be diesel-hauled.

The present city of Salisbury has grown up round its majestic Gothic cathedral, which was built between 1220 and 1226, and houses one of the four original copies of Magna Carta. The old town of Sarum, whose history is traced back to pre-Roman times, lay 2 miles to the north. Five miles further north still is the famous assembly of standing stones known as Stonehenge, popularly believed to be the remains of a Druidical temple, but whose origins have never been established with certainty. On the railway side, the town is another meeting-place of Western and Southern Regions—indeed, the Western used to have its own station (the remains still stand alongside the present one) and engine shed; the latter is on the right, west of the station, and now houses two ancient Southern engines which are being preserved as museum pieces. Nowadays the visiting W.R. engines, which may be as large as "Castle" and "County" 4-6-0s, are serviced at the Southern locomotive shed, on the left at the west end of the station. Incidentally, all Southern trains to and from the west stop at Salisbury, partly because the Southern alone of British Railways has never laid down any watertroughs from which engines can replenish their water supplies whilst running at speed; whilst we are at rest, therefore, our engine will be refilling its tender.

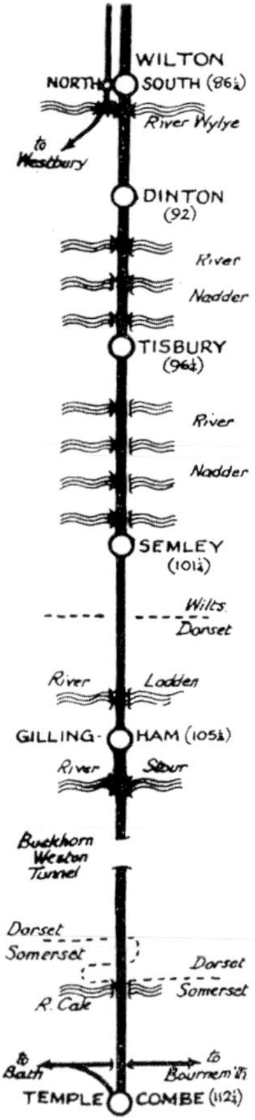

The exit from Salisbury is a sharp climb, mostly at 1 in 115, up to milepost 85¼. Soon after comes a sharp curve through Wilton, a town that has given its name to a type of carpet it was the first to manufacture, although its celebrity nowadays rests mainly on sheep-rearing. From this point the railway follows a mainly uphill path through the beautiful Nadder valley to a summit at Semley. Worth watching for is the great 16th Century tithe barn on the right just before Tisbury station; it is over 200 ft. long. At Semley there begins the amazing switchback of steep gradients for which this line is famous and which will cause our speed to alternate from the very fast, as our engine charges downhill to get a run at the next bank, to the somewhat slow, as it blasts its way up to another summit. The market town of Gillingham, for example, is at the foot of a sharp descent of 1 in 100-130 from Semley, and of a climb culminating in 1 in 100 to the 742 yd. Buckhorn Weston Tunnel; at the entrance to this tunnel the line swoops downhill again at 1 in 90/100—speed should be in the 80's at the bottom of this dip—only to charge uphill again at the same inclination through Templecombe to milepost 113½.

Templecombe is an interesting junction on two levels with the cross-country line of the former Somerset & Dorset Joint Railway, which carries through traffic from the Midlands and the North to Bournemouth via Bath. S. & D. trains cannot run straight into Templecombe station; they run beneath our route at right-angles as we approach the station, which they have to gain by reversing back into it up a spur line from their low level.

Then, after a stretch of level beyond Milborne Port, home of rural leather-making and the centre of a thriving dairy-farming area, the line sweeps downhill again through Sherborne, beginning with a mile at 1 in 80 where the speed will be whipped up into the 80 m.p.h. range. The ruins of a Norman castle, where once Sir Walter Raleigh lived and where he is alleged to have smoked his first pipe, overlook the railway from a hillock on the left as you approach the station; on the other side of the line the tower of the Abbey Church of St. Mary the Virgin, a fine example of the Perpendicular period, dominates the town, but the buildings of the famous boys' public school are not so easy to discern.

The railway avoids the busy town of Yeovil, which is served by a branch from Yeovil Junction, whence the main line begins another climb at 1 in 150-140 to milepost 126¼. After 4 miles of undulating gradients an even steeper climb begins below Crewkerne, through which station the train is battling with three miles uphill at 1 in 80; at Crewkerne, famous for its weaving and sailmaking, the sails for Nelson's *Victory* were manufactured. This ascent is followed by 13 miles of fast downhill running down the picturesque Axe valley to Axminster, the noted carpet making town. About two miles before Axminster, the railway is bridged by the ancient Fosse Way, the great Roman road which ran all the way from Lincoln through Newark, Leicester and Bath to Exeter. Between Axminster and Seaton the railway reaches its nearest point to the South Coast; just before Seaton Junction there is a brief glimpse of the sea left down the Axe valley.

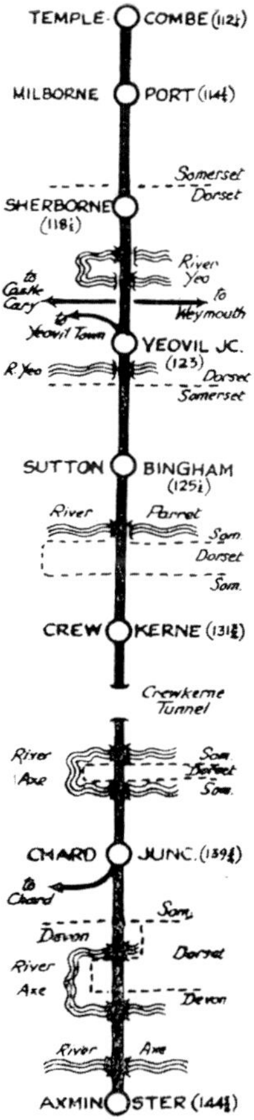

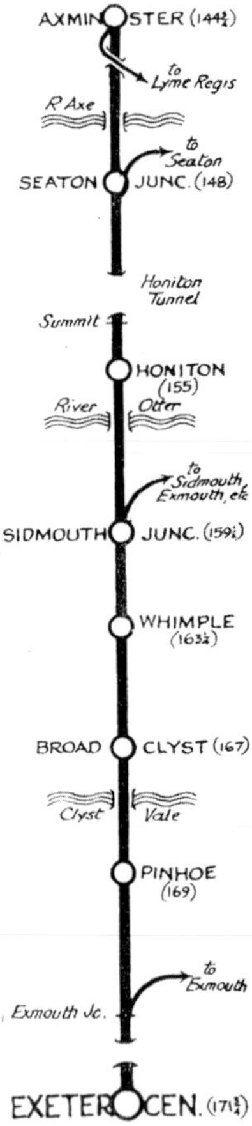

At milepost 146¼, between Axminster and Seaton, there begins one of the best-known inclines on British Railways, the arduous Honiton bank, 8 miles long and graded at 1 in 80 for nearly the whole of its final 4½ miles. From Seaton Junction, in the shadow of the 567 ft. Shute Hill (on the right), the train battles up the beautiful valley of the Umborne Brook. Near the top of the bank this stream crosses from left to right beneath us and disappears up a wild-looking valley. Soon afterwards we plunge into the 1,353 yd. Honiton Tunnel, at the other end of which is the summit of the bank. Now follows another swift descent of nearly five miles at 1 in 80-100 through Honiton station, beyond which there is an attractive view of this ancient lace-making town on the right. Suddenly our rush downhill is ended as the brakes are applied for Sidmouth Junction. This station is sited " in the wilds ", and owes its name and existence purely to the fact that it is the terminus of the branch from the main line to Sidmouth, over 8 miles away.

Nearly 2 miles from Sidmouth Junction the line sweeps downhill again at between 1 in 100 and 200 through the cider apple orchards around Whimple to Broad Clyst, beyond which point it turns uphill again at 1 in 100 through Pinhoe. The housing estates on the outskirts of Exeter come into sight on the left and soon we have a good view of Exmouth Junction motive power depot on the right (notice the great lattice tower in the shed yard with a signal arm projecting from it; this is used as a test for enginemen's sight). After a short 263 yd. tunnel we pass within the shadow of the Exeter City F.C. grandstands (on the left) at St. James Halt and then brake to a standstill at Exeter Central.

As a result of the accidents and machinations of Victorian railway history Southern trains to the West Country have to pass through the Western Region St. David's station as well as their own at Central; moreover, in pursuance of an ancient agreement between the old L.S.W.R. and G.W.R., every Southern passenger train except one in the early morning still has to stop at St. David's as well as Central. The oddity of it all is that the Southern trains to Plymouth arrive in St. David's facing in the opposite direction to W.R. trains for the same destination, and then run for just over a mile up the W.R. main line towards London before diverging left on to their own route at Cowley Bridge Junction. The connecting line between Central and St. David's, which is almost a semi-circle, is one of the steepest on any British main line; right from the platform end at Central it goes " over the top " at 1 in 37 down through a short tunnel. In the reverse direction most trains have to be assisted at the rear—and some goods trains double-headed as well—up the hill from St. David's. This results in another practice very rare in this country. On such days as a summer Saturday, when traffic up and down the bank is continuous, there is often not time to return these banking engines from Central to St. David's on their own without holding up westbound traffic. Sometimes, therefore, returning bankers are coupled on to the front of a train leaving Central for St. David's, where they are run off into a siding ready for their next banking job; this means that you will occasionally see a train cautiously descending the hill with three or even four engines at the front end!

The Southern traveller through Exeter sees little of the beautiful and historic city until he has emerged from the tunnel on the way down to St. David's. Then the Norman towers of the superb cathedral can be seen on the brow of the hill behind him; the West Front of this building, which was erected between 1280 and 1369, is one of the most ornate in the country and is covered with statuary. Little remains of the neighbouring castle, known as Rougemont and built by William the Conqueror, which stood in what is now a pleasant park overlooking Central station on the left as you arrive from London; on the opposite side of the railway here the forbidding edifice is the County gaol.

At Exeter we shall have changed our engine, be it a steam " Merchant Navy " Pacific or a diesel-electric, and it is probably a "West Country" or "Battle of Britain" Pacific—a lighter machine

EXETER CATHEDRAL, known to Devonians as the Cathedral of St. Peter's, dominates the heart of Exeter. The Cathedral, which is one of the largest in England, is hidden by the narrow streets of the city, but the Close has been described as the most delightful in Britain. This is the great Nave of Exeter Cathedral.

[*Crown Copyright*

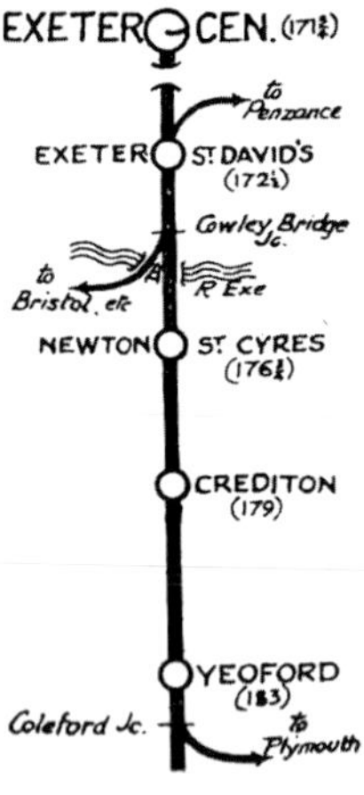

than a "Merchant Navy", which the track west of Exeter is not built to carry—which resumes our journey. Plymouth, Bude and Padstow passengers face an almost unbroken climb from very near sea level on the banks of the Exe river to a summit at Meldon, 950 ft. up in the wild country on the edge of Dartmoor, over 26 miles away. Ilfracombe and Torrington passengers share the gentle beginning of this ascent through the lush meadowland of the Yeo valley to Crediton, and the steeper climbing thence to the cattle-farming centre of Yeoford, but just beyond Yeoford their ways separate at Coleford Junction.

From Copplestone the Ilfracombe and Torrington portions of the "ACE" enjoy a downhill spin all the way to the shores of the Taw Estuary at Barnstaple. This descent is on single track from Copplestone to Umberleigh, broken by crossing loops at the intermediate stations. If you lean

[PADSTOW AND PLYMOUTH PASSENGERS NOW TURN TO PAGE 23]

out of the window you will see that at each of these crossing places the engine-crew hand over to the signalman one token and collect from him another. Except on branches worked with only one engine in steam, it is always the practice on single line sections of British Railways that a token system reinforces the usual signalling and safety arrangements, to prevent any mischance of two trains being admitted simultaneously to the same section and meeting head-on. Where traffic is light, trains are arranged to alternate in each direction and only one of these tokens—known as a " tablet " or " staff " according to shape—exists, which must be in the possession of a driver before he can enter the section concerned. In most cases, as there may be considerable traffic and more than one train may be proceeding in the same direction successively, it is obviously impracticable to have a single token, which would have to be manhandled back to the starting point of the section between the passage of each train. A number of tokens are then provided, but these are issued from special machines, one at each end of the section and linked electrically to ensure that between them they are in possession of all the tokens save one only, which is held by the driver of the train occupying or about to occupy the section. This latter is the method in force on each of the sections between Copplestone and Umberleigh.

At Lapford, home of a great dried-milk factory, the railway joins the beautiful wooded valley of the Taw river, flanked by hills rising to 600 ft. in height, and the rest of the journey down to Barnstaple Junction is through glorious scenery. At Barnstaple

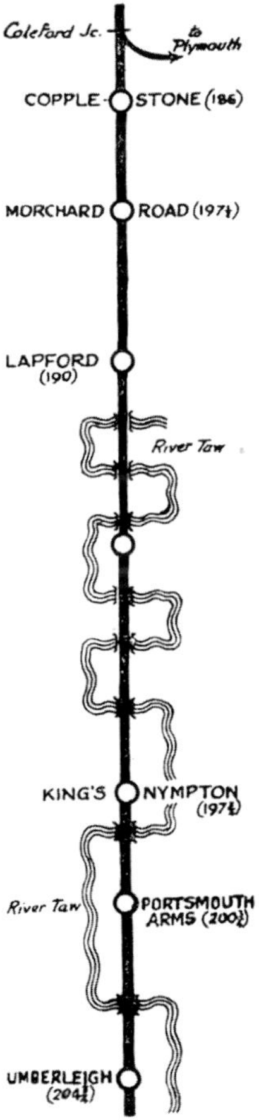

19

CLIMBING MORTEHOE BANK—Pacific No. 34062 17 *Squadron* makes the ascent of the stiff 1 in 40 incline from Braunton, helped in rear by Class " N " 2-6-0 No. 31840, with the " Devon Belle " (now discontinued). [*W. J. Armstrong*

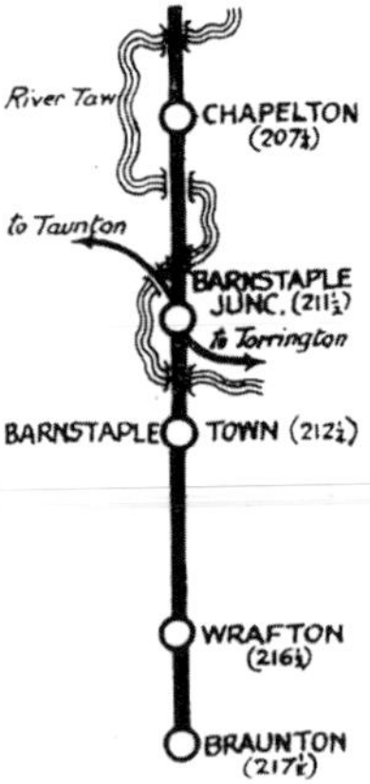

Junction Bideford and Torrington trains take the left bank of the Taw, while Ilfracombe trains curve very sharply right across the river to the other shore, which they follow as far as Wrafton. A big R.A.F. jet fighter station flanks the railway on the left at the approach to Wrafton; an interesting story attaching to this airfield is that during the last war a German bomber landed here after raiding Swansea, its pilot being under the impression that he had crossed the English instead of the Bristol Channel and that he was over the then friendly territory of France! As the train nears Braunton, you will glimpse Crow lighthouse at the end of Saunton Sands.

The last 9 miles from Braunton to Ilfracombe are in the shape of a great gable, with the peak at Mortehoe. Each slope of the gable is extremely steep and the heavier trains usually require the services of an assistant engine. For the first two miles from Braunton the gradient ranges from 1 in 81 to 1 in 100, but for the next 3 miles or so the railway curves up a wooded valley at from 1 in 40 to 1 in 45, reaching a summit over 600 ft. above sea level near Mortehoe. At the approach to Mortehoe there is indeed a tempting glimpse of the blue Atlantic far below near Woolacombe, and—in clear weather—the distant outline of Lundy Island out to sea. The descent to Ilfracombe is even more precipitate, for the gradient is 1 in 36 for two miles. After a short tunnel, there is a fine prospect of the town and the sea below the railway, which runs into a wind-swept terminus almost at the very edge of the cliffs.

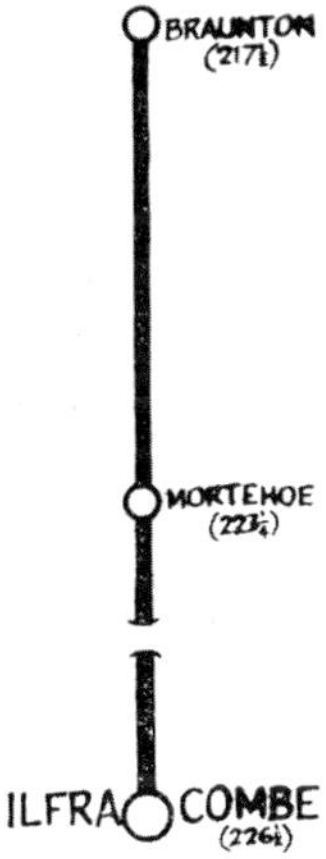

CROSSING THE TAW at Barnstaple, "West Country" Class Pacific No. 34020 *Seaton* heads a train from Ilfracombe to Exeter. [Donald Kelk

22

Beyond Coleford Junction trains for the North Cornwall coast and Plymouth begin serious climbing at gradients ranging from 1 in 77 to 1 in 100 all the way up to Meldon, except for one or two very short downhill " breathers ". When the Yeo river has been crossed between Bow and North Tawton, the great Tors of Dartmoor can be seen on the left, with Cawsand rising to a height of 1,750 ft., and the railway runs gradually nearer to them. After a sharp right-hand curve over the East Okement River viaduct, we run into Okehampton station, high above the attractive little town.

Facing Page: OKEHAMPTON from the railway. The engines in the shed yard are Pacific No. 34017 *Ilfracombe* and Class " T9 " 4-4-0 No. 30712.
[*R. E. Vincent*

Beyond Okehampton we pass on the left the great Meldon Quarry, which supplies stone ballast for permanent way work throughout most of the Southern Region; the ballast is ferried away in trains of large bogie wagons specially built for the job. Then comes perhaps the great moment of the journey, as the train suddenly leaps over the West Okement river 130 ft. above the ground on the 183 yd. long Meldon Viaduct (*see page* 2). To the left the view expresses all the savage beauty of Dartmoor as we look up the glen of the rushing stream to the towering shape of Yes Tor, 2,028 ft. up and the second highest Tor of the moors; it hides the most lofty, High Willhayes—which is only 11 ft. higher—from our view. Beyond the viaduct the North Cornwall line diverges to the right and, after a mile of further climbing in cutting, the Plymouth line reaches the Southern's highest summit, 950 ft. above sea level.

[PLYMOUTH PASSENGERS NOW TURN TO PAGE 25]

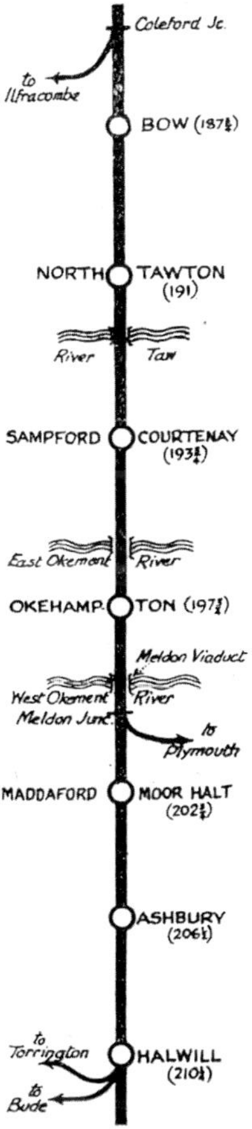

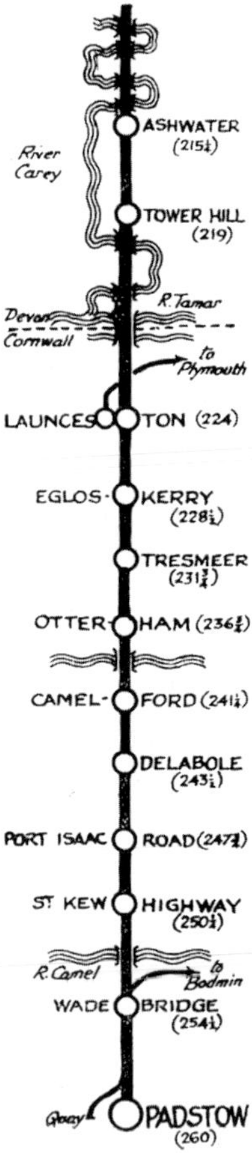

The North Cornwall line is single throughout, except for various crossing loops. When we have parted company with the Bude line at Halwill we begin a swift descent of 1 in 73-82 for three miles, after which the slope eases and then turns uphill for a mile at 1 in 94 before Launceston. The ancient Norman castle, once the seat of the Earl of Cornwall, crowns the hill overlooking the two adjoining stations. Now the railway climbs again, at first gently and then at 1 in 73-78 through Tresmeer, to the wild country north of Bodmin Moor, rich in the legends of King Arthur; once again we reach a summit 800 ft. above sea level at Otterham. Camelford is the station for Tintagel; nearby is Slaughter Bridge, where tradition has it that King Arthur fought his last battle.

From Camelford the railway once more rushes headlong downhill, on gradients ranging from 1 in 73 to 1 in 88, to the outskirts of Wadebridge. At the start of this descent the line skirts a vast slate quarry, 400 ft. deep, and you will see the slate wagons beginning their journey into the depths of the earth. The 333 yard Trelil Tunnel, the only one on this section, bestrides the line between Port Isaac Road and St. Kew Highway. From Wadebridge station the railway runs through the town to the water's edge, and the journey ends with a delightful amble down the estuary of the Camel, with the golden sands of Roch at its mouth soon coming into sight and the houses of Padstow huddled round the town's narrow streets on the left bank. Finally the line swings sharply northward across a tributary of the Camel by a fine girder bridge of three 130 ft. long spans, to its Padstow terminus at the water's edge.

From Meldon summit the railway begins a long, sharply winding descent, mostly on gradients steeper than 1 in 100, almost to the level of the Tavy river near Saltash, but broken by a 1½-mile climb out of Tavistock as the railway climbs out of the Tavy and into the Tamar valley. As soon as we have emerged from the cutting beyond Meldon summit wonderful views open out on all sides. To the left the ramparts of Dartmoor are still high—Great Links and Kitty Tor are both better than 1,900 ft. above sea level; to the right we look out over rolling country to distant Bodmin Moor. Another Norman castle will be noticed on the right, rising above the cottages of Lydford, home of a mint in Saxon times and up to Tudor days one of the West Country's most important boroughs. Between Lydford and Brentor the view to the left is filled by the great flank of Gibbet Hill, 1,035 ft. high, where gallows stood until Victorian days and where many of the infamous Judge Jeffreys' victims were put to death.

As we draw out of Tavistock station over a bridge high above the roofs of the town, the Tavy drops away below us in a wooded valley. Beyond it on the left are the receding moors, the high wireless mast on Hessary Tor pinpointing the bleak country round Princetown and Dartmoor gaol, 7 miles away. Soon after we have threaded the 593 yd. Shillamill Tunnel through the ridge separating the two valleys, you will notice ahead on the right the graceful and lofty stone viaduct by which the Callington branch from Bere Alston crosses the deep Tamar valley; nowadays this magnificent structure carries a very light service, but it was built in times when there was rich traffic from the nearby Cornish tin and

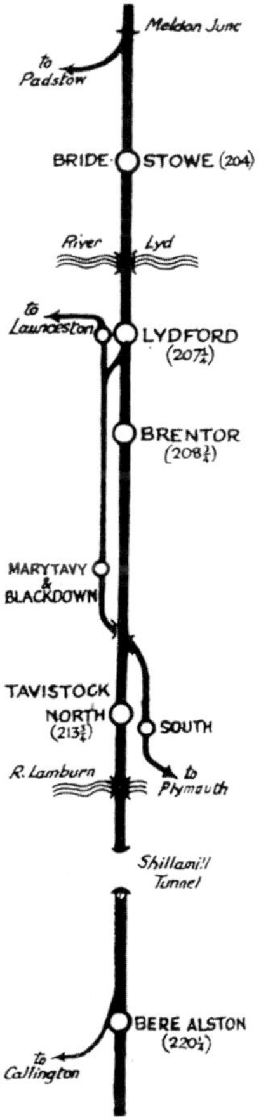

CALSTOCK VIADUCT, the graceful structure carrying the Callington branch over the Tamar, which can be seen from Plymouth trains as they approach Bere Alston. [*B. A. Butt*

copper mines to the then port of Calstock below it; there was a lift alongside the viaduct to transfer loads from the railway down to the water's edge.

From Bere Alston the railway descends the crown of the ridge down to the meeting point of the Tavy and Tamar, and there is a lovely prospect to the left over rolling country to the Plym valley round Bickleigh. At length the railway reaches very nearly to water level beyond Bere Ferrers, where it bridges the Tavy on a nine-span viaduct 1,480 ft. long. This bridge pales into insignificance, however, beside the majestic Royal Albert bridge at Saltash, which carries the Western Region main line from Plymouth to Penzance high above us into Cornwall; this structure is 2,200 ft. long and its railway 110 ft. above the water.

Now our line curves away from the river. The somewhat depressing suburbs of Devonport sprawl on both sides of the railway until it dives into two tunnels beneath Devonport Park and emerges in the impressive, turreted station of Devonport. A half-mile further on we join the Western Region main line to Penzance—the same line we encountered at Exeter—and once again we are heading the "wrong way"; for any W.R. train that passes us in the *opposite* direction will have come *from* London to the West Country, as we have done. We follow the W.R. main line through that Region's principal Plymouth station, North Road, for some distance in the London direction; then we take one side of the triangle adjacent to the big W.R. Plymouth engine shed at Laira (which you will see on the left), and make our way to the Southern's own terminus at Friary, near the centre of the city.

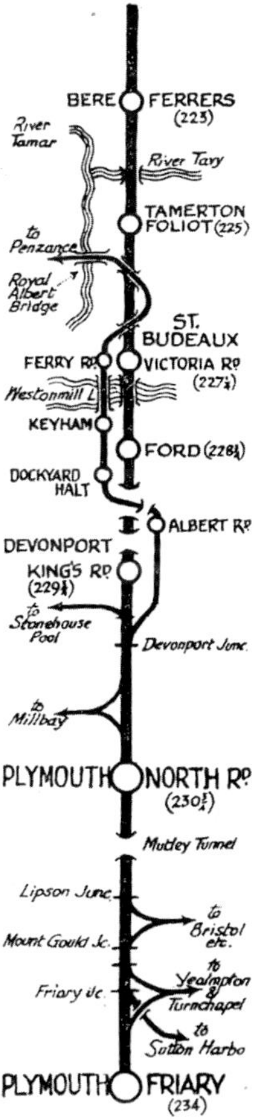

" MERCHANT NAVY " Class 4-6-2 No. 35005 *Canadian Pacific.* [*L. Elsey*

The " ACE's " Locomotive

If the " ACE " is steam-hauled on the day of your journey it will be by one of the three-cylinder Bulleid Pacifics of the Southern—probably by one of the larger " Merchant Navy " class from Waterloo to Exeter and by one of the slightly smaller " West Country " or " Battle of Britain " engines west of Exeter. The " Merchant Navy " type was introduced in 1941, the smaller engines from 1945 onwards.

BULLEID PACIFIC DIMENSIONS

	" Merchant Navy "	**" West Country " " Battle of Britain "**
Locomotive Weight:	94 tons 15 cwt.	86 tons 0 cwt.
Boiler Pressure:	280 lb.	280 lb.
Cylinders (diam. × stroke):	(3) 18 in. × 24 in.	(3) $16\frac{3}{8}$ in. × 24 in.
Driving Wheel diameter:	6 ft. 2in.	6 ft. 2 in.
Tractive Effort:	37,515 lb.	31,050 lb.

" MERCHANT NAVY " CLASS NUMBERS AND NAMES

35001	Channel Packet	35006	Peninsular & Oriental S.N. Co.	35010	Blue Star
35002	Union Castle	35007	Aberdeen Commonwealth	35011	General Steam Navigation
35003	Royal Mail	35008	Orient Line	35012	United States Line
35004	Cunard White Star	35009	Shaw Savill	35013	Blue Funnel
35005	Canadian Pacific				

35014 Nederland Line
35015 Rotterdam Lloyd
35016 Elders Fyffes
35017 Belgian Marine
35018 British India Line
35019 French Line CGT
35020 Bibby Line
35021 New Zealand Line
35022 Holland-America Line
35023 Holland-Afrika Line
35024 East Asiatic Company
35025 Brocklebank Line
35026 Lamport & Holt Line
35027 Port Line
35028 Clan Line
35029 Ellerman Lines
35030 Elder Dempster Lines

"WEST COUNTRY" AND "BATTLE OF BRITAIN" CLASS NUMBERS AND NAMES

34001 Exeter
34002 Salisbury
34003 Plymouth
34004 Yeovil
34005 Barnstaple
34006 Bude
34007 Wadebridge
34008 Padstow
34009 Lyme Regis
34010 Sidmouth
34011 Tavistock
34012 Launceston
34013 Okehampton
34014 Budleigh Salterton
34015 Exmouth
34016 Bodmin
34017 Ilfracombe
34018 Axminster
34019 Bideford
34020 Seaton
34021 Dartmoor
34022 Exmoor
34023 Blackmore Vale
34024 Tamar Valley
34025 Whimple
34026 Yes Tor
34027 Taw Valley
34028 Eddystone
34029 Lundy
34030 Watersmeet
34031 Torrington
34032 Camelford
34033 Chard
34034 Honiton
34035 Shaftesbury
34036 Westward Ho
34037 Clovelly
34038 Lynton
34039 Boscastle
34040 Crewkerne
34041 Wilton
34042 Dorchester
34043 Combe Martin
34044 Woolacombe
34045 Ottery St. Mary
34046 Braunton
34047 Callington
34048 Crediton
34049 Anti-Aircraft Command
34050 Royal Observer Corps
34051 Winston Churchill
34052 Lord Dowding
34053 Sir Keith Park
34054 Lord Beaverbrook
34055 Fighter Pilot
34056 Croydon
34057 Biggin Hill
34058 Sir Frederick Pile
34059 Sir Archibald Sinclair
34060 25 Squadron
34061 73 Squadron
34062 17 Squadron
34069 229 Squadron
34064 Fighter Command
34065 Hurricane
34066 Spitfire
34067 Tangmere
34068 Kenley
34069 Hawkinge
34070 Manston
34071 601 Squadron
34072 257 Squadron
34073 249 Squadron
34074 46 Squadron
34075 264 Squadron
34076 41 Squadron
34077 603 Squadron
34078 222 Squadron
34079 141 Squadron
34080 74 Squadron
34081 92 Squadron
34082 615 Squadron
34083 605 Squadron
34084 253 Squadron
34085 501 Squadron
34086 219 Squadron
34087 145 Squadron
34088 213 Squadron
34089 602 Squadron
34090 Sir Eustace Missenden, Southern Railway
34091 Weymouth
34092 City of Wells
34093 Saunton
34094 Mortehoe
34095 Brentor
34096 Trevone
34097 Holsworthy
34098 Templecombe
34099 Lynmouth
34100 Appledore
34101 Hartland
34102 Lapford
34103 Calstock
34104 Bere Alston
34105 Swanage
34106 Lydford
34107 Blandford Forum
34108 Wincanton
34109 Sir Trafford Leigh-Mallory
34110 66 Squadron

Introducing the rest of the

famous trains SERIES

1. The Elizabethan (E.R. and Sc. R.)
2. The Royal Scot (L.M.R. and Sc. R.)
3. The Cornish Riviera Express (W.R.)

Each book follows the same general format and is fully illustrated with diagrams and photographs. The series will be extended.

6d.
EACH

Ian Allan Ltd

CRAVEN HOUSE • HAMPTON COURT

famous trains — 5

The

SOUTH WALES PULLMAN

PADDINGTON — SWANSEA

(Western Region)

by

G. FREEMAN ALLEN

Ian Allan Ltd

THE "SOUTH WALES PULLMAN" tops the 8½-mile climb to Badminton, headed by "Castle" Class 4-6-0 No. 5074 *Hampden*. [G. F. Heiron

Introduction

AMERICAN travellers by the " South Wales Pullman " will not need to be told that the Pullman idea originated in their country in the mid-19th Century. Across the Atlantic as elsewhere in the early days of railways, accommodation for passengers was usually cramped and primitive, especially where night travel was involved. For an American by the name of George Pullman these things were nothing like good enough. One or two railways had turned out sleeping cars of a sort by 1860—Pullman himself had been allowed by the Chicago & Alton line to remodel one of their carriages into his first effort at a sleeping car—but they were very humdrum vehicles by comparison with the luxurious car *Pioneer*, which Pullman constructed in 1864.

The *Pioneer* was something entirely new, a foot wider and two and a half feet taller than any other carriage of its day and palatial in its interior appointments. Unfortunately it was so massive that few American railways of the time were fit to use it, and it looked like being a white elephant. But then it was specially requested for use on President Lincoln's funeral train after his assassination in 1865, and thereafter Mr. Pullman found many enquirers after his new luxury car. Railways set to work to enlarge their bridges and tunnels to take such a big vehicle, and soon Pullman founded the Pullman Palace Car Co. to turn out, not only sleepers, but luxury dining and parlour cars as well. By the end of the century the Pullman concern owned and operated almost all the sleeping cars operating on the American continent, and to-day over 7,000 Pullmans are running in the U.S.A.

In 1872 Mr. James Allport, general manager of Britain's Midland Railway, toured the U.S.A. and was greatly impressed with Pullman comfort. As a result of his reports on his return home, the Midland Railway imported a number of American-type Pullman parlour and sleeping cars, and thus the first Pullmans seen in this country went into service between St. Pancras, London, and Bradford in June, 1874; in the following year a day Pullman car service was put on between St. Pancras and Liverpool. The Great Northern soon followed the Midland lead with the introduction of Pullman sleepers on its night trains between Kings Cross, London, and Scotland, while in December, 1881, the London Brighton & South Coast Railway pioneered Britain's first regular all-Pullman car train, the fore-runner of to-day's "Brighton Belle".

A British Pullman Car Company was formed in 1882 and acquired by Mr. (later Lord) Davison Dalziel in 1907; from him the present Pullman Car Company took over stock, cars and goodwill in 1915. By then the Pullman was well established on many British railways as the height of luxury day travel—the last British Pullman sleeping cars were withdrawn from the old Highland Railway in 1907—and Pullman cars, instead of being imported in sections from the U.S.A. and reassembled over here, as the earliest had been, were being built to what has become the traditional British Pullman outline, either by the works of the railways operating them or by outside carriage builders. The 1923 grouping and the 1948 nationalisation of British Railways made little difference to Pullman services in this country, and although in 1954 the British Transport Commission acquired the equity capital of the Pullman Car Co., it still functions as an independent concern, maintaining the high standards of service and special luxury that have made "Pullman" a national byword for comfort in travel.

"The South Wales Pullman"

THE Great Western Railway was one of the few in Britain which saw little of Pullman cars. Knowing the American visitor's justified predilection for Pullman cars, the G.W.R. introduced them on its Ocean Liner boat trains between Plymouth and London in the summer of 1929 and in the same year put on an all-Pullman train between London and the Devon Coast, the "Torquay Pullman"; but in the following year both these Pullman services ceased and the cars were later transferred to the Southern Railway for use on the latter's boat trains between Southampton and Waterloo.

The "South Wales Pullman" made its debut with the summer service of 1955, as a luxury express for the many men of industry who shuttle between their London offices and thriving South Wales. Leaving Paddington at 9.55 a.m., the "South Wales Pullman" stops at Newport, Cardiff and Port Talbot and reaches Swansea at 2 p.m.; at 4.35 p.m. it sets out again for London, making the same stops as in the down direction, and is due into Paddington at 8.45 p.m.

The Route of "The South Wales Pullman"

NOTE: The figures in brackets after station names indicate mileages from Paddington.

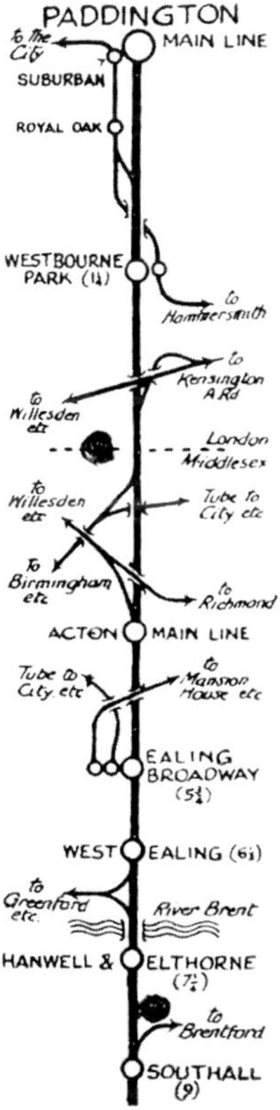

OUR journey begins beneath the great arch of Paddington station, designed by Brunel after the style of Paxton's Crystal Palace for the 1851 Exhibition and erected in 1854. The first few miles of the trip are not exactly attractive, as we thread a path through the gaunt terraces and tenements of West London and past the extensive carriage sidings of Old Oak, where our train was cleaned and prepared for its journey. Just before Westbourne Park the electric line of London Transport from the City to Hammersmith crosses beneath us. Near Old Oak sidings and also on the right is the big Old Oak Common locomotive depot, which services the motive power for trains out of Paddington. A "flying junction" allows engines and carriage stock to cross to the down side from Old Oak over our heads, thus avoiding interference with the main line. Acton is also the location of a great freight yard, connected by cross-London railways with the other main lines out of the capital to North, East and South; a heavy transfer goods traffic is worked over these orbital lines, and you will possibly notice engines of the London Midland, Eastern and Southern Regions in the Acton goods yards.

The Western exit from London is one of the most encouraging of any from the capital so far as the driver is concerned, for the line is either dead level or very faintly against the engine all the way to Swindon; this is part of the old London-Bristol main line of Brunel, who spared no

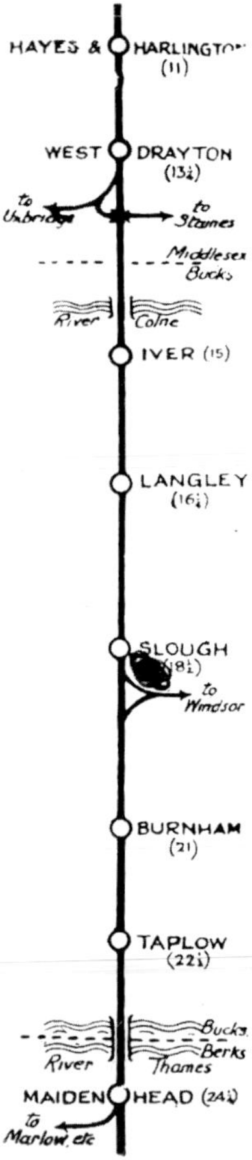

expense to avoid undue gradients. Thus we shall be gathering speed swiftly as we cross the Brent river and Uxbridge Road—the continuation of London's celebrated shopping centre, Oxford Street—on the lofty Wharncliffe Viaduct, near Hanwell. Rightwards there is a distant view of Harrow-on-the-Hill, crowned by its parish church spire, beneath the shadow of which is the famous public school that educated Byron, Sir Winston Churchill and many another famous man. Beyond Hanwell on the left is the great A.E.C. motor works, where many of London's buses—and the Western Region's diesel railcars—amongst other vehicles, have been manufactured.

Southall is another busy goods centre, with yards served by their own engine shed (on the left), for we are in the midst of the extensive industrial areas of West London and passing factories labelled with the names of many famous products; one of the biggest is the E.M.I. plant, home of His Master's Voice and Columbia gramophone records, which adjoins the line on the right just beyond Hayes station.

Beyond Langley there will be a view on the left-hand horizon of Windsor Castle, and we shall have frequent glimpses of it as far as Maidenhead; Windsor is about 2 miles from our route at Slough, a busy junction and industrial centre with its own locomotive depot (on the left beyond the station), which is the terminus of many suburban services from London. On the other side of Slough there is a distant view of Burnham Beeches, the last relics of an ancient forest. The Thames is approaching us from the left and just before Maidenhead we cross the wide river on a graceful bridge, from Buckinghamshire into Berkshire.

A.T.C IN ACTION—W.R. 2-6-0 No. 5380 at Southall passes over an A.T.C. ramp and whistles, for the neighbouring distant signal is on and a horn has sounded in the engine's cab. [*P. Ransome-Wallis*

The Thames valley is prone to mist, but even in thick fog Western expresses are able to keep moving at a good pace quite safely thanks to Automatic Train Control, or A.T.C. for short. At each " distant signal ", the warning signal which tells a driver whether he must be prepared to halt at the next "stop" signal, a ramp is laid between the running rails. A contact beneath the locomotive buffer beam strikes the ramp as the engine passes over it; if the distant signal is showing a caution aspect the ramp is dead, a loud horn blasts in the engine cab and automatically the brakes are partially applied as a warning to the driver, but if the signal is showing clear, the ramp is electrified, sounds a cheerful bell on the footplate to reassure the driver, and the train can proceed in security.

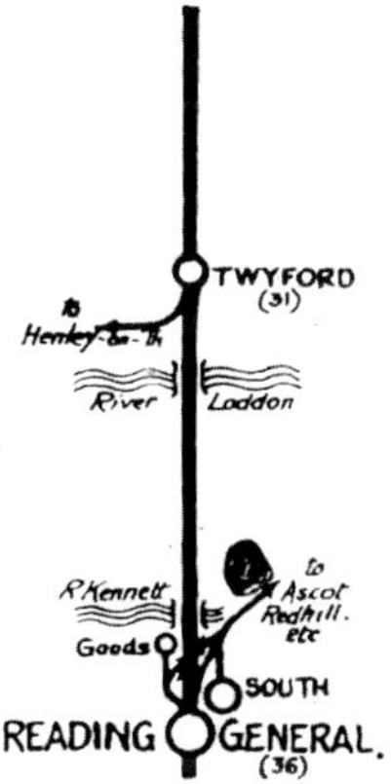

PICKING UP WATER AT SPEED—W.R. "County" Class 4-6-0 No. 1004 *County of Somerset* on a down Didcot train takes refreshment from Goring troughs [*R. Russell*

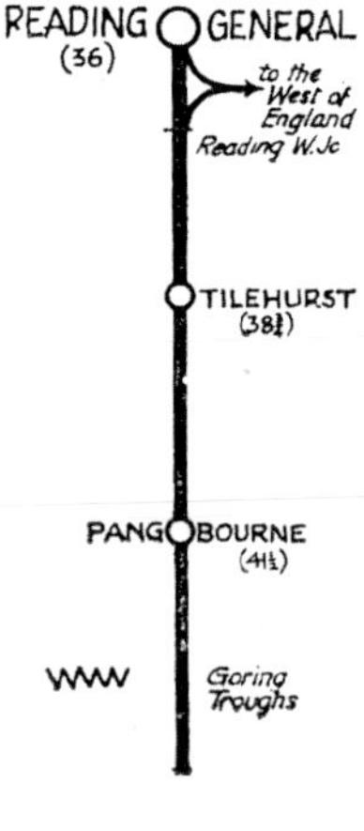

Southern electric and steam trains are soon running parallel with us on the left, past Huntley & Palmer's big biscuit works, into their own station at Reading, while we forge through the bigger Western station and part company with the main line to Taunton, Devon and Cornwall, which bears left at the end of the station platforms. There is a good view on the left of the Reading locomotive depot in the " V " of this junction.

The first few miles of the journey beyond Reading, once we have cleared the town's suburban outskirts, are extremely picturesque, for the railway takes the wooded valley breached by the Thames between the Chiltern Hills, on the right, and the Berkshire Downs, on the left. As we leave Reading the high ground of Caversham

Heights, overlooking one of the river's finest reaches, is conspicuous on the right.

Between Pangbourne and Goring our " Castle " class locomotive picks up water on the move. Its tender holds no more than 4,000 gallons of water, whereas its boiler consumes it at the rate of 40-50 gallons per mile, so that a tenderful is insufficient for a non-stop run to our first halt, at Newport. To save the train having to stop specially for water, therefore, water troughs are spaced out at suitable intervals along the route; after Goring, we shall come to others at Chipping Sodbury and Magor. As his train approaches the troughs, the fireman lowers a sharp-bladed scoop beneath the tender that cuts into the water in the troughs, forcing it up at high velocity into the tender. Fine judgment is necessary to withdraw the scoop before the tender is overfull, or an overflow will burst out of the opening at the top of the tender, spattering unwary passengers in the first one or two Pullmans of the train who have their ventilators open.

Apart from the rolling Berkshire downs away to the left, the scenery is flat and featureless beyond Goring and the railway, after a stretch of level past the water-troughs, resumes its steady but gentle climb to Swindon on gradients mostly between 1 in 754 and 1 in 1508. On the right beyond Cholsey are the first signs of Didcot's busy railway activity in Moreton Cutting sidings, where you may notice a Southern Region engine, since this yard is the transfer point of some freights between the S.R. and the Midlands via Oxford and Banbury; the latter route curves away to the right at the busy junction of Didcot, whose motive power depot is also to the right of the sta-

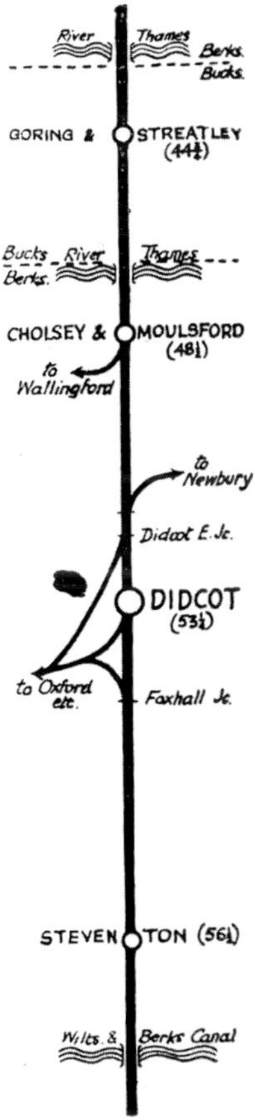

9

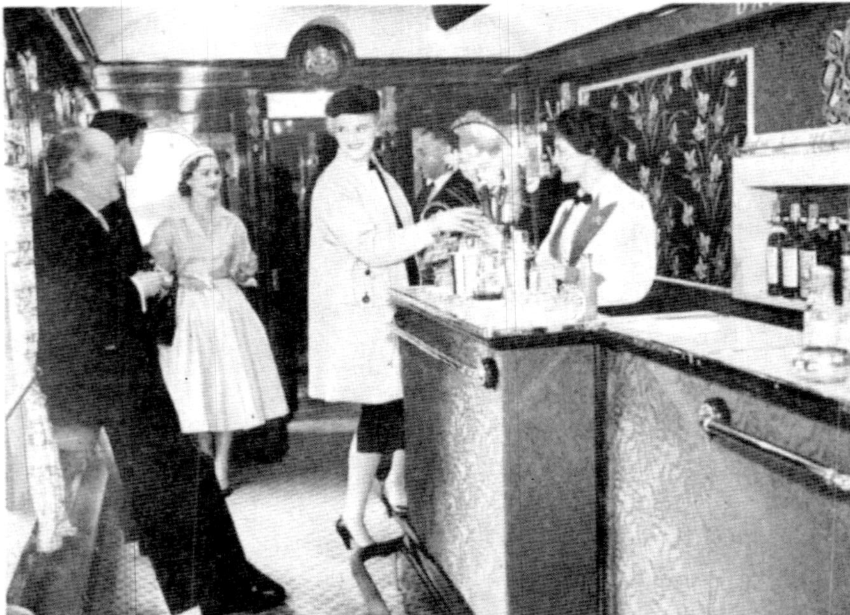

TIME FOR A REFRESHER?—An attractive hostess is waiting to serve you with an *aperitif* in the elegant Daffodill Bar of the "South Wales Pullman." [Fox Photos

10

tion. Beyond the station first a big Army Ordnance Depot, then a large R.A.F. store depot occupy many acres of ground.

Near Steventon there is to be seen on the left an interesting raised causeway, dating back to the old days when roads became a morass in wet weather. Wantage Road was the terminus of a fascinating steam tramway which linked the main line station with the town of Wantage, and ran alongside the public road for most of its length. This little standard gauge system, $2\frac{1}{2}$ miles long and independently owned, was the first steam tramway in Great Britain to be used for passenger traffic. It was opened in October, 1875, but closed to passenger traffic in July, 1925. Its remaining goods traffic was taken off in December, 1945, and the rails removed, but its tiny 0-4-0 tank engine *Shannon*, built for a Bedfordshire railway in 1857 and acquired by the Wantage Tramway in 1878, is preserved in a place of honour on the down (left hand) platform of Wantage Road station. Beyond Challow look out on the left-hand side for the White Horse of Uffington cut out of the chalk downs, marking the site of the battle of Ashdown in 871; it was allegedly made by the soldiers of King Alfred to mark his victory over the Danes.

Although Swindon as a market town is at least eight centuries old and there is mention of it in the Domesday Book, its present importance and size dates from the mid-19th Century. In 1841 Swindon had about 2,500 inhabitants, but in June of that year Brunel's London-Bristol line of the Great Western Railway was completed through the town. Because Swindon was a convenient division point of the route for operating purposes, as well as the junc-

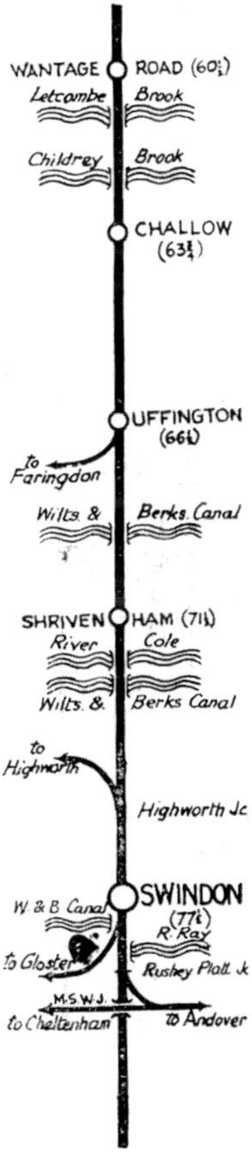

SEVENTY MILES AN HOUR STANDING STILL—Western Region 4-6-0 No. 7916 *Mobberley Hall* hard at work, but quite stationary, on the test plant rollers at Swindon works [*British Railways*

12

tion with the railway to Gloucester and Cheltenham, the Locomotive Carriage and Wagon Superintendent of the time, Sir Daniel Gooch, selected the town as the site for a central locomotive works and repair depot. The original buildings, which began full operation in January, 1843, still form part of the great industrial plant now covering 155 acres and employing nearly 6,000 on the annual construction of 100 or more new engines and the repair of over 1,000. The G.W.R. built a fine housing estate for its workers south of the line—not only that, but also St. Mark's Church (whose vicar's salary the railway paid for the first five years of its life), a cricket ground (now a public park) a shopping centre and gardens between the housing estate and the works. The gardens, unfortunately, can no longer be seen, for in later years the land was taken over to accommodate a large carriage works. All these and other railway activities in Swindon, one of Britain's three great railway towns, now occupy about 12,000 of a population that in just over 100 years since the railway's coming has swollen to 70,000.

Alongside Swindon station on the right is part of the carriage and wagon works. Just beyond the western ends of the station platforms an alternative route to South Wales veers away to the right on its way through the Cotswolds to Gloucester and Cheltenham, with Swindon motive power depot to its right, while on our left we may glimpse some part-finished coaches outside the body-building and paint shops of the carriage works, with St. Mark's church just beyond them. To the right we find the great locomotive works filling the view. In front of it there will be lines of slightly shabby-looking engines awaiting repair, and others shining with the spotless new paint that speaks of overhaul completed. You may like to know that on any Wednesday except in the first fortnight of July there are conducted tours of this great factory, starting from the entrance to the tunnel which runs from the housing estate under the main lines to the works.

One of the most intriguing buildings at Swindon is obscured from our view as we speed past. This is the Test House, where a big locomotive can be mounted on rollers and worked up to the highest speeds while it is still stationary. The engine is coupled to testing instruments and various parts of it to dials and gauges which record its efficiency. By varying the resistance the rollers offer to the engine's driving wheels, the Test House engineers can simulate all types of load and gradient and obtain a complete record of the engine's performance in varying conditions.

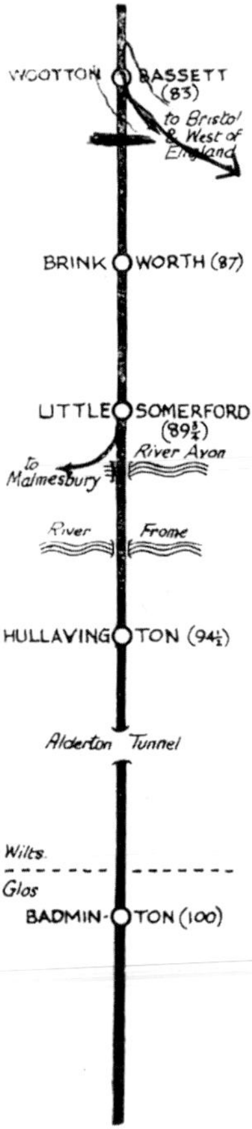

Beyond the outskirts of Swindon our route strikes the first downhill stretch of any length, at 1 in 660, but there is no chance of high speed for we are soon slowing to curve away to the right from the Bath-Bristol main line at Wootton Bassett, although the turn-out is so finely engineered that the limit is no lower than 50 m.p.h. In earlier days South Wales traffic had to follow the Bath line, with which we have just parted company, making a tedious detour via Bristol which exasperated many South Wales travellers; as a result of their complaints, and also to open up an alternative route to Bristol itself via Filton that would relieve the busy Bath line, the G.W.R. completed our present Badminton line in 1903, shortening the South Wales run by 10 miles.

The foot of the 1 in 300 descent from Wootton Bassett is reached just before Little Somerford. Hereabouts great R.A.F. transport aircraft may fly low over the "South Wales Pullman" for the big Lyneham airfield is only a few miles away to the south; on occasion one may glimpse parachute exercises over the surrounding country. A mile beyond Hullavington a brook is carried high over the railway on a narrow iron aqueduct, the first of several under which we pass on this route. Our engine will now be working hard on the long climb of 8½ miles at 1 in 300 through Hullavington and the 506 yards-long Alderton Tunnel to Badminton, in the heart of the pleasant country hunted by the Duke of Beaufort's hounds.

At Badminton there begins the long descent, commencing with nearly 11 miles of 1 in 100 down, which will drop the line nearly 550 ft. in height in the next 18 miles

CHIPPING SODBURY TUNNEL—" Castle " Class 4-6-0 No 5029 *Nunney Castle* emerges with the westbound "Pembroke Coast Express". [*G. F. Heiron*

NOTE

On subsequent pages, the maps of the "South Wales Pullman's" route indicate by initials the pre-1923 ownership of certain lines which cross the train's route. The key is as follows:

A.D.R. ..	*Alexandra (Newport and South Wales) Docks and Railway.*
Mid. R.	*Midland Railway.*
N. & B. R.	*Neath and Brecon Railway.*
P. T. R.	*Port Talbot Railway.*
R. & S. B. R.	*Rhondda and Swansea Bay Railway.*
Rhy. R.	*Rhymney Railway.*
T. V. R.	*Taff Vale Railway.*

15

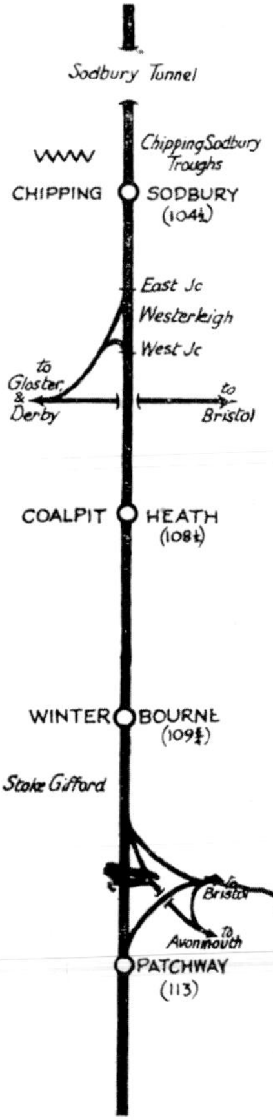

to lower it sufficiently to pass *under* the River Severn. Soon cutting walls rise steeply and we plunge into Chipping Sodbury Tunnel under the Cotswolds (this tunnel, just over 2½ miles long and the fifth longest in Britain, is often mistaken by the unwary for the Severn Tunnel!). Incidentally, if you want to check our speed, keep watch on the right-hand, or " up " side, for the mileposts. These are spaced at intervals of a quarter-mile, and each shows a mileage figure, or a mileage figure and below it " 1 ", " 2 " or " 3 ", indicating an additional " ¼ ", " ½ " or " ¾ " mile. If you count the number of seconds the train takes to cover a quarter-mile between any two of these posts and divide the answer into 900, the result will be your speed in miles per hour, e.g. a quarter-mile covered in 15 seconds equals 60 m.p.h. As far as Severn Tunnel Junction these posts indicate mileage from London by the route we are following; from there onwards they show mileage from London via the Gloucester route, which diverged at Swindon and was the first through route opened from London to South Wales.

Near Winterbourne we cross three sizeable viaducts, the biggest of them 265 yards long and 90 ft. above the ground, and then speed slackens for the important Stoke Gifford Junction, where we take a right-hand curve away from the Bristol line and head direct for the Severn. On the left are the countless buildings and the airfield of the vast Bristol Aeroplane works at Filton.

Soon after Patchway the steep descent to the Severn Tunnel begins. Between this point and Pilning the up and down tracks are independent of each other, so as to allow trains climbing away from the tunnel

16

LUXURY ON WHEELS—The interior of a typical first class Pullman car, showing the comfortable individual armchairs.

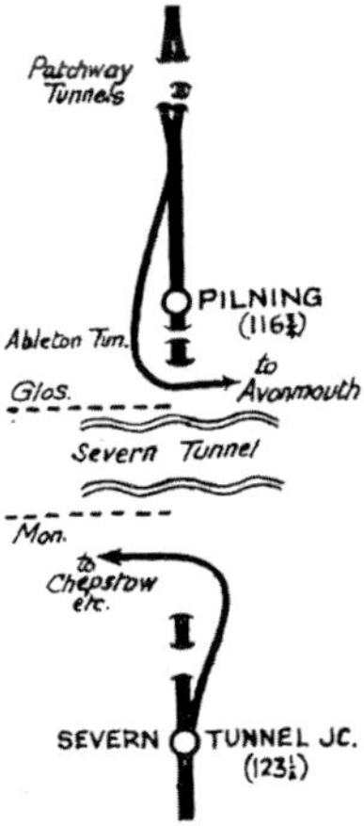

an unbroken ascent of 1 in 100 for just over 3 miles, instead of the changing grades of the down line, which culminate in 1¼ miles of 1 in 68 on the Welsh side of the 1,243 yds.-long tunnel astride the bank (the corresponding tunnel on the up line is exactly a mile long). The down line was the original one to Pilning, the track being doubled and the new up line laid when the Severn Tunnel was completed in 1886. From Pilning both lines drop at 1 in 100 into the Severn Tunnel and on to a point two miles inside it and 144 ft. *below* sea level, where, after a short level stretch, the railway begins to climb out of the depths up a steady 1 in 90 gradient.

17

SEVERN TUNNEL JUNCTION—2-6-2 tank No. 3177 (*centre*) has just uncoupled from the freight on the right, after assisting it through the Severn Tunnel. The freight on the left has travelled down the west bank of the river from Gloucester through Chepstow. [*R. J. Doran*

Before the Severn Tunnel was opened, London-South Wales travellers had to make a circuitous trip via Kemble and Gloucester, a route still followed from Swindon by Western Region trains to and from South Wales on one or two Sundays in the year when the tunnel is closed for maintenance (and also by the London-South Wales night trains). It was in 1872 that the G.W.R. eventually decided to tunnel under the Severn estuary to create a more direct route to Newport and beyond, after several years of meditating the problem and an alternative suggestion to bridge the Severn, which is 2¼ miles wide at the spot where the railway crossing was to be made. After nearly 13 years' arduous labour, during which the workings were three times flooded, twice by a powerful fresh water spring that has ever since been kept at bay by a permanent pumping station, this great example of British engineering was completed in 1886 at a cost of just over £1,800,000. Apart from London's Tube tunnels, it is the longest in the country and measures 4 miles 628 yards from portal to portal. Because of the steep gradients through the Severn Tunnel, all freight trains take the assistance of a pilot engine in both directions between Pilning and Severn Tunnel Junction. The two tracks through the Severn

Tunnel are some of the busiest on the Western Region. Not only do they carry the bulk of the rail traffic between South Wales and England, but also the flow between the West of England and the North-West, which joins the "South Wales Pullman's" route from Bristol on the Stoke Gifford triangle and leaves it on another triangular junction just outside Newport to head for Hereford and Shrewsbury; in summer especially, when thousands of North Country people are making for the Devon and Cornwall coasts, this cross-country traffic is very heavy. There is ample evidence of the extent of the freight traversing the tunnel in the extensive Severn Tunnel Junction marshalling yards, which line both sides of the main line as it climbs up after its under-water descent. Almost all the freight to and from South Wales is cleared in these sidings, which are served by their own locomotive depot (on the left), housing nearly 100 engines, including diesel shunting locomotives. Beyond Severn Tunnel Junction, our route is almost level as it crosses low-lying moors that are often flooded. In the left distance the chimneys and derricks of Avonmouth, the port of Bristol, can be discerned across the Severn. There is a conspicuous sign now of our approach to Newport, the lofty Transporter Bridge across the Usk, which can be seen ahead to the left; this structure is 645 ft. long and 175 ft. high above the river.

After the route to the North-West has curved away forming one side of the Maindee triangle, the "South Wales Pullman" crosses the Usk on a fine girder bridge. It is worth keeping an eye on the river's farther shore, on the left, for the

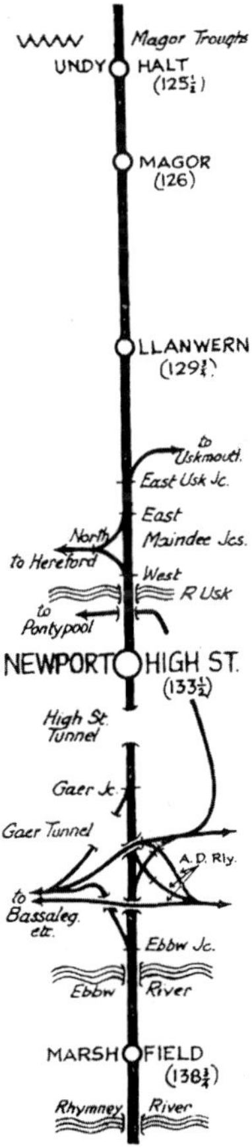

20

Above. NEWPORT STATION — "Brittannia" Pacific No. 70025 *Western Star* heads west with the 1.55 p.m. Paddington-Fishguard express

[H. J. Davies

Right. RURAL ST. FAGAN'S — An up freight approaches the station, headed by 2-8-0 tank No. 4290

[J. C. Flemons

ruins of Newport's 12th Century castle, before we halt in the town's handsomely spacious station. Both Newport and Cardiff owe their present-day size and industrial importance to the fact that each bestrides the mouth of a group of river valleys descending from the high-lying South Wales coalfields. In the peak period of foreign demand for Welsh steam coal from 1850 to the early 1920's —the outstanding year was 1913, when 38 million tons were exported—Welsh companies hurried to build lines from the pits down to the coast, and in the 75 miles of the South Wales main line between Newport and Kidwelly there are 30 junctions with branches diverging either into the hills or toward the coast, whilst four more lines cross the main route on the level. At various times over 60 different railway companies operated systems in the Welsh coalfield and there were 16—aside from the invading L.N.W. and Midland companies—still independent for the G.W.R. to absorb in the 1923 grouping. Every valley running up into the Welsh mountains had its own railway; in some cases there were competing lines on different sides of the same valley.

After we have threaded the 742 yards-long High Street Tunnel beyond Newport, lines diverge rightward down which there flowed before 1923 L.N.W. trains from the Sirhowy Valley, Brecon & Merthyr traffic from the Rhymney Valley and beyond, coal trains of the Alexandra Docks & Railway Co. (the owner of Newport Docks), as well as heavy traffic from Ebbw Vale on tracks which the G.W.R. had taken over from the Monmouthshire Railway in 1880. Nowadays this last line is worked by some of British Railways' latest heavy 2-10-0 freight locomotives, which deal with the loads of ore that have to be hauled up the steep gradients of the valley to the big Ebbw Vale steelworks. These engines operate from the big motive power depot you will see on the right at Ebbw Junction. On the left stretch Newport Docks, occupying the neck of land between the Usk and Ebbw rivers, with the Transporter Bridge towering above them.

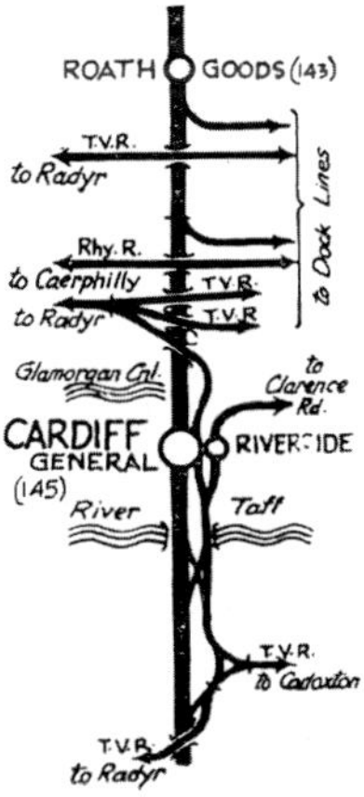

From the outskirts of Newport to Cardiff the railway strikes an almost dead level path through rather featureless landscape, except that beyond St. Mellons we catch a glimpse of the broad Severn Estuary before we cross the Rhymney river. As we approach Cardiff, Wales' largest city and the county town of Glamorgan, the docks, once the busiest coal-exporting port in the world, can be seen on the left. It was the second Marquess of Bute who initiated the spread of this great port, by constructing the dock now known as West Bute in 1839. Then, with the South Wales coal boom, came the independent railways to encourage further growth. After the opening of the Taff Vale Railway from Merthyr in 1841 (later it tapped the Aberdare, Rhondda and other valleys), the East Bute Dock was added, and following the arrival of the Rhymney Railway in 1858, the Roath basin and dock were built in 1874 and 1887 respectively. Traffic soon became so intense —in the immediate pre-World War I period, 250 trains daily were passing through the hub of the Taff Vale system, Pontypridd—that the Taff Vale eventually opened docks on the other side of the river estuary at Penarth, while the Barry Railway in 1884 obtained powers to open up a completely new dock area on Barry Sound, 7 miles from Cardiff. The other major independent system to serve Cardiff was the Cardiff Railway, an adjunct of the port owners who had inherited the Bute empire; the Cardiff Railway was formed in 1885 and added the South Bute Dock to its system in 1907.

To-day there are over 5 miles of quays and many industries have established premises close at hand, which have added their quota of tracks to an already complex railway system. The great Dowlais steel-works of Messrs. Guest, Keen & Baldwins adjoins the Roath Dock, and grain ships are constantly unloading cargoes for Messrs. Spillers big plant; timber traffic is heavy at the Bute Docks, and a big fleet of fishing trawlers operates from West Bute Docks. There are many other heavy industries in the city itself, which boasts some of the finest public buildings in the British Isles, including the Welsh National Museum, the County Hall and the University College of South Wales. These are in Cathays Park, to the right of the station and beyond the prominent grandstands of the rugby football ground of Cardiff Arms Park. The principal motive power depot of the Cardiff area, Canton shed, adjoins the line on the left as we leave the General station.

From Ely the railway begins a gradual ascent up the valley of the Ely river, culminating in $2\frac{1}{2}$ miles mainly at 1 in 106 to 187, before the summit is reached just east of Llanharan. On the right look out for the charming thatched cottages and the whitewashed Tudor castle of St. Fagan's, which is now a Welsh Folk Museum. Then, after the Barry line has bridged our route, the towering aerial of the B.B.C. Television transmitter at Wenvoe is conspicuous on the left. Apart from the pits and their tips which incongruously scar the landscape at Llanharan, an isolated outpost of the southern outcrop of the coalfield, the fertile plain of south Glamorgan which we are now traversing is still unspoiled by industry and given over to agriculture. Its market town is Bridgend, which also developed as a shopping centre for the mining folk of the Llynvi, Garw and Ogmore valleys; these strike northward into the hills noticeable on the right as we leave Bridgend. Nowadays only 10 of the 30 odd collieries working in the South Wales boom are still operating, and you will notice the extensive light industry that has sprung up in Tremains Trading Estate, served by its own unnamed station, at the approach to Bridgend. Bridgend station is approached from both directions on curves over which a 40 m.p.h. speed restriction is in force. The railway which crosses over us east of Bridgend enables traffic between the mining valleys already mentioned via Tondu and the docks at Barry to avoid Bridgend station.

The railway descends quite sharply from Llanharan through Pencoed, the gradient ranging mostly from 1 in 126 to 1 in 157 for just over $3\frac{1}{2}$ miles and now, after 3 miles of

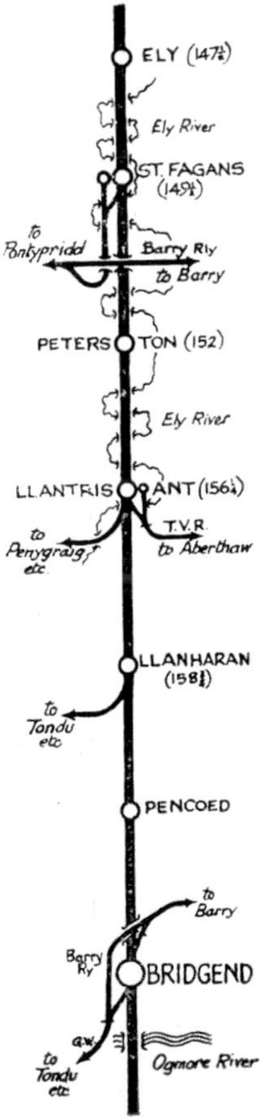

MARGAM STEELWORKS fills the background of this picture, which shows an up South Wales express headed by "Castle" class 4-6-0 No. 4091 *Dudley Castle*. [P. Ransome-Wallis

level track to just beyond Bridgend station, the line climbs again at 1 in 132-163 to Stormy Siding, just before Pyle. There is an abrupt descent at 1 in 93 from this point through Pyle, after which the slope eases to 1 in 139 to the foot of the bank before a stretch of level running alongside the sand dunes of Margam Moors. On the inland side of the railway soon after leaving Pyle one can clearly see the modern Margam Abbey rising above the trees at the foot of a hill, which reaches a height of 1,130 ft. above sea level. On the other side of the line the view is soon filled by the great modern Abbey works of the Steel Company of Wales. Opened in 1951, the three plants comprising this concern are now the largest steel-producers in Europe, turning out over 1½ million tons every year; much of the output is processed at the new strip mills at Llanelly. One of the buildings of Abbey works is three-quarters of a mile long.

Beyond the Margam steelworks the docks of Port Talbot, on the estuary of the Avon, or Afan river, come into sight on the left. Port Talbot was a harbour long before the South Wales boom and the appearance of railways (there is evidence that wool was shipped from there as long ago as the 13th Century), but the modern installations and port of to-day were not begun until the end of the last century. Since then modern industry has developed at Port Talbot and adjoining the docks, in addition to the Margam works (to which ore is ferried direct by transporter grabs) are the Port Talbot steelworks of Guest, Keen & Baldwins and a copper smelting works of the Rio Tinto Co., amongst others.

After leaving Port Talbot, while hills

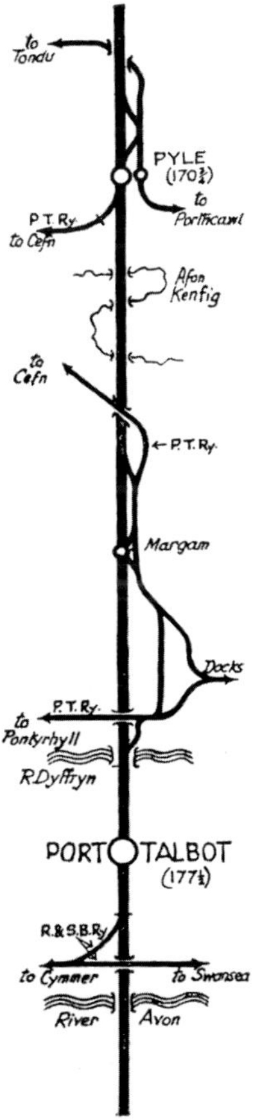

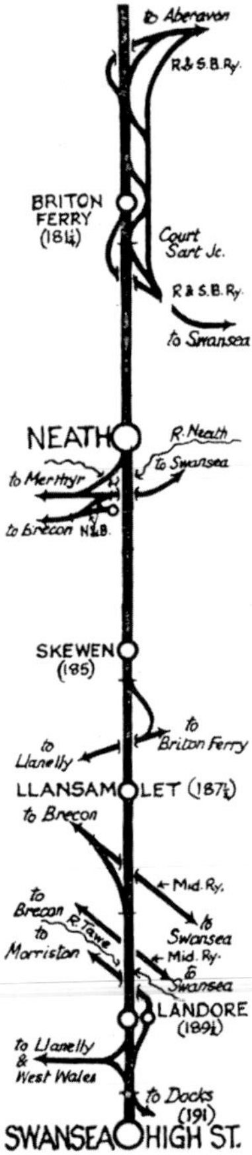

crowd the railway on the right, there is conspicuous ahead on the left the flaming chimney of the Anglo-Iranian oil refinery on the other side of a ridge of hills separating us from Swansea. Beyond Briton Ferry the railway turns inland to curve round the head of the Neath river estuary through Neath itself, an ancient town whose Cistercian abbey and castle, built in the 12th Century, are to the right of the railway. Neath also has age-old associations with the metallurgical industry and copper smelting was carried on in the town as long ago as the late 16th Century; tinplate, steel and other heavy metal industries are also prominent. As we leave Neath there is fine view to the right up the river valley towards the hills above Resolven, chief among them the 1,560 ft. high Cefn Mawr, towards which there extends the fascinating railway that cuts across almost the whole Welsh coalfield, tunnelling through hillsides and striding across the valleys by a superb series of viaducts—including the 200 ft. high and 1,650 ft. long Crumlin Viaduct—to Pontypool Road.

After we have slowed to the permitted maximum of 40 m.p.h. over Neath's reverse curves, we climb at 1 in 99 to 88 for 2 miles to a summit just beyond Skewen, after which the line drops down at 1 in 91 to 106 through Llansamlet and again, after a short uphill section, down a very steep bank from Landore, past Swansea's principal engine shed (on the right), into Swansea's terminal High Street station. Just before Landore we cross the Tawe river on a fine viaduct, a third of a mile long.

The town of Swansea, filling a deep valley and clambering up its 600 ft. high sides has been nicknamed the "Metallurgical

LANDORE VIADUCT—A local leaves Swansea for the east [J. N. Westwood

Metropolis ". Copper smelting became its chief industry in the 19th Century, and to-day the big I.C.I. copper refineries occupy many acres at Landore, while the town is equally famed for the vast quantities of tinplate turned out in the district, not to mention other metal industries. The first dock was built in 1847 and to-day there are over 6 miles of quays, where the latest development is special equipment by which tankers discharge oil direct from Queen's Dock by pipeline to the Anglo-Iranian refinery at Llandarcy, 4 miles away; King's Dock, covering 221 acres, is one of the largest in the world. All this commercial activity, however, is separated from the town itself, a happy mixture of old and new, ranging from the 14th Century castle to the fine Civic Centre and Brangwyn Hall, with their conspicuous tower, in Victoria Park. A remarkable panorama of the town and its industry is obtained from the heights above, a view ranging from Port Talbot to Mumbles and across the Channel, in good weather, to the North Devon coast from Minehead to Ilfracombe. But Swansea is not all commerce and suburbia. The trams of the Swansea & Mumbles Railway, oldest passenger-carrying line in the world, lead the way to the charming holiday country of the Gower peninsula, with its magnificent cliffs, secluded beaches and old-world villages.

CLOSE-UP of "Castle" Class 4-6-0 No. 7000 *Viscount Portal* [G. F. Heiron

MOTIVE POWER OF THE

"South Wales Pullman"

"CASTLE" CLASS 4-6-0 DIMENSIONS

Weight: *Locomotive*—79 tons 17 cwt. *Tender*—46 tons 14 cwt.
Boiler Pressure: 225 lb. per sq. in.
Cylinders (4)*:* 16in. diameter × 26in. stroke.
Driving Wheel Diameter: 6 ft. $8\frac{1}{2}$ in. *Tractive Effort:* 31,625 lb

"CASTLE" CLASS 4-6-0 NUMBERS AND NAMES

No.	Name	No.	Name	No.	Name
4037	The South Wales Borderers	4082	Windsor Castle	4093	Dunster Castle
4073	Caerphilly Castle	4083	Abbotsbury Castle	4094	Dynevor Castle
4074	Caldicot Castle	4084	Aberystwyth Castle	4095	Harlech Castle
4075	Cardiff Castle	4085	Berkeley Castle	4096	Highclere Castle
4076	Carmarthen	4086	Builth Castle	4097	Kenilworth Castle
4077	Chepstow Castle	4087	Cardigan Castle	4098	Kidwelly Castle
4078	Pembroke Castle	4088	Dartmouth Castle	4099	Kilgerran Castle
4079	Pendennis Castle	4089	Donnington Castle	5000	Launceston Castle
4080	Powderham Castle	4090	Dorchester Castle	5001	Llandovery Castle
4081	Warwick Castle	4091	Dudley Castle	5002	Ludlow Castle
		4092	Dunraven Castle	5003	Lulworth Castle

5004	Llanstephan Castle
5005	Manorbier Castle
5006	Tregenna Castle
5007	Rougemont Castle
5008	Raglan Castle
5009	Shrewsbury Castle
5010	Restormel Castle
5011	Tintagel Castle
5012	Berry Pomeroy
5013	Abergavenny Castle
5014	Goodrich Castle
5015	Kingswear Castle
5016	Montgomery Castle
5017	The Gloucestershire Regiment 28th, 61st
5018	St. Mawes Castle
5019	Treago Castle
5020	Trematon Castle
5021	Whittington Castle
5022	Wigmore Castle
5023	Brecon Castle
5024	Carew Castle
5025	Chirk Castle
5026	Criccieth Castle
5027	Farleigh Castle
5028	Llantilio Castle
5029	Nunney Castle
5030	Shirburn Castle
5031	Totnes Castle
5032	Usk Castle
5033	Broughton Castle
5034	Corfe Castle
5035	Coity Castle
5036	Lyonshall Castle
5037	Monmouth Castle
5038	Morlais Castle
5039	Rhuddlan Castle
5040	Stokesay Castle
5041	Tiverton Castle
5042	Winchester Castle
5043	Earl of Mount Edgecumbe
5044	Earl of Dunraven
5045	Earl of Dudley
5046	Earl Cawdor
5047	Earl of Dartmouth
5048	Earl of Devon
5049	Earl of Plymouth
5050	Earl of St. Germans
5051	Earl Bathurst
5052	Earl of Radnor
5053	Earl Cairns
5054	Earl of Ducie
5055	Earl of Eldon
5056	Earl of Powis
5057	Earl Waldegrave
5058	Earl of Clancarty
5059	Earl St. Aldwyn
5060	Earl of Berkeley
5061	Earl of Birkenhead
5062	Earl of Shaftesbury
5063	Earl Baldwin
5064	Bishop's Castle
5065	Newport Castle
5066	Wardour Castle
5067	St. Fagans Castle
5068	Beverston Castle
5069	Isambard Kingdom Brunel
5070	Sir Daniel Gooch
5071	Spitfire
5072	Hurricane
5073	Blenheim
5074	Hampdem
5075	Wellington
5076	Gladiator
5077	Fairey Battle
5078	Beaufort
5079	Lysander
5080	Defiant
5081	Lockheed Hudson
5082	Swordfish
5083	Bath Abbey
5084	Reading Abbey
5085	Evesham Abbey
5086	Viscount Horne
5087	Tintern Abbey
5088	Llanthony Abbey
5089	Westminster Abbey
5090	Neath Abbey
5091	Cleeve Abbey
5092	Tresco Abbey
5093	Upton Castle
5094	Tretower Castle
5095	Barbury Castle
5096	Bridgwater Castle
5097	Sarum Castle
5098	Clifford Castle
5099	Compton Castle
7000	Viscount Portal
7001	Sir James Milne
7002	Devizes Castle
7003	Elmley Castle
7004	Eastnor Castle
7005	Sir Edward Elgar
7006	Lydford Castle
7007	Great Western
7008	Swansea Castle
7009	Athelney Castle
7010	Avondale Castle
7011	Banbury Castle
7012	Barry Castle
7013	Bristol Castle
7014	Caerhays Castle
7015	Carn Brea Castle
7016	Chester Castle
7017	G. J. Churchward
7018	Drysllwyn Castle
7019	Fowey Castle
7020	Gloucester Castle
7021	Haverfordwest Castle
7022	Hereford Castle
7023	Penrice Castle
7024	Powis Castle
7025	Sudeley Castle
7026	Tenby Castle
7027	Thornbury Castle
7028	Cadbury Castle
7029	Clun Castle
7030	Cranbrook Castle
7031	Cromwell's Castle
7032	Denbigh Castle
7033	Hartlebury Castle
7034	Ince Castle
7035	Ogmore Castle
7036	Taunton Castle
7037	Swindon

495/247/20/11/58 *Published by Ian Allan, Ltd., Craven House, Hampton Court, Surrey and Printed by Crampton & Sons Ltd., Sawston, **Cambridge**.*

famous trains — 6

The

QUEEN OF SCOTS

KINGS CROSS — LEEDS — EDINBURGH — GLASGOW (QUEEN ST.)

(Eastern, North Eastern and Scottish Region)

by

G. FREEMAN ALLEN

Ian Allan Ltd

LEAVING LEEDS—Class "A1" 4-6-2 No. 60134 *Foxhunter* climbs through the Leeds suburb of Holbeck on its way to London with the southbound "Queen of Scots" [*Eric Treacy*

Introduction

ALTHOUGH the name " Queen of Scots " did not come into the railway language until 1928, the service which it graces had been in process of development since the railway grouping of 1923. The latter event brought into L.N.E.R. hands a number of Pullmans which the Great Eastern had been sprinkling into several of their trains since the First World War ended, but without noticeable profit. The L.N.E.R. conceived the idea of using them to open up a new luxury service to Newcastle via Leeds and Harrogate, which appeared in the timetables for the first time in the summer of 1923.

The " Harrogate Pullman ", as it was named, soon attracted good patronage and in the summer of 1925 its itinerary was extended to Edinburgh. In the autumn of that year its route was changed, so as not to compete with a new Leeds and Bradford Pullman service just inaugurated, and it now ran non-stop over the 198¾ miles between Kings Cross and Harrogate—but by a decidedly unusual route; instead of taking the Leeds line at Doncaster, it travelled a little further to Shaftholme Junction and then made its way through Knottingley, Ferrybridge and Church Fenton to join its present route to Harrogate at the approach to Crimple Viaduct. For three years the express followed this path, until in May, 1928, the companion " West Riding (*now* Yorkshire) Pullman " was altered to an afternoon, instead of a morning departure from London, and the Harrogate train could resume the normal route via Leeds; not only that, but the latter, equipped with a brand-new all-steel train and extended to Glasgow, was given the proud title of " Queen of Scots ". Up to 1935 the famous Ivatt Atlantics were usually at the head of the train between London and Leeds and put up some of the best speed performances of which even these remarkable engines were capable.

The load is usually one of 10 cars weighing some 400 tons between Kings Cross and Leeds, where two are detached, leaving eight for the rest of the journey. A Copley Hill Class " A1 " Pacific works the train between Kings Cross and Leeds in both directions, a Neville Hill (Leeds) Class " A3 " Pacific between Leeds and Newcastle in both directions, a Heaton (Newcastle) Pacific—the class may vary—the down train between Newcastle and Glasgow and a Haymarket Pacific the up train between Edinburgh and Newcastle.

NOTE: The figures in brackets after station names indicate mileage from Kings Cross.

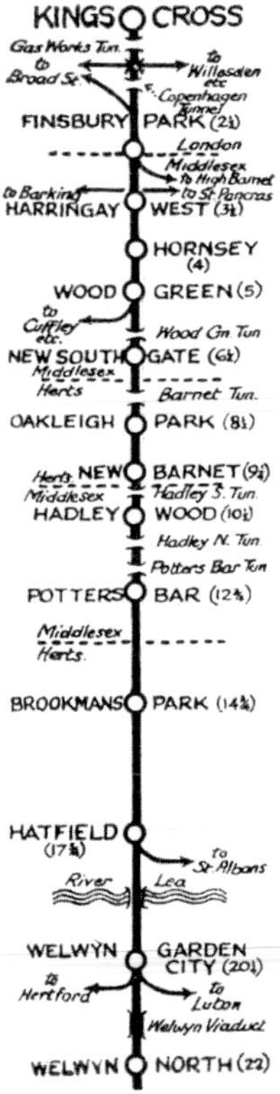

The Route of The Queen of Scots

THE start from Kings Cross is hard on the engine, for as soon as it plunges into the murky Gas Works Tunnel (528 yds. long), just beyond the platform, it is tackling a gradient of 1 in 107, which continues through the succeeding Copenhagen Tunnel (594 yds. long). Between these two tunnels, on the left, are the lines leading to Kings Cross goods yard and motive power depot. The gradient eases past the carriage sidings at the approach to Finsbury Park and turns downhill as we pass Ferme Park goods yard and Hornsey, with its freight engine shed on the right; but before we reach Wood Green the engine resumes uphill work, now at 1 in 200, which does not end until we top the summit at Potters Bar, 12¾ miles out. Wood Green is dominated on the left by Alexandra Palace, erected in 1875 after an earlier structure, completed two years previously, had been destroyed by fire; the latter had been put up as a result of complaints that the Crystal Palace was inaccessible to North Londoners. and, like the Crystal Palace, had been constructed of exhibition hall materials—in this case, those of the Grêat Exhibition held at South Kensington in 1861. Alexandra Palace, now the home of the B.B.C's London television transmitter, was named after the then Princess of Wales, wife of the future King Edward VII.

Beyond Wood Green are two more tunnels, 705 and 605 yds. long respectively, and soon there are the first signs of open country as we approach Hadley Wood.

4

Three more tunnels, 384, 232 and 1,214 yds. long respectively, bring us to the summit at the recently modernised and enlarged Potters Bar station, whereafter the "Queen of Scots" gathers speed on the descent of 1 in 200-350 to Hatfield. The tall masts on the right are those of the B.B.C's sound radio transmitter at Brookmans Park. Beyond Hatfield the line turns uphill again at 1 in 200, broken by a section of level across the stately viaduct carrying the railway 100 ft. high above the Mimram valley at the approach to Welwyn North, to a summit north of the second Welwyn Tunnel.

At Langley, between Knebworth and Stevenage, our Pacific locomotive picks up water on the move, for even the 5,000 gallons capacity of its massive tender is not adequate for the 185¾ miles of our first stage, to Leeds, since the boiler consumes 40-50 gallons per mile. So, from water troughs laid between the running rails at intervals of 50-100 miles, the engine crew replenish their supplies by lowering a sharp-bladed scoop, which cuts into the water, forcing it up at high velocity into the tender.

Stevenage is the start of an almost unbroken 17-mile sweep downhill through the busy junction of Hitchin (the engine shed is on the right alongside the station) to the Ouse valley beyond Sandy. Our speed may well touch 90 m.p.h. before our driver has to observe the 70 m.p.h. restriction round curves at Offord.

The county town of Huntingdon, an agricultural centre, was the birthplace of Oliver Cromwell, and at one time his family had their home in Hinchingbrooke House, the stately building on rising ground to the left of the railway, which is now the seat of

PULLMAN AT PETERBOROUGH—Class " V2 " 2-6-2 No. 60832 heads the down " Yorkshire Pullman " out of Peterborough (North) station. Peterborough Cathedral is seen on the extreme left, the chimneys of Fletton brickyards on the extreme right of the horizon. [*P. J. Lynch*

the Earls of Sandwich. Huntingdon marks the commencement of a 3 miles' climb at 1 in 200 to Leys summit, after which the railway descends once more, also at 1 in 200, for just over 4 miles through Abbots Ripton to a stretch of level through Holme. Then the chimneys of the London Brick Company's extensive kilns make an avenue for us, indicating the approach to Peterborough.

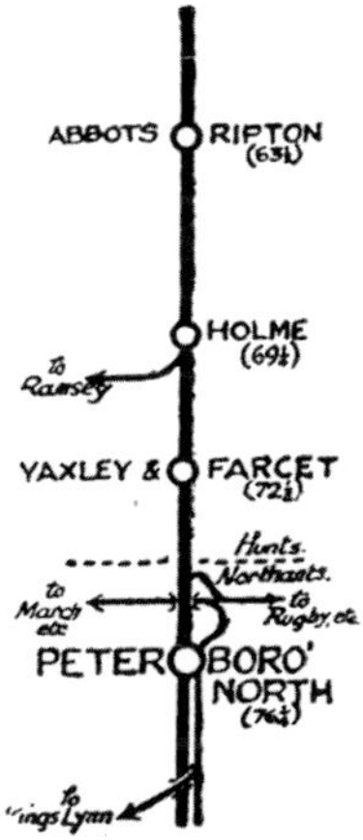

Peterborough is an expanding industrial city on the banks of the Nene river, which we cross on a fine girder bridge, slowing to take the awkward reverse curve through the North station at the regulation 20 m.p.h. This curve and the limited accommodation of the station are a serious hindrance to operations on the main line; under modernisation, the station is to be rebuilt and extended westwards, so that through trains will have a much straighter path and be able to pass at speed.

In future years, therefore, passengers will have a more fleeting glimpse than now of Peterborough's cathedral, seen to the right as we approach the station. The cathedral was nearly two centuries building; hence the choir, tower and nave, built between 1117 and 1193, are of Norman style, while the great west front, seen from the train, which was put up between 1200 and 1250, is in the Early English style. As to industry, the city's activities include the production of silk, clothing and textiles, mustard and engineering. It is not primarily these industries, but Peterborough's focal position on lines radiating to East Anglia and the Midlands, as well as the main line to the north, which account for the size of the big New England freight yard and locomotive depot, home of over 150 locomotives, to be seen on the right as we leave the city.

After our engine has taken up more water from Werrington troughs, we begin at Tallington the long climb to Stoke summit, 345 ft. above sea level and the highest point reached by the "Queen of Scots" south of the Scottish border. Stoke bank is over 15 miles long and gradually steepens from 1 in 440 to 1 in 178; since its curves are few and gentle, it forms in the reverse direction the finest railway racing ground in Britain,

"A.T.C."

A driver at the controls of a Class "A4" Pacific. On the right is the A.T.C. ("Automatic Train Control") visual indicator and apparatus.
[*P. Ransome-Wallis*

BETWEEN New Barnet and Huntingdon on the route of the "Queen of Scots" there is being installed an automatic train control (A.T.C.) that is under test with a view to its adoption as standard throughout British Railways. The purpose of the apparatus is to warn the driver of the aspect of signals he is passing, to reinforce his own observation. Between the running rails at the approach to every distant signal are two inductors, one a permanent magnet, the other an electro-magnet which is not energised when the signal is "on"; when the signal is "off", it automatically cuts in a current which energises the electro-magnet to throw a force directly contrary to that of the permanent magnet. If the distant is "on", the permanent magnet acts on a receiving apparatus beneath the engine which then makes a brake application, and in the cab sounds a horn and operates a visual reminder to catch the driver's attention; if the distant is "off", the live electro-magnet influences the engine's receiver in such a way that a reassuring bell is sounded in the cab. This A.T.C. apparatus is now being extended to the whole length of main line between Kings Cross and Grantham.

To-day speeds of at least 90 m.p.h. down Stoke bank are frequent. Incidentally, if you want to check the " Queen of Scots' " speed, time the number of seconds it takes to cover any quarter of a mile from the mileposts on the left of the track (on the right after Berwick) and divide the result into 900; your answer will be the speed in miles per hour.

The top of Stoke bank is marked by our entrance into the 880 yds. Stoke Tunnel, through which we accelerate on a long descent to the Trent Valley, beginning with 5 miles of 1 in 200 down to the manufacturing town of Grantham, dominated by the 285 ft. spire of its St. Wulfram parish church. Pacifics predominate among the locomotives grouped round the motive power depot to the left of the station, for many expresses halt at Grantham to change engines. As we speed through the station, we may catch our first glimpse of one of British Railways' new diesel trains, which now provide the service between Grantham and Nottingham—a route followed for a year by the predecessor of to-day's " Yorkshire Pullman ", the " Sheffield Pullman ", when it was introduced in June, 1924.

After the 987 yds. Peascliffe Tunnel, the down gradient is again 1 in 200, but it gradually flattens out to level track by the time we cross the Trent at Newark. Between Newark station and the bridge is a rarity in this country, a flat crossing of two main lines; the crossing is still controlled by the signalbox on the intersecting Nottingham-Newark line, which was built by the Midland Railway before our route came into being; in olden days, therefore, Midland trains took precedence over even the lordliest East Coast Route expresses.

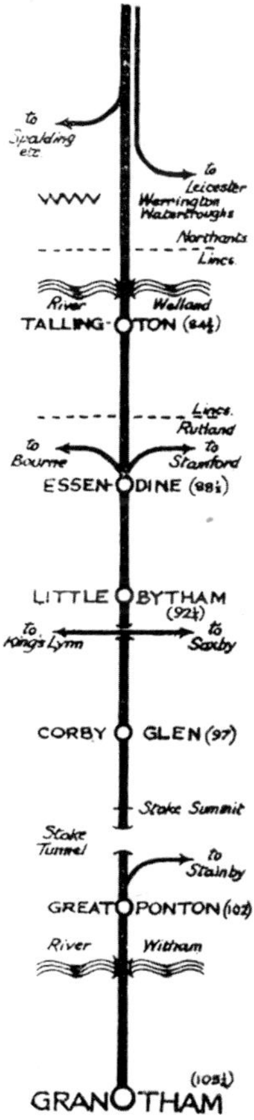

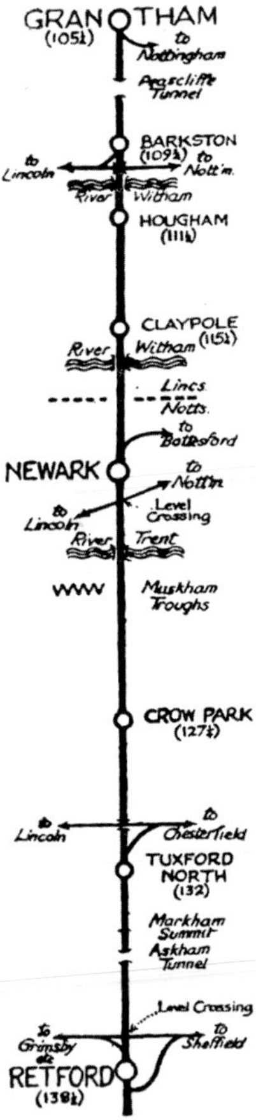

From Crow Park to Retford our route skirts the eastern fringe of the Dukeries, destination of many day-trippers from the Midlands seeking the beauties of Sherwood Forest and the many parks and ancient houses which give the district its name; the latter include Clumber Park, seat of the Duke of Newcastle, Welbeck Abbey, family home of the Duke of Portland, and Thoresby. On the other side of the line, a glance to the right after Crow Park on a clear day may discern Lincoln Cathedral, as the railway climbs at 1 in 200 up to Dukeries Junction, south of Tuxford; the railway enthusiast will glimpse Tuxford shed on the left at this junction. Then, from the short Askham Tunnel (57 yds.) there is a descent at 1 in 200 and 1 in 178 to Retford, approached over another flat railway crossing. On this crossing there occurred years ago a remarkable near-disaster when the driver of a northbound Scottish express, approaching Retford with a clear road, saw a goods train ambling straight across his path in the Lincoln direction; with no distance in which to stop his train, the quick-thinking driver of the express accelerated, cutting the goods clean in two and saving his own train at the expense of two or three wagons splintered to matchwood. Modern signalling equipment, of course, guards against the possibility of such conflicting train movements to-day.

Another of England's stately homes, Serlby Park, stands on the left at the approach to Scrooby, meeting place of the Pilgrim Fathers who sailed to America in the *Mayflower* and who assembled in the old manor house close to the line near the

GRANTHAM SHED—A bird's-eye view. On the left are several freight 2-8-0s and in the foreground several Pacific locomotives. [*P. H. Wells*

station. From Scrooby troughs there is a three-mile " hump " at 1 in 198 to Piper's Wood, on the county boundary, and soon afterwards we reach the tangle of junctions and yards at the approaches to Doncaster. Doncaster motive power depot is on the right south of the station.

Doncaster was the most important centre of the old Great Northern Railway. Here it handed over East Coast Route trains to the North Eastern Railway's care (the actual boundary was at Shaftholme Junction, just north of the station) and rubbed shoulders with the trains of five other pre-grouping companies (G.C., G.E., L. & Y., L.N.W. and Midland) working in over the many cross-country routes radiating from the town. Moreover, in 1853 the G.N.R. built to the west of the station its locomotive and carriage works, which over the years have been extended from the original

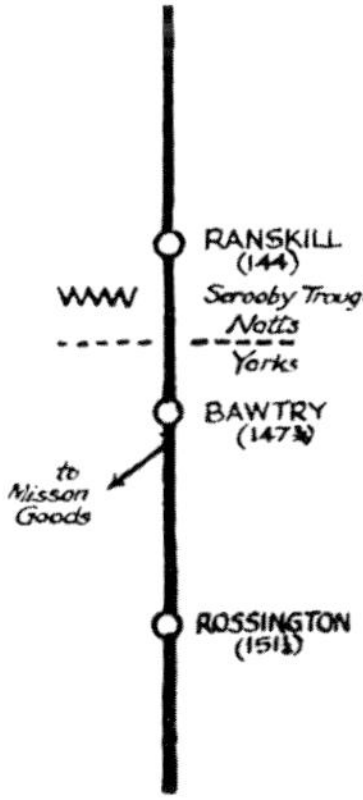

11

DONCASTER—Class " A4 " 4-6-2 No. 60026 *Miles Beevor* pulls out of the station with a Leeds-Kings Cross express. The works are out of the picture to the left. [*J. Cupit*

11½ acres of buildings to to-day's 85 acres (not counting the Carr wagon works, on the left of the main line south of the station). Doncaster station has been modernised since the war and in particular its signalling is now entirely colour-light, operated from two all-electric signal cabins north and south of the station, instead of the former six. Instead of tugging at the old-type levers, the Doncaster signalmen have only to flick little thumb switches, some of which will set up a complicated route through a whole series of points—simultaneously proving that it is safe to do so—at a single turn. Above the control panel a vast diagram of the station layout indicates the movement of every train by coloured lights, while " train describers " flash the trains' descriptions on to illuminated screens as their approach is advised by neighbouring signalboxes. In the old days, every train passing through Doncaster required, on an average, ten lever movements in the station's two boxes; in the new cabins each train needs no more than the twist of 3 or 4 thumb switches. The large town is the centre both of a wide agricultural area and also of the South Yorkshire coalfield.

From Doncaster our route lies through the great South Yorkshire coalfield and the scenery on to Leeds is dominated by pithead towers, chimneys and slagheaps. After a level section of track the railway begins to climb from Carcroft, first at 1 in 440, but steepening to 1 in 150 from South Elmsall up to the summit near Nostell, whereupon we drop down at 1 in 150 to Sandal and the Calder valley. A curving viaduct of 94 arches leads us into Wakefield, county town of the West Riding and a cathedral city. A 30 m.p.h. speed restriction through the

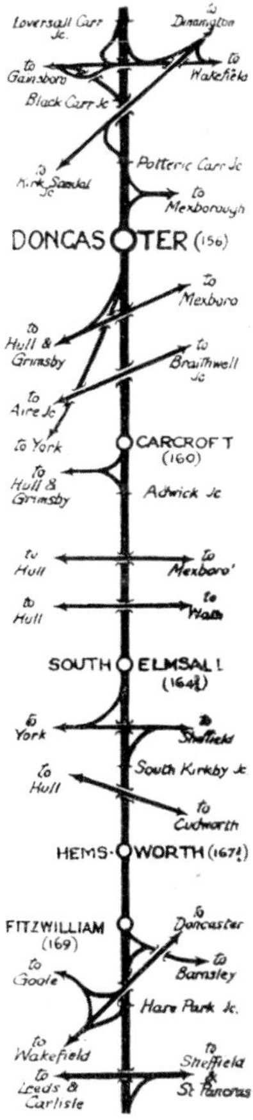

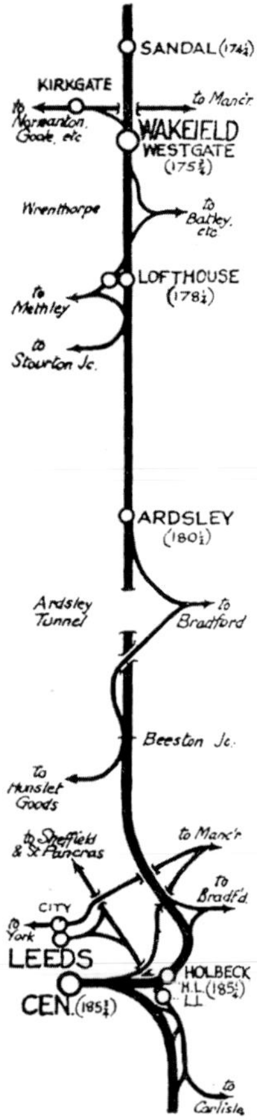

Westgate station is an unhelpful start to the long climb to Ardsley now facing the engine; this begins with over 2 miles at 1 in 100 to Lofthouse, after which the gradient eases no more than a fraction, to 1 in 122. Ardsley is a busy freight centre, with important marshalling yards occupying many acres and a locomotive depot serving them on the right. The summit divides the Calder Valley from Airedale, into which the " Queen of Scots " now descends on a 1 in 100 gradient that takes us to Beeston and the outskirts of Leeds' busy railway area.

The Leeds United football ground is noticeable on the right before we cross the Manchester-Leeds main line. Then, away to the right, a smoke haze leads the eye to one of Leeds' principal motive power depots, Holbeck, serving the old Midland main line from London's St. Pancras station to Carlisle. Our own route now curves sharply right, past the engine shed providing motive power for the Kings Cross-Leeds main line, Copley Hill, on the left, and descends sharply—the gradient is 1 in 50 for a short stretch—into Leeds Central terminus. Here a fresh engine from Neville Hill shed is attached to the rear of the train, for at Leeds Central the " Queen of Scots " has to reverse.

Restarting from Leeds Central, the " Queen of Scots " retraces its steps towards London for a short way, then bears right away from the Doncaster line to descend to Holbeck (Low Level). Here it joins the tracks emerging from Leeds City, which carry London Midland traffic for Scotland via Carlisle, and for Bradford. Soon we diverge rightward from this route and strike the stiff climb through the suburbs of Leeds up Heading-

CLIMBING THROUGH THE WOODS to Bramhope Tunnel, Class "A3" 4-6-2 No. 60074 *Harvester* heads the southbound "Queen of Scots" out of Wharfedale. [*J. Woolfenden*

THROUGH THE COALFIELDS—Class " A3 " 4-6-2 No. 60039 *Sandwich* approaches Lofthouse with the 3.5 p.m. Leeds-Kings Cross express. [*J. B. Welldon*

CROSSING THE URE at Ripon—Class " D49 " 4-4-0 No. 62748 *The Southwold* and Class " A3 " 4-6-2 No. 60086 *Gainsborough* double-head a Newcastle-Liverpool express. [*A. Mayor*

ley bank, which begins with ¾-mile at 1 in 130 and then steepens to 1 in 100 for the next 4½ miles to the summit in the woods beyond Horsforth. Just beyond the summit the train plunges into Bramhope Tunnel, 2 miles 234 yards long—the seventh longest in the country—and the gradient alters sharply to 1 in 94 downhill for 2¾ miles. Speed must be restricted on the descent, however, for just beyond the tunnel there is a sharply-curved triangular junction at Arthington.

What a contrast now in the scenery since we were last in the open air! We went underground from the suburbs of Leeds; now we have emerged from a rampart of wooded hills into beautiful Wharfedale, looking right towards the Princess Royal's home at Harewood, one of the many ancient mansions and churches in the valley, and left towards Otley and Ilkley. The railway winds across the river and is now engaged in a 3¾ miles' climb at 1 in 185-195 through Weeton. Soon after passing Pannal, look ahead and to the left for a superb view through a wide cleft in the hills of the 31-arch Crimple viaduct, 615 yds. long and 116 ft. above the ground. Now our speed is greatly reduced, for we approach this viaduct on one of the sharpest main line curves in the country, making a left-hand turn of 90 degrees at the junction with the Church Fenton-Wetherby line, onetime route of the " Queen of Scots " (*see page* 3). Below us as we cross the viaduct is the path of the original Leeds Northern Railway, now abandoned, which diverged from our present route at Pannal and circled the east of Harrogate via Starbeck.

From Crimple Viaduct there is a mile of testing uphill work at 1 in 91 to the cutting

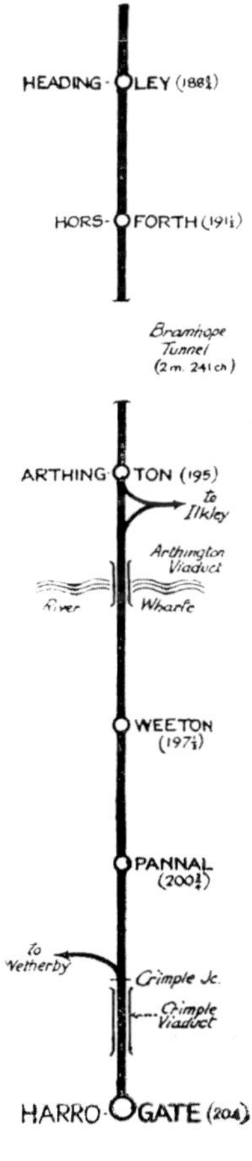

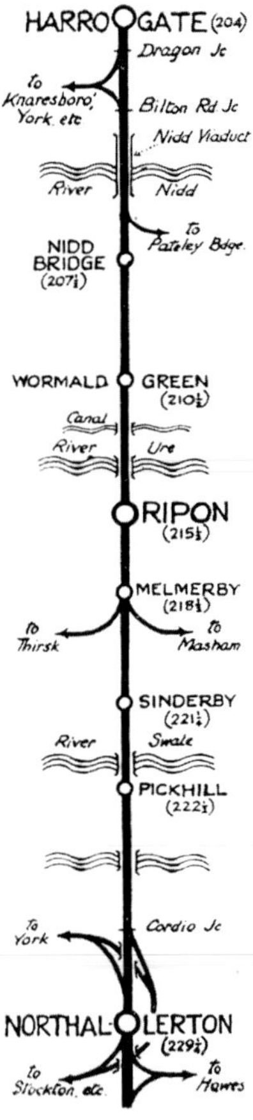

which takes the railway through the Stray, a sweeping common on the fringe of Harrogate, our next stop. Harrogate is probably the country's most fashionable inland resort, thanks mainly to the medicinal value of its natural saline, sulphur and chloride of iron springs, but also to its bracing situation over 400 ft. up in the foothills of the Pennines and the ready access from it to the beauties of the Yorkshire moors and dales.

The restart from Harrogate is down 1½ miles of 1 in 66 to Bilton Road Junction, but our speed over the curve there must be restricted to 40 m.p.h. A lofty viaduct carries us over the Nidd river, deep in a picturesque wooded gorge on the right, and after Nidd Bridge the descent is resumed, steepening to 1 in 133 for 3 miles beyond Wormald Green to the outskirts of Ripon. This is a charming cathedral city on the Ure river, with old-world narrow streets through which the curfew is still sounded every night when the Wakeman blasts his horn at the Mayor's house and the town cross. The stately cathedral, seen on the left as we approach the station, was built between 1150 and 1250 and was restored by Sir Gilbert Scott in the mid-19th Century. A special attraction of Ripon is the remarkably well-preserved remains of Fountains Abbey, a 12th Century Cistercian monastery, at Studley Royal, south-west of the city. Onwards from Ripon the running is almost level through farmland backed by the distant Hambleton Hills on the right, to Northallerton.

At Northallerton, an agricultural centre which is the county town of Yorkshire's North Riding—and another place where the quaint curfew custom still persists—we rejoin the four-track East Coast main line in a finely laid-out series of burrowing and flying junctions which enable trains to pass between the Leeds and Stockton routes, from Newcastle to York or vice versa, or between the Newcastle and Leeds lines, with the minimum of interference to conflicting streams of traffic. The whole layout is signalled by colour lights and is under the control of a single all-electric cabin, similar to those at Doncaster. The railway enthusiast will like to know that Northallerton's small locomotive depot is on the left alongside the station at a lower level. The next 14¼ miles to Darlington are on easy gradients and offer little spectacular, except for the rolling Cleveland Hills on the right as we leave Northallerton.

As the "Queen of Scots" slows to its stop in Darlington Bank Top station, you will glimpse the historic *Locomotion No. 1*, George Stephenson's celebrated engine built in 1825 for the Stockton & Darlington Railway, the world's first to use steam traction; with another S. & D. engine it stands proudly on a pedestal on the station platform at the head of the south end bays. Moreover, after the restart we make contact with the route these engines used, for a mile north of Darlington our main line strikes its third flat crossing, this time with the track of the Stockton & Darlington Railway itself, now used only for goods traffic. It is fitting that this birthplace town of railways should still maintain a locomotive works, which lies north of Bank Top station on the left. Many other engineering firms have their plant at Darlington.

For 10 miles from Darlington the "Queen of Scots" climbs gradually across broad

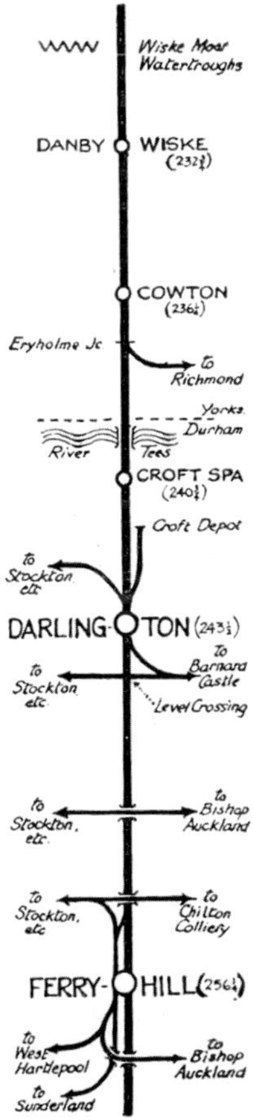

DURHAM VIADUCT—Class "A1" 4-6-2 No. 60127 *Wilson Worsdell* rides high above the city with a northbound express. [K. Field

moorland and through the Durham coalfield to a summit 292 ft. above sea level at Bradbury, after which it dips down to cross the Wear river on Croxdale Viaduct; as we cross this stately structure the towers of Durham cathedral are visible ahead on the right, and soon we have a superb view of this stately Norman edifice after the train has climbed up from Croxdale to another high viaduct at the approach to Durham station. In the cathedral are interred the remains of the Venerable Bede and of St. Cuthbert; the latter's body was removed to this spot for fear of Viking raids by the monks of Lindisfarne in 995, and around the tomb there grew a mediaeval fortress city on the rocky eminence 70 ft. above the river. The cathedral was erected in the late 11th Century, after William the Conqueror had ventured north on a punitive expedition; he it was who in 1072 built the castle to the left of the Cathedral.

Near Plawsworth there will be some fast running on the 1 in 150 descent to Chester-le-Street, beyond which the gradient is easier but still downhill to the outskirts of Newcastle at Low Fell. Worth watching for on this section are: Lumley Castle, seat of the Earl of Scarborough, on the right at Plawsworth; the Penshaw Monument, seen on a hill to the right after Chester-le-Street, which is a 100 ft. long replica of the Grecian Temple of Theseus and honours the first Earl of Durham; and beyond it the present Earl's seat, Lambton Castle.

About ½-mile beyond Bensham we curve left past Gateshead engine shed (on the right) on to the King Edward VII bridge over the Tyne, 112 ft. above the water. To the right downstream is the much older High Level Bridge, used by both road and

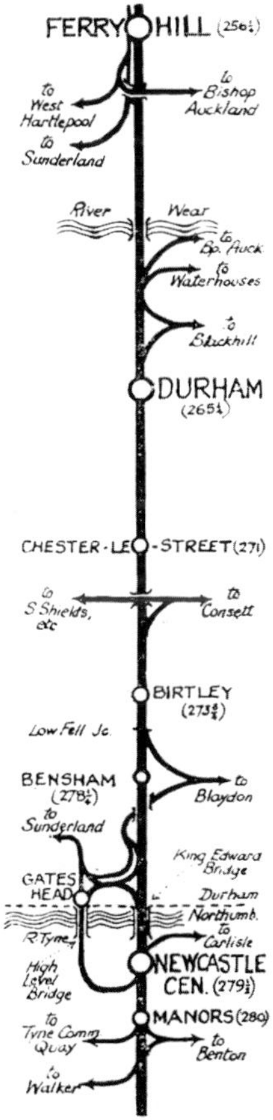

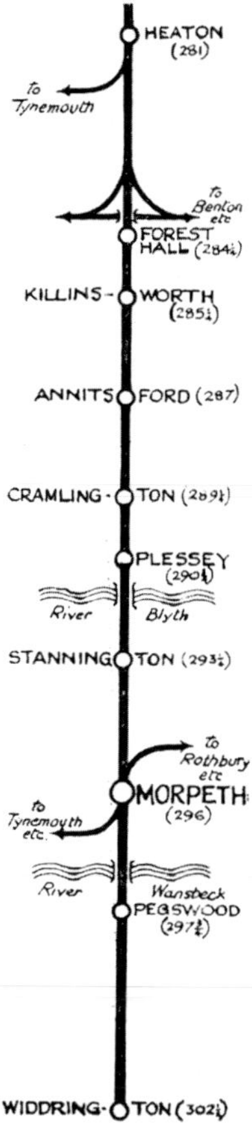

railway and beyond that, first a low level swing bridge and then the graceful Tyne Road Bridge, completed in 1928. After its stop in Newcastle's 15-platform Central station, the " Queen of Scots " pulls out in the shadow of the Norman castle erected by Henry II in 1172, which stands in the " V " of the junction with the tracks curving away to the right to cross the High Level Bridge. On the left the 193½ ft. lantern tower of Newcastle cathedral, where John Knox once occupied the pulpit, is conspicuous. Newcastle is 8 miles from the sea, but the largest ships can sail up to its quays and yards, where that grand old Cunarder and Blue-Riband-holder *Mauretania*, amongst other ships, was built. To-day, besides dealing with a great volume of cargo, Newcastle is the principal port for the Norwegian tourist traffic.

Newcastle's other important motive power depot, Heaton, is on the right beyond the station of the same name. The " Queen of Scots " is now climbing more or less continuously until Cramlington, after which the gradients undulate to Alnmouth. At Killingworth an old ivy-covered house adjoining the line was once the home of George Stephenson; he it was who fashioned the sundial over the door. The remnants of another Norman castle, built soon after the 1066 Conquest, are to be seen on the left before Morpeth, where we come within sight of the North Sea. Better known is Warkworth Castle, visible on the right after Acklington in a bend of the Coquet river, which runs down from Rothbury Forest in the lee of the 1,447 ft. high Tosson Hill away to the west. An old Saxon fortress once stood on the site of Warkworth Castle, which was built in 1159

THE HIGH LEVEL BRIDGE AT NEWCASTLE, with the castle visible on the left. Crossing the bridge is Class " A2/2 " 4-6-2 No. 60501 *Cock o' the North* with a York-Newcastle train. [*K. Field*

and conferred by Edward III as a family seat on the Percy house, a clan celebrated in the lore of the Border country.

From the stately viaduct over the Aln at Alnmouth (pronounced " Alemouth "), the engine faces 4 miles of 1 in 170 up Longhoughton bank to Little Mill, but soon after enjoys a " breather " on 2½ miles of 1 in 150 down gradient through Christon Bank. Beyond Chathill one may glimpse the 2,000 ft. high hills at the eastern end of the Cheviot range if the weather is clear. On the coast beyond Lucker it is worth looking out for Bamburgh Castle, erected as long ago as 541 by King Ida, while out at sea one soon notices the lighthouse of the Farne islands, two miles offshore, from one of which Grace Darling and her father made their epic rescue. Another historic island

Above: CLIMBING COCKBURNSPATH BANK to Grantshouse—Class " A2 " 4-6-2 No. 60534 *Irish Elegance* on the southbound " Queen of Scots " [*C. J. B. Sanderson*
Below: TAKING WATER from Lucker troughs—Class " A1 " 4-6-2 No. 60152 *Holyrood* on a Kings Cross-Glasgow express. [*I. W Armstrong*

is Lindisfarne, or Holy Island, standing offshore from Beal, where one of the earliest Christian missions to Britain was founded by St. Aidan in the 7th Century.

At Goswick there begins a long climb of some 22 miles up to the flanks of the Lammermuir Hills at Grantshouse, broken by two level or slightly downhill sections through Tweedmouth and Ayton. Beyond Tweedmouth we have our first glimpse ahead of the 28-arch Royal Border Bridge over the Tweed at Berwick, built by Robert Stephenson in 1847-50 and opened by Queen Victoria; it is 2,160 ft. long and 126½ ft. above the water. Downstream to the right is the graceful ferro-concrete Royal Tweed Bridge, carrying the Great North Road, which was opened by the then Prince of Wales in 1928, and beyond that the ancient stone bridge it replaced. Berwick station stands on the site of the town's old castle, witness of many a Border struggle since it was first sacked by William the Conqueror. The actual Anglo-Scottish boundary is three miles further north and is marked by an attractive lineside sign.

Beyond Berwick the railway hugs the rocky coastline and there are some magnificent prospects to the right as the engine attacks the 4 miles of 1 in 190 up to Burnmouth. After the respite at Ayton comes the final 7½ miles up, mostly at 1 in 200, to Grantshouse and the summit; then the "Queen of Scots" threads the 267 yds. Penmanshiel Tunnel in the cleft between the 1,283 ft. Heart Law on the left and the 803 ft. Meikle Black Law on the right. Speed is increasing rapidly for the next 4½ miles are downhill at 1 in 96 to a stretch of level beyond Innerwick, but then the descent is resumed on easier grades through Dunbar.

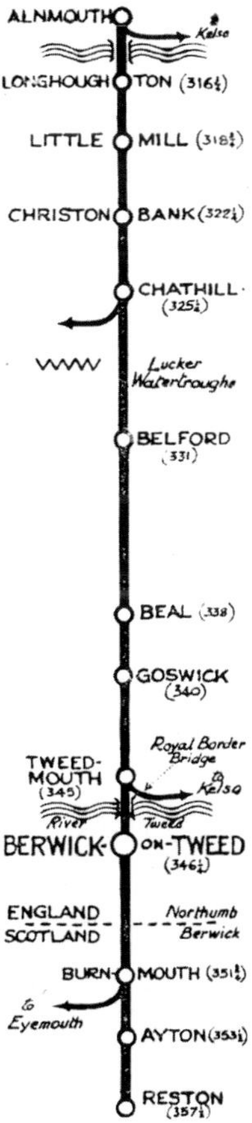

25

PRINCES STREET GARDENS, EDINBURGH—A freight from the Glasgow line approaches Waverley station; high up on the left is the castle. [B. *Lockey*

Between Dunbar and Drem there are frequent glimpses out to sea of the once volcanic Bass Rock, 3 miles offshore, where Cromwell consigned many of his Scotch Covenanter captives to prison. Further up the coast the conical outline of North Berwick Law, 614 ft. high, stands guard above the famous golfing town, while inland, on the other side of the line, is the 724 ft. Traprain Law.

At Longniddry Junction the sea drives up close to the railway again, and if it is a clear day, you will see the line of the Fifeshire hills on the other shore of the Firth of Forth. Garleton Hill, some two miles to the left of the railway, is topped by the Hopetoun Monument, erected in 1824 in memory of the Earl who took over command of British troops at the Battle of Corunna, in Spain, after the death of Sir John Moore. The famous Battle of Prestonpans in 1745 was fought in the country between the railway south of that station and the coast; there is visible evidence of it in a monument to the left of the line, erected to a colonel who was killed in the struggle. Pinkie House, where Bonnie Prince Charlie slept after the battle, can be seen on the right just before Inveresk.

We are now nearing Edinburgh. Beyond the Braid Hills on the left, the unmistakeable outline of Arthur's Seat, that 822 ft. high mass of volcanic rock overlooking Edinburgh, is coming into sight. Soon after passing the popular seaside resort of Portobello, the railway enthusiasts will be keeping a look-out for St Margaret's engine shed. Then the engine is climbing the last steep $1\frac{1}{2}$ miles of 1 in 78 through Calton Tunnel and beneath the walls of the city gaol into the great Waverley station.

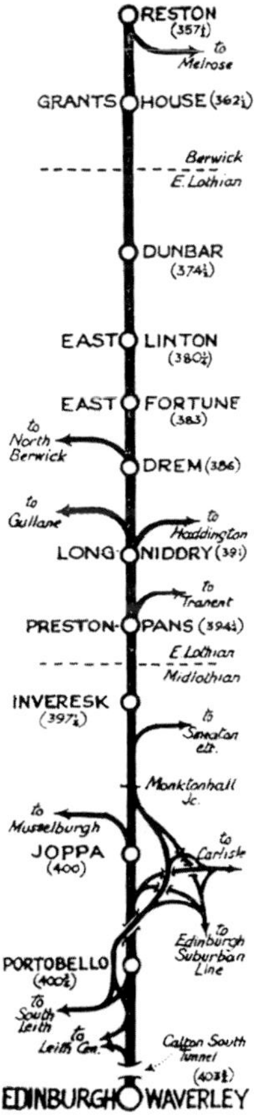

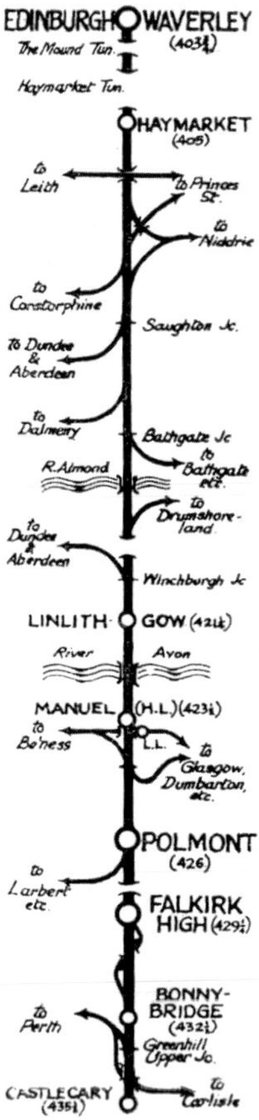

Restarting from Waverley station, the train is immediately enclosed in the 124 yds. tunnel beneath the Mound, once the city's refuse dump but now ground proudly occupied by Scotland's National Gallery; alongside the railway on the right are the gardens adjoining Princes Street, while on the left the ground climbs steeply to the ramparts of Edinburgh Castle. After the 1009 yds. long Haymarket South Tunnel those looking for Haymarket engine shed will see it on the right, before the Aberdeen line diverges on its way to the majestic Forth Bridge, of which we shall soon catch a distant glimpse, also on the right. The line to Glasgow is little short of level as far as Cowlairs, thanks to the lavish construction of viaducts and embankments by its original engineers. Beyond Bathgate Junction we cross the Almond river on a $\frac{5}{8}$-mile viaduct of 36 arches, approached by $\frac{1}{2}$-mile of embankment on each side, over which there is a 30 m.p.h. speed restriction. Winchburgh Tunnel, before Linlithgow, is 372 yds. long, and beyond it one notices on the right Binns Tower, where the Royal Scots Greys Regiment was raised in 1681; a little further on is the Hope Monument, raised to a general killed in the Indian Mutiny. There is another 23-span viaduct beyond Linlithgow, carrying the railway over the Avon river and, beyond the 845 yds. long Falkirk Tunnel, yet another with a central span of 130 ft., over what were once the locks of the Union and Forth & Clyde canals. Falkirk is a heavy industrial town, the centre of a district rich in coal and iron, at which the "Queen of Scots" stops in the down direction.

The last notable viaduct is just before Castlecary, a structure of eight 50 ft. spans carrying the railway over the road to Stirling. Beyond the station the railway crosses the line of the wall erected by the Romans from the Forth to the Clyde in the 2nd Century. One of Scotland's largest marshalling yards, Cadder, covers many acres alongside the main line between Lenzie and Bishopbriggs, and then the sight of Eastfield motive power depot is a warning of our approach to the steep descent into Glasgow's Queen Street terminus from Cowlairs, home of a locomotive, carriage and wagon works established in 1842 and still busily at work.

The builders of the Edinburgh-Glasgow railway planned a high level terminus, but strong opposition from the owners of the Forth & Clyde Canal, which the railway would have had to bridge, decided them to avoid a protracted battle for their original scheme and tunnel below the waterway; hence the precipitous 1 in 41 incline by which the railway descends, partly through a 999 yds. long tunnel, to Queen Street station, Glasgow. In the earliest days trains were hauled up the bank from the terminus by cable operated by a stationary winding engine at the summit; not until 1909 was the cable apparatus abandoned in favour of banking engines, which are still used. Sometimes late-running trains are stopped at Cowlairs and their main line engine removed in favour of a shunting engine, which eases the train down the hill to Queen Street; this practice lessens track occupation on the double track incline, since the incoming main line locomotive can proceed straight to nearby Eastfield shed, while the shunting engine is conveniently placed to bank the train out of Queen Street when it is due to depart.

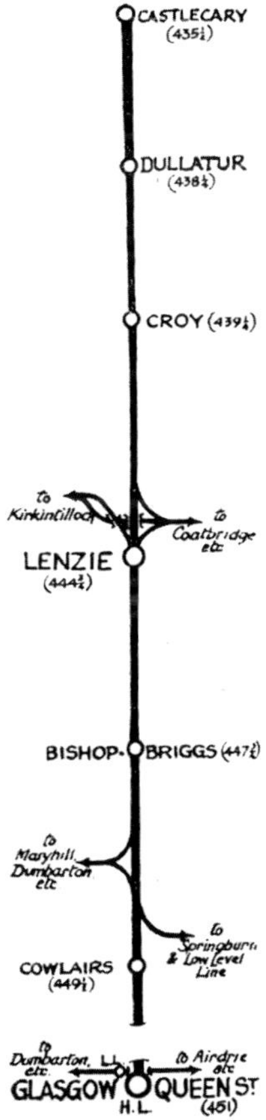

Published by Ian Allan, Ltd. Craven House, Hampton Court, Surrey and Printed by Crampton & Sons, Ltd., Sawston, Cambridge

famous trains — 7

The

ROYAL WESSEX and BOURNEMOUTH BELLE

WATERLOO—BOURNEMOUTH, SWANAGE & WEYMOUTH

(Southern Region)

by

G. FREEMAN ALLEN

Ian Allan Ltd

DIESEL-HAULED—The "Bournemouth Belle" at speed near Farnborough behind diesel-electric locomotive No. 10201.
[*R. D. Swift*

Introduction

BEFORE the days of corridor trains on the old London & South Western Railway, single Pullman cars were included in several expresses between Waterloo and Bournemouth. Since there was no access to them from other vehicles while the train was in motion, you had to be a Pullman passenger if you wanted any refreshment in the course of the journey. With corridor trains came the railway's own restaurant cars and Pullmans disappeared from the Bournemouth line, not to return until the 1930's, when the Southern Railway put on a Sunday all-Pullman train between London and Bournemouth. The popularity of the service was soon apparent, and in 1936 the Southern was prompted to make it a daily train, named the " Bournemouth Belle ".

At first the " Belle " was non-stop to Bournemouth Central, but soon a Southampton stop was inserted in the schedule in both directions. Coming up, the " Bournemouth Belle " before the war boasted the fastest timing of any express between Southampton and Waterloo, being booked to cover the 79.2 miles in 85 minutes as part of a two-hour dash up from Bournemouth Central. The express was withdrawn from the timetables in the Second World War, but when it reappeared in the autumn of 1946 the two-hour booking up from Bournemouth was reinstated. Post-war loads soon increased, however, and the timing has since been lengthened to 2 hours 10 minutes down and 2 hours 5 minutes up.

The " Royal Wessex " is the post-war descendant of a celebrated pre-war flier, the Southern's " Bournemouth Limited ". The latter name was bestowed in 1929 on a non-stop train between London and Bournemouth that soon became a star of the Southern timetables. In the years immediately before the Second World War the Southern " Schools " 4-4-0s were the principal engines used on this express, which was the country's most testing assignment in those days for a four-coupled engine, since the 11-coach " Bournemouth Limited " was booked to run the 107.9 miles from Waterloo to Bournemouth in 116 minutes down and only two minutes more in the return direction. The express was withdrawn in 1939 and, although its early morning path up from Weymouth and afternoon path down from Waterloo were used again from October, 1945, by a train later named the " Royal Wessex " in honour of the 1951 Festival of Britain, non-stop running between London and Bournemouth has not been resumed.

The Route to Weymouth

THE start from Waterloo is the most interesting of any from London termini. The railway runs for most of the way to Clapham Junction on an embankment or over bridges among the city's rooftops, and parallel with the Thames as far as Vauxhall. Thus, as the train winds out of the station over the sharp curves at the approach to Waterloo, there is a wonderful view to the right of the Houses of Parliament, Big Ben and Westminster Abbey across the river; on the Waterloo bank the big red-tiled roof of County Hall, headquarters of the London County Council, is conspicuous and, a short distance further on, you will notice the tree-hedged Lambeth Palace, home of the Archbishop of Canterbury. At the approach to Vauxhall, the long facade and dome of the Tate Gallery can be glimpsed on the other side of the Thames, but on the other side of Vauxhall the right-hand view is taken up by the big Nine Elms goods station.

NOTE: The figures in brackets after station names indicate mileages from Waterloo.

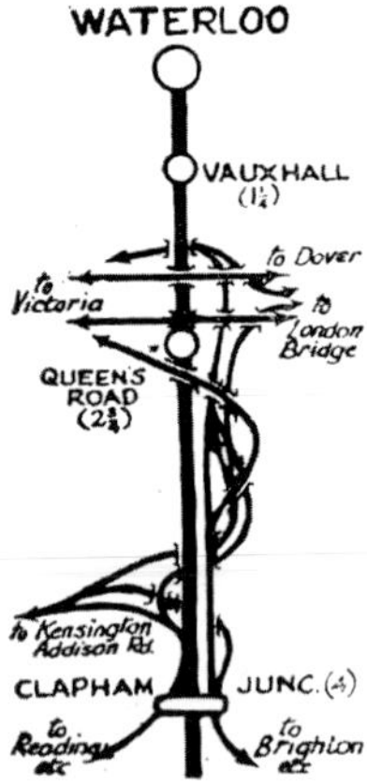

Railway enthusiasts will be looking left, however, for a sight of Nine Elms locomotive depot and then, just after the Victoria-Kent Coast main line has bridged us, for Stewarts Lane locomotive depot on a level below us. On the other side of the line the majestic chimneys of Battersea Power station, a great modern edifice designed by Lutyens, lazily disgorge white smoke.

Now we are among the maze of junctions and carriage sidings at the approach to Clapham Junction, where the Victoria-South Coast line sweeps down from the left to run parallel with us through the busiest station in the world. Over 2,000 trains pass through its platforms every weekday, and at the morning or evening rush-hour there is not a moment when you can stand on its platforms and not see a train approaching, leaving or standing at the station.

The big factory-like building close to the

4

lineside on the right as we approach Wimbledon is the Durnsford Road power station, supplier of current to the electric lines into and out of Waterloo; electric trains are stored in the car sheds just beyond it. Wimbledon is the terminus of District line trains of London Transport, which occupy platforms on the right of the station. If you are travelling in summer, the riot of colour in Carter's seed-testing beds will catch your eye on the left after Raynes Park. Here and at all the branch line junctions on this route as far as Hampton Court Junction, beyond Surbiton, you will see one reason why the Southern can run its expresses so smartly out of London, despite the intense suburban service In every case interference with main line traffic is avoided by carrying the branch line over by a flying junction or burrowing it under the main line to join the up or down slow line from Waterloo, according to whether the branch is coming in from the left or right of us, instead of laying it right across the main lines on the flat. Naturally, flying or burrowing junctions are a more expensive way of doing things than ordinary flat junctions, but in the long run they pay tremendous dividends in keeping heavy traffic moving efficiently, as the Southern, which has made extensive use of them in the London area, knows to its profit.

Beyond Malden the chimneys of the modern Kingston Power station can be seen on the horizon to the right. On the other side of the track, you will notice Sandown Park racecourse beyond Esher; this is one of the well-known trio of racecourses in this area, the other two being Hurst Park and Kempton Park.

5

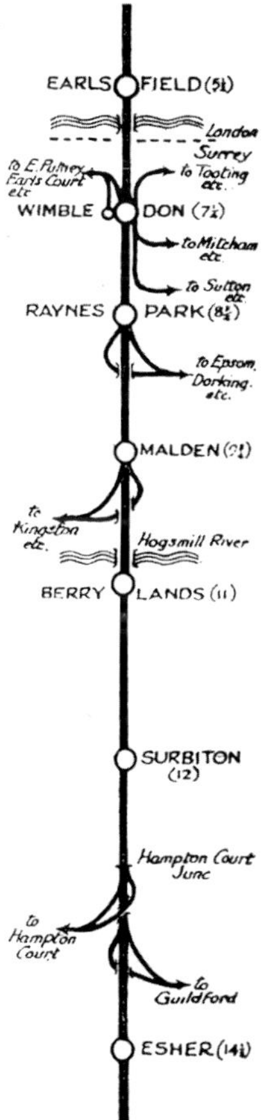

IN THE LONDON SUBURBS—*Above*: The down "Bournemouth Belle," headed by "Britannia" Pacific No. 70009 *Alfred the Great*, passes Durnsford Road power station and electric car sheds. *Below*: Diesel-electric locomotive No. 10000 speeds the down "Royal Wessex" through Wimbledon [*P. F. Winding, R. Russell*

As the railway emerges from a long cutting at Weybridge, you will see on the left the remains of the famous Brooklands racing track, where in days gone by many a Southern express was paced by cars on the straight which paralleled the railway. Now the centre of the circuit is taken over by the Vickers-Armstrong aircraft works, and perhaps there will be a glimpse of a four-jet Valiant bomber amongst the Viscount and Viking airliners which are usually dispersed round the airfield. Hitherto the exit from Waterloo has been more or less level, but at West Byfleet there begins a long climb of some 10½ miles at from 1 in 314 to 1 in 387 to a summit beyond Brookwood at milepost 31.

Incidentally, if you want at any time to check the distance you have travelled from Waterloo, it is continuously shown on these mileposts, which are spaced out at quarter-mile intervals by the trackside on the left; one, two or three dots or bars after the figure shown on the milepost indicate an additional ¼, ½ or ¾ mile, though in some places the fractions are printed as such. You can use these mileposts to check the speed of your train. If you time the number of seconds you take to cover the quarter-mile between any two of these posts and divide the result into 900, the answer will be your speed in miles per hour, e.g. a quarter-mile covered in 12 seconds equals 75 m.p.h. Don't confuse the mileposts with the numbers shown on metal discs on the bridges you pass over or under, by the way; the latter are purely the reference numbers by which the bridges are known to railwaymen. The other little trackside posts, on the left, with two arms inclined at varying angles like the

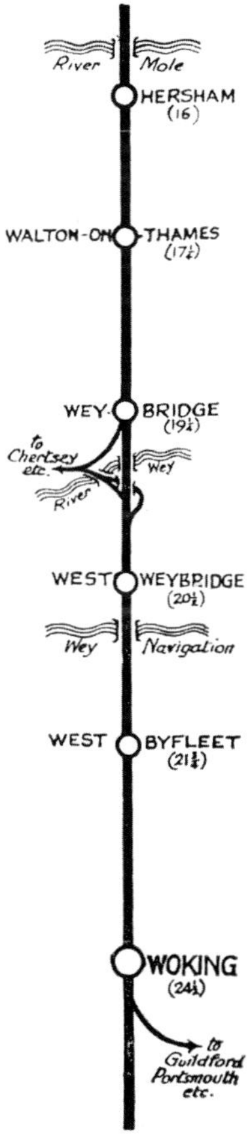

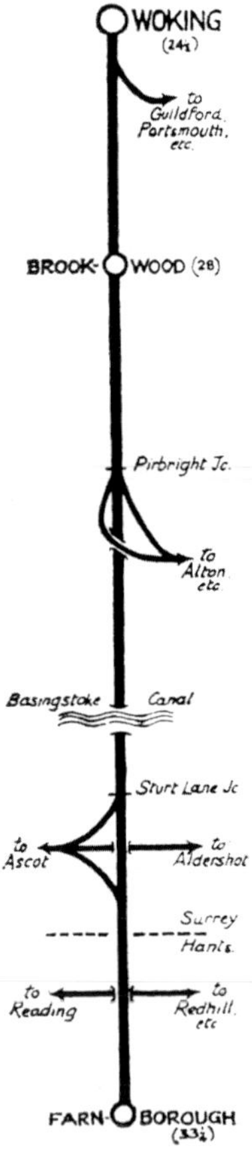

hands of a clock, indicate a change of gradient; e.g., a post with the arms at "twenty to four" with the minute hand marked "400" and the "hour hand" 200, indicates a change of incline from a rise of 1 ft. up in every 400 ft. along to 1 ft. down in every 200 ft. along.

Apart from its interest as a busy railway junction, a novel feature of Woking is the mosque you will notice on the left. The famous Necropolis lines the left side of the track before Brookwood; in days gone by special funeral trains were run to this cemetery from Waterloo. We are in Army territory now, with Pirbright Common on the left, the Bisley rifle ranges beyond the trees to our right and the line to nearby Aldershot diverging by another flying junction: just beyond this junction you will see the Basingstoke Canal on the right, and soon it crosses the railway on an aqueduct.

An interesting feature of the 23½ miles from Woking to Basingstoke is that they are controlled by one of the earliest fully automatic signalling installations in Britain; hence the fact the signals are semaphores, whereas modern automatic installations use powerful colour lights of the type that signalled our way out from Waterloo to Hampton Court Junction, beyond Surbiton. Except at junctions, where obviously a signalman must be retained to route the trains on to their respective lines, the trains protect themselves. The basis of the system is that the two rails of each track act as outward and return leads from a source of weak electric current to the signalling apparatus and back, each track being insulated into sections controlled by a signal. When a train enters a section, it forms a short circuit for the current, which, instead of reaching the signal, hops across to the opposite line straight away. This change in the current flow sets the signal to danger. It will stay at danger until the train has cleared the section, which will be long enough to leave a safe headway between it and any following train, whereupon the signal will clear again. This "track circuiting", as it is called, is the basis, not only of automatic signalling, but also of the safety devices in modern signal-boxes, where it is used to lock apparatus and prevent signalmen accepting trains into sections already occupied.

From milepost 31 to a point 2 miles from Basingstoke the track is level or slightly against the engine. The market town of Basingstoke is an important junction, where we are joined by the cross-country route from the Western Region at Reading, which contributes a considerable amount of traffic from the Midlands for Portsmouth and Southampton; some of these through trains are worked through to their destinations by Western Region locomotives. Basingstoke engine shed, by the way, is on the right just beyond the station. At Worting Junction, 2½ miles beyond Basingstoke, we cross from the Salisbury and Exeter line to the Bournemouth route, which soon begins to curve away to the left, while the up Bournemouth line sweeps across the tracks to the West Country on the Battledown flyover bridge. The point-work at Worting Junction is finely engineered for high-speed running. In the westbound direction Bournemouth trains can cross over smoothly at 50 m.p.h., while coming up they sweep on to the up Exeter line from the flyover at a mile a minute.

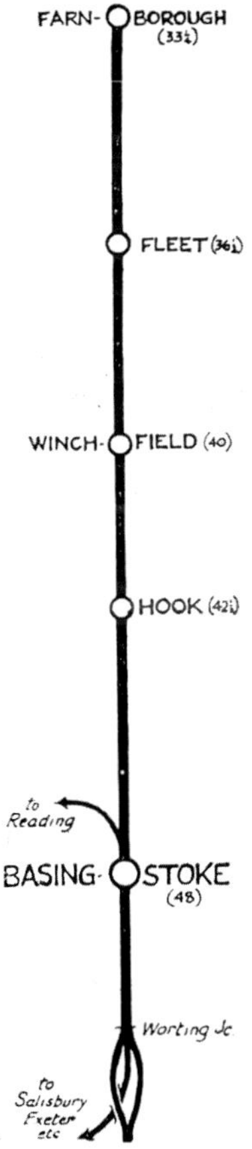

Right : ON THE BATTLE-DOWN FLYOVER—An up Bournemouth express climbs to the bridge over the Exeter main line west of Basingstoke. The engine is Pacific No. 34093 *Saunton*
[*T. E. Williams*

Below : Pacific No. 35012 *United States Line* speeds past Shawford Junction with the 1.30 p.m. Waterloo-Weymouth.
[*R. C. Riley*

The 200-yard Litchfield Tunnel marks the end of the intermittent climbing since West Weybridge and the railway now sweeps downhill from the chalk downs, straight as a die, for 16 miles to Allbrook Junction, Eastleigh, over a wonderful racing stretch and a superb piece of engineering by the old London & Southampton Railway as long ago as 1840; except for a slight variation for a mile or so on the London side of Winchester, the slope is an uninterrupted 1 in 252 down all the way. Extensive works were necessary to provide such a fine piece of track, of course; deep cuttings and three tunnels—Litchfield and two more, 265 and 200 yards long respectively, at the approach to Micheldever—had to be dug, the earth excavated being used for high tree-lined embankments beyond Micheldever. As a result, the section from Litchfield tunnel to Winchester was not completed until a year after the route had been finished between Waterloo and Basingstoke, and Southampton and Winchester; during that year passengers had to detrain and cross the gap in road coaches. In later years the cutting between the last tunnel and Micheldever station was still further widened to procure chalk for extensions of Southampton docks, and now there is room for numerous sidings there.

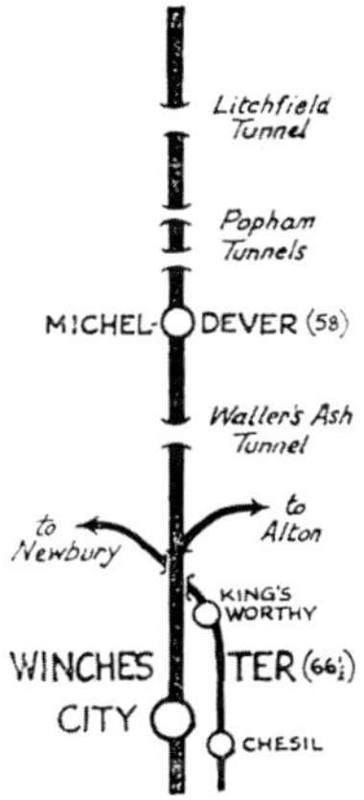

After the 400 yards-long Waller's Ash Tunnel and the junction with the Alton line we hurry through Winchester on the "Bournemouth Belle", but stop there if we are travelling on the "Royal Wessex". We must look back after we have emerged from the cutting beyond the station for the best view of this historic city, the virtual capital of England in Anglo-Saxon times, when the kings of Wessex ruled the whole country. Under King Alfred it became a great centre of learning—many years later, in 1387, William of Wykeham founded there one of the country's greatest public schools, south of the cathedral close—and Canute governed the country from Winchester. Alfred, Canute and other Saxon kings were buried in a minster Alfred founded north of the cathedral, known as Hyde Abbey, of which a gateway and other traces survive. The Norman kings were also fond of Winchester, and every Easter William the Conqueror, who kept his treasure in the city, wore his crown in state in the cathedral, the longest (550 ft.) in England; its low, square tower and long roof can be seen in the left distance. Patron saint of the cathedral, which was erected between 1070 (the Norman tower and transepts) and 1360 (the Perpendicular nave), is St. Swithin, whose name is best known for the association of his feast-day with a meteorological superstition. Conspicuous on the left as we leave the city is the 328 ft.-high St. Catherine's Hill, the site, it is believed of the earliest settlement here in prehistoric times.

We now have the company of the Itchen river on the left as we hurry through Shawford to Allbrook Junction, where serried ranks of sidings on the left denote our approach to the railway town of Eastleigh, the main centre for locomotive and carriage construction on the Southern Region. The carriage and wagon works was established on the down side of the diverging Portsmouth line in 1890, and the locomotive works was set up in the "V" of the Portsmouth line and our Bournemouth route, alongside the locomotive depot, in 1909; in those days, of course, the owner of the works was the London & South Western Railway, which previously had its plant at Nine Elms London. The works cover 81 acres, but although coaching stock is still constructed here, locomotives are not and the locomotive plant is given over entirely to repair work, principally on the former Southern Railway classes which were built here before nationalisation, notably the celebrated Bulleid Pacifics which haul the "Bournemouth Belle" and the "Royal Wessex." Eastleigh locomotive depot possesses a few Bulleid Pacifics and several "Lord Nelson" 4-6-0s amongst its allocation, whose principal duties are to work the boat trains between Southampton and Waterloo. Beyond the works on the left you notice Eastleigh airport, which serves Southampton, and its associated works of such well-known firms as Vickers-Armstrong and Saunders-Roe.

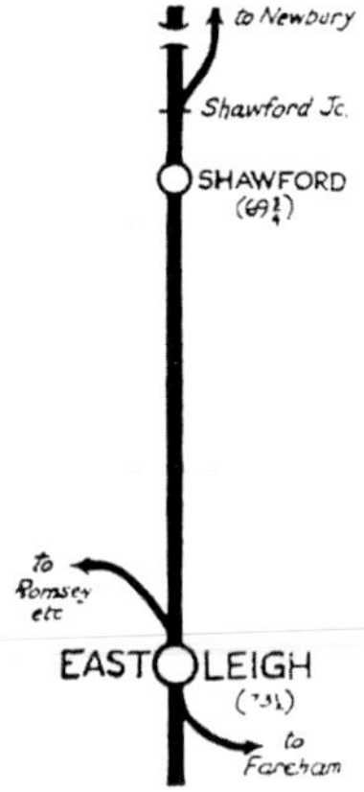

EASTLEIGH—*Above* : Pacific No. 35018 *British India Line* passes the station on the down "Royal Wessex" *Below* : Inside the works, showing a Bulleid Pacific under repair with most of its air-smoothed casing removed. [*L. Elsey, R. H. Clark*

1

THE OCEAN TERMINAL AT SOUTHAMPTON—The *Queen Mary* is tied up at the quay and a 'Lord Nelson" 4-6-0 is leaving with a boat train. [P. *Ransome-Wallis*

The descent continues more gently from Eastleigh, but at St. Denys, where the Itchen river has swollen to a wide estuary in the area of the old Roman port of Clausentum, we begin to slacken speed for Northam Junction. Here we curve very sharply right, almost at walking pace, away from the line to Southampton Old Docks, thread a short tunnel and soon come to a stand at Southampton Central, overlooked on the right by the lofty tower of Southampton's modern civic centre. On the Southern Region there are no water troughs from which our engine can replenish its tender whilst on the move, as on other Regions of British Railways, so that the engine crew will use our waiting time at Southampton to take on water.

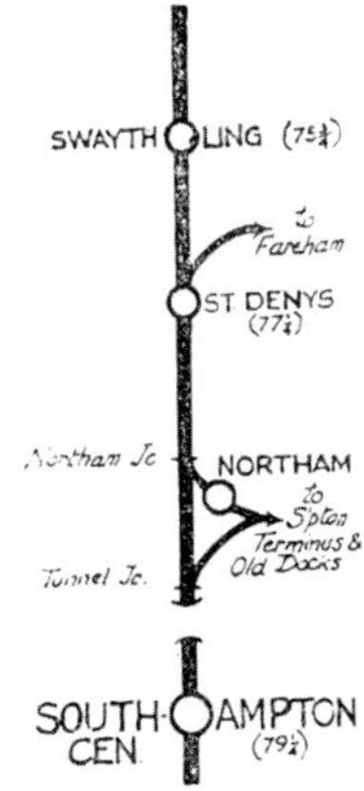

Our chances for a glimpse of some of the great ocean liners come as we pull out of Southampton Central. Looking back on the left we shall probably see in the distance the funnels of ships tied up in the Old Docks on the bank of the Itchen, which date from the first half of the last century. Southampton is one of the world's finest natural harbours, well sheltered and with the advantage of two channels to the sea, either by Spithead or the Needles—a fact which possibly accounts for its odd double high tide, the second high water following the first within about two hours—and it has been used as a port since mediaeval times, when it was an outlet for the wool trade of Winchester. The growth of London as a port in Tudor times affected Southampton's prosperity, and its modern well-being dates from the completion of the London & Southampton Railway in 1840. Plans for the Old Docks were drawn up by that railway's engineer, Francis Giles, and sufficient construction had been completed by 1843 to enable Southampton to take over from Falmouth the distinction of being the country's principal steamship port. During the rest of the century further extensions were made, but they so severely extended the finances of the Southampton Dock Co. that in 1892 the London & South Western Railway, successor of the original Southampton line and constituent of the later Southern Railway, was persuaded to

SOUTHAMPTON CENTRAL STATION—"The Bournemouth Belle", headed by Pacific No. 35014 *Nederland Line*, is ready to leave.

purchase the docks. So it came about that the continuous deep water quay which parallels the railway for 1½ miles on the left as we leave Southampton was constructed by the enterprising Southern Railway, in justified anticipation of increased traffic. Between 1928 and 1933 407 acres of mudland between the River Test and the railway were reclaimed and two million tons of concrete were poured into what are known as the New Docks, where the largest Atlantic liners usually berth nowadays. On the quayside a magnificent Ocean Terminal building, with escalators between its comfortable lounges and the boat train platform was completed in 1950. The largest Southern Pacifics can work their boat trains into and out of the Ocean Terminal, which they reach from Millbrook. Between the quay and the main line are extensive sidings and a carriage shed, as well as the conspicuous Rank flour mills near the town and, further west, General Motors' factory.

Possibly we shall have a close-up of one of the great British liners as we come to the end of the docks, where the main line passes close to the tip of the largest graving dock in the world. Opened by King George V in 1933 and named after him, it is 1,200 ft. long, 165 ft. wide and 59 ft. deep, and it can accommodate—and does, at regular intervals—the largest British ships, up to the *Queen Elizabeth*. Once they are safely enclosed in the dock, its 58 million gallons of water can be pumped out in four hours, so that the ship's hull and screws can be checked and repainted.

Beyond the graving dock on the left is the Southern Region's Redbridge sleeper depot, where one of the three quaint Class "C14" 0-4-0 tanks, No. DS77, works as a shunter; these three engines, with driving wheels no bigger than 3 ft. in diameter, were originally the motor units of steam railcars built by Drummond for the L.S.W.R. in the first decade of the century. Then we cross the broad estuary of the Test river on a causeway and, after Southampton's industrial suburb of Totton, bid farewell to the branch which curves away leftward to Fawley, known the country over for its great oil refinery, the "Silver City". The exit from Southampton is on level track to this point.

Now we are in the historic New Forest, and probably some of the sturdy little wild ponies of the forest are grazing in the clearings close to the track. There are some 1,500 of these animals, whose forbears are often claimed to have come to England from Spain with the Armada, and they belong to the people of the forest, the commoners, who own or rent land in it.

Lyndhurst Road is the station for the

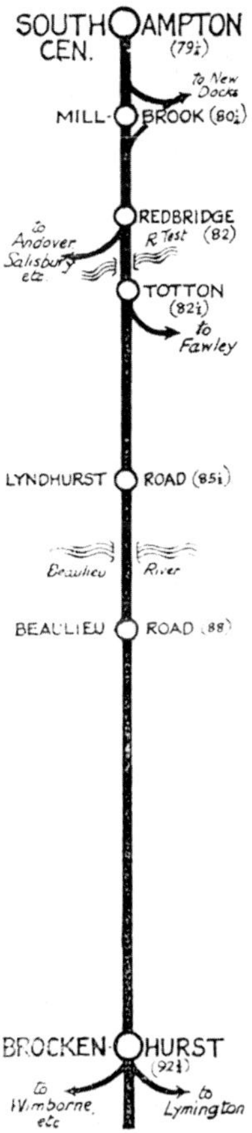

LEAVING BROCKENHURST—The "Royal Wessex", headed by Pacific No. 35010 *Blue Star*. [R. C. Riley

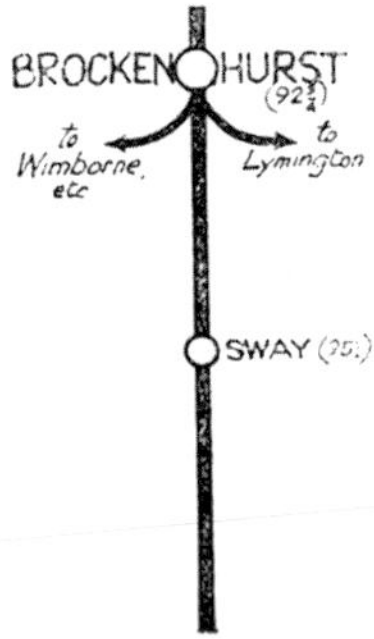

recognised "capital" of the New Forest, the old town of Lyndhurst, with its antlered hall where the green-uniformed Verderers meet regularly to administer the laws of the forest. Beaulieu Road station, the summit of a steep hump at 1 in 150, is well provided with cattle pens, for every summer an auction sale of the forest ponies is held here. The ruins of Beaulieu Abbey, built by King John, are some way distant to the left and are not visible from the line. Incidentally, the correct pronunciation of Beaulieu as "Bewley" is not so inexplicable as it appears, but a reminiscence of Saxon days, when the settlement was named "Beolea" ("bee meadow"); the town's present name originated with the Normans.

Just before Brockenhurst there begins a

steep climb mainly at 1 in 103 to 176 to a summit near Sway. Brockenhurst, one of the New Forest's show towns, is also the junction for the original line to Dorset. When the London & Southampton Railway was opened, Bournemouth was little more than a village, so that when an extension to Dorchester was laid down in 1847 the route chosen was via Wimborne—the line which diverges to the right beyond Brockenhurst and rejoins us again at Hamworthy Junction. It was 1870 before there was a railway to Bournemouth, which was an extension of a branch from Ringwood to Christchurch that has long since been abandoned, and 1888 before the route our train now follows from Lymington Junction, Brockenhurst, was completed to Bournemouth via Sway. In summer the old route via Wimborne is still used by some Saturday trains for Weymouth or Swanage, which thus avoid the busy Bournemouth area.

Beyond Sway a 200 ft. high ferro-concrete tower stands out amongst the trees on the left. This hideous structure, a landmark for miles around, was erected nearly 90 years ago by an eccentric retired barrister named Andrew Peterson, who was anxious to demonstrate in this way the potentiality of concrete. He left a request that his body should be buried in the tower and that a light should be kept burning at its summit to act as a beacon for shipping in the distant Solent. His first behest was carried out, but naval authorities forbad the second, considering the beacon would cause more confusion than confidence among sailors. Not surprisingly the tower has ever since been known as Peterson's Folly.

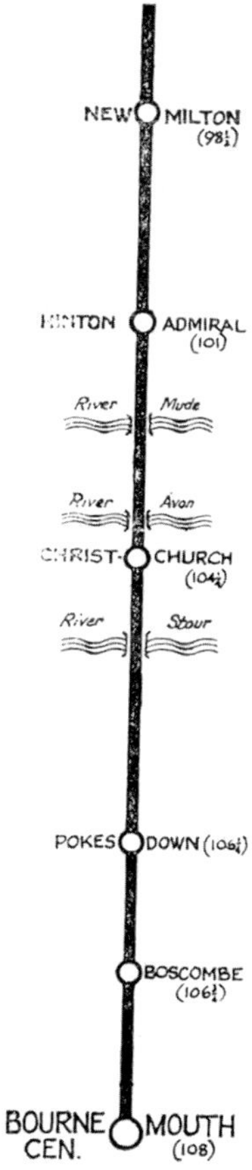

BOURNEMOUTH CENTRAL—Pacific No. 34108 *Wincanton* leaves with the up "Royal Wessex". [*W. N. Lockett*]

About a mile beyond New Milton the railway sweeps downhill at gradients varying from 1 in 103 to 1 in 300, through Hinton Admiral, where a search of the lefthand horizon for the wireless masts on Hengistbury Head may lead us to a glimpse of the sea beyond, if the weather is clear. Then the brakes are applied, for there is a speed restriction over the curve through Christchurch, the tower of whose famous 11th Century priory is easily picked out on the left; this building is said to have the most perfect mediaeval interior preserved in the country. The Christchurch speed restriction prevents the driver from taking a run at the awkward 1½ miles of 1 in 99 uphill which follow as far as Pokesdown, where the gradient eases but is still upward through Boscombe to the approach to Bournemouth Central Station.

The many attractions of Bournemouth as a seaside resort are not visible from the railway, which emerges from the roofed-over vault of Bournemouth Central in a deep cutting. The principal Bournemouth motive power depot adjoins the Central station at the country end, on the right. Some 2 miles from the Central station the high ground on both sides of the railway falls away into the upper Bourne valley, where there is a triangular junction, two sides of which are on high arched viaducts.

Here, at Gasworks Junction, the "Bournemouth Belle" turns left, past the small Somerset & Dorset section engine shed at Branksome, and completes almost a semicircle, making tracks for the terminus of Bournemouth West. The last stage into the station is down a steep falling gradient of 1 in 60, past extensive carriage sheds and sidings on the left.

Weymouth-bound "Royal Wessex" passengers continue straight ahead at Gasworks Junction, but they will catch a glimpse of Branksome shed, and probably of a Midland 4-4-0 or two, on the left as they make for Branksome station and the steep bank down through Parkstone to Poole. The descent begins at 1 in 130 just before Branksome station and soon steepens to 1 in 60 through Parkstone station, high above the town and offering a fine view of Parkstone Bay to the left. The foot of the bank is at the approach to the causeway across an inlet of Parkstone Bay.

Parkstone bank is a difficult obstacle for up trains, since they cannot take a rush at it; for those that do not stop at Poole are subjected to a severe speed restriction over the sharp curve on which Poole station is built, and then have only a mile of level track over the causeway in which to regain speed. In winter the Weymouth trains are not usually so heavy as to embarass their engines on this incline, but in summer it is a different matter; then many up trains have the assistance from Poole of a banking engine, which is not coupled to the rear of the train, so that it can drop off beyond Branksome and return light to Poole without the necessity to halt the main train to uncouple it. Poole is an interesting old town, which once carried on a thriving

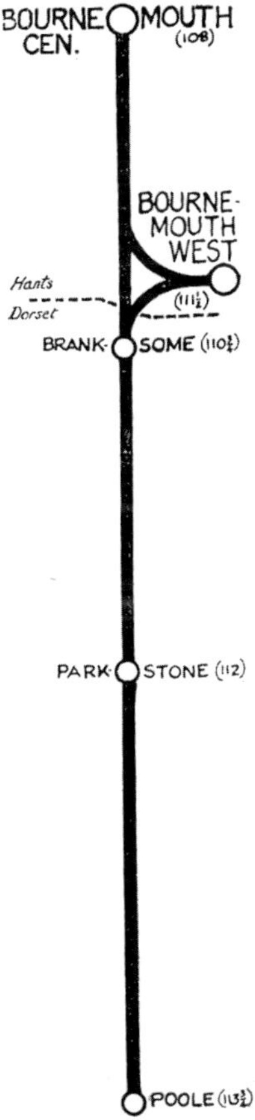

21

CORFE CASTLE—Pacific No. 34005 Barnstaple passes with a summer Waterloo-Swanage Express [J. F. Aylard

transatlantic shipping trade, but to-day's larger craft are unable to take advantage of its fine natural harbour because of sand-banks at its entrance.

Hamworthy Junction, beyond another causeway across Holes Bay, is at the summit of a slight hump, but otherwise the going is more or less level through Holton Heath, where a vast naval explosives factory occupies many acres on the right-hand side to Wareham. The rather hum-drum surroundings of Wareham station are misleading, for the town itself, some distance away, has traces of an encircling Roman wall in its earthen ramparts.

From Worgret Junction, a mile beyond Wareham, a picturesque branch turns away south-eastwards, cutting across the Purbeck Hills to Swanage. Marble was once excavated from these hills, but that is now exhausted; beneath the marble, however, lay china clay, which is still mined extensively. The branch climbs sharply, mainly at 1 in 80, across moorland, with the high ground of Creech Heath on the right, to Corfe Castle. At the approach to the station the train passes the ruins of Corfe Castle high above the line on a hillock to the right. The castle dates from Norman times, although there are traces of an earlier Saxon settlement, and guarded this gap in the Purbeck hills; it was frequently the residence of King John, as well as the prison of some earlier monarchs, and served its last military duty as a Parliamentary stronghold against the Roundheads, who eventually sacked it in 1646. From Corfe Castle the branch turns downhill, mainly at 1 in 78, through more attractive moorland scenery, dominated by the 650 ft. high Codlington Hill on the left, to Swanage.

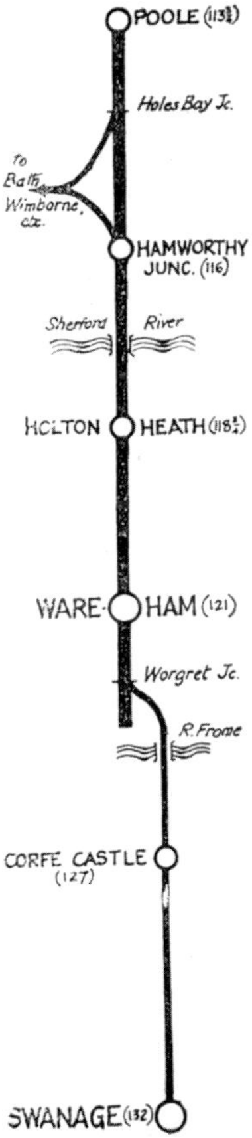

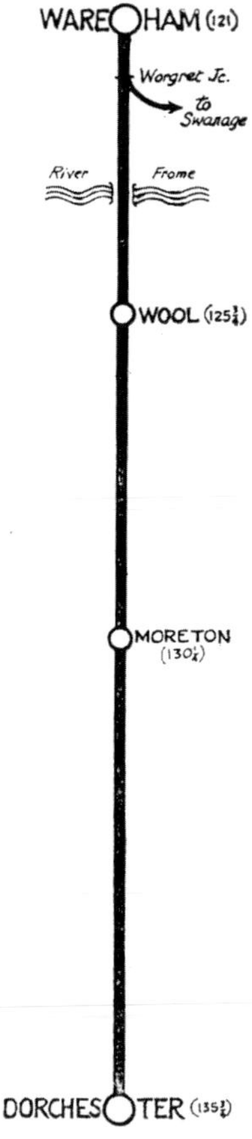

From Wareham the engine of a Weymouth train faces a long pull uphill almost to Dorchester, with a short downhill respite beyond Worgret Junction and two more after Moreton. The railway is climbing up the valley of the river Frome, running along the southern edge of the sweeping Dorset heathlands which, as " Egdon Heath ", figure in the novels of Thomas Hardy. At the approach to Wool one can see on the right the Manor House associated with Hardy's *Tess of the D'Urbervilles.* On the other side of the railway, hard by a weir on the river, are the ruins of Bindon Abbey. Beyond Wool we travel along the southern edge of Bovingdon Camp, and now the gradient steepens to 1 in 200 and finally 1 in 100 up to Moreton. Lawrence of Arabia is buried in a simple grave in Moreton churchyard, while the heart of Thomas Hardy is enshrined in the church at Stinsford, a village to be seen on the right of the railway two miles from Dorchester.

The layout of Dorchester station is one of the most curious in the country, for its up platform is a terminus, laid well away from and at an angle to the down platform, which is sited on the double track curving away leftward to join the former Great Western route to Weymouth from Westbury via Yeovil. The reason for this curiosity is that when the London & Southampton Railway was extended to Dorchester in 1847, the builders were aiming eventually for Bridport and not Weymouth, and terminated their line facing in the direction of Bridport in what is now the up platform and adjacent sidings. Later the Bridport idea was strongly opposed; moreover, in 1857 the Great Western Railway's line to Weymouth was built right across its path,

DORCHESTER SOUTH—Class "N15" 4-6-0 No. 30739 *King Leodegrance* arrives with the 2.20 p.m. Weymouth-Andover Junction; it will run past the cameraman, then back into the up platform, on the right. [*R. C. Riley*

and the G.W.R. wanted no competition in the area.

An agreement was reached that the G.W.R.—then, of course, a broad gauge system—should lay mixed gauge track from Dorchester to Weymouth, so that the standard gauge trains of the Southampton company could use the route from Dorchester as well as G.W. trains; in return, the Southampton company laid in mixed gauge for 8 miles on the Wareham side of Dorchester—a pointless bargain, for there is no record that a G.W. train ever used the broad gauge lines on the east of Dorchester. What is now the Southern main line to Weymouth was then laid as a connection from the approach to Dorchester South station's up platform to the G.W.R. beyond it. A down platform was later built inside the sharp curve of this spur, but a new up platform was never built; as a result, trains from Weymouth for the Bournemouth direction have to run past the down platform and then back into the up platform. What are now carriage sidings between the main line and the up platform were part of the original terminus, which was shrouded by an all-over roof. The locomotive depot is on the left of the main line, at the London end of the station.

HALT

Dorchester, county town of Dorset, is the successor of a Roman country town of considerable size and importance, for it was the intersecting point of several roads. There are many relics of Roman civilisation in the neighbourhood; indeed, not far frcm the South station are the remains of an old Roman amphitheatre. "Casterbridge", the town well-known in Thomas Hardy's novels, is based on Dorchester.

Out of Dorchester the railway begins to drop sharply at 1 in 117 but soon begins a steep climb at 1 in 91 to the 700 yds.-long Bincombe Tunnel. On the right is the unmistakable outline of the 432 ft.-high hill topped by Maiden Castle, or "Mai-dun".

Above left: CLIMBING OUT OF WEYMOUTH—The 9.20 a.m. Weymouth-Waterloo, double-headed by a Class "K10" 4-4-0 since scrapped and Class "H15" 4-6-0 No. 30524, climbs the 1 in 55 past Upwey Wishing Well Halt. [*R. W. Beaton*

Below left: TRAIN IN THE STREET—W.R. 0-6-0T No. 1370 hauls a Channel Islands boat train slowly through the streets of Weymouth from the quay to the station. [*I. S. Pearsall*

Archaeologists have traced life on this hill back as far as 4,000 years ago. After many vicissitudes Mai-Dun had become a citadel housing, we are told, some 4,000 people behind its ramparts. From the train the banks of the fortifications can be clearly seen cascading down the hillside from its crown. When the Romans came, they began to erect their own settlement on the site of the present Dorchester, and Mai-Dun lost its colony, although about 375 A.D. the Romans set up a temple on its north side, to which latter-day finds of gold and other relics bear witness.

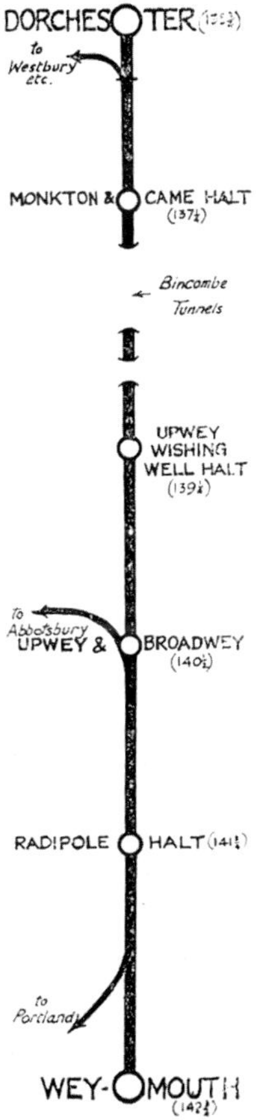

27

At the entrance to Bincombe Tunnel you may notice an odd siding between the up and down tracks and connected to both of them. This is used by assistant engines which have banked trains out of Weymouth and dropped off after emerging from the tunnel, for the climb out of Weymouth is one of the steepest on British main lines. From the Dorchester end of Bincombe Tunnel the railway falls for some 3 miles at 1 in 50 to 1 in 74, the gradient then easing somewhat as the terminus comes into sight. As we leave the tunnel, picturesque Upwey village is in a hollow to the right; the tiny station carries the odd name of Upwey Wishing Well Halt, for the Wey rises nearby in a celebrated wishing well. To the left is the 531 ft. high Bincombe Hill and ahead our first glimpse of the sea. Soon we are passing the Weymouth engine sheds on the left and slowing to a halt in the terminus, with our engine's buffers almost brushing cars in the street beyond, so close are the buffer-stops to the roadway.

Pullman Cars

These are the named Pullman cars operating on Southern Region steam-hauled trains:

ALICANTE
AQUILA
ARGUS
ARIES
AURORA
CAMILLA
CARINA
CASSANDRA
CHLORIA
CLEMENTINA
CORAL
CORUNNA
CYGNUS
DAPHNE
EMERALD
FINGALL
FLORA
FLORENCE
GLENCOE
GROSVENOR
HAWTHORN
HERCULES
HIBERNIA
IBIS
ISLE OF THANET
JUNO
LATONA
LEGHORN
MAID OF KENT
MALAGA
MEDUSA
MIMOSA
MINERVA
MONACO
MONTANA
MYRTLE
NEPTUNE
OCTAVIA
ONYX
ORION
ORPHEUS
PALERMO
PALMYRA
PEGASUS
PENELOPE
PERSEUS
PHILOMEL
PHOENIX
PLATO
PORTIA
RAINBOW
REGINA
ROSALIND
ROSAMUND
ROSEMARY
RUBY
SAPPHIRE
SAPPHO
SAVONA
SCOTIA
SEVILLE
SORRENTO
SUNBEAM
THEODORA
TOPAZ
VALENCIA
ZENOBIA

famous trains — 8

The

IRISH MAIL

EUSTON—HOLYHEAD

(London Midland Region)

by

G. FREEMAN ALLEN

Ian Allan Ltd

Class "7MT" Pacific No. 70045 makes for Holyhead with the down "Irish Mail." Photographed near Bagill, on the shores of the Dee, with Messrs. John Summers' steelworks conspicuous on the skyline across the river. [*R. J. Blenkinsop*

Introduction

THE " Irish Mail " service is now over 100 years old. It was on June 18th, 1849, that the first service bearing this title left Euston with mails for Ireland at what has since become the train's customary departure hour of 8.45 p.m. At that time Robert Stephenson's great Britannia tubular bridge over the Menai Strait was not completed, so the train had to be terminated at Menai Bridge and its mails and passengers transferred to road vehicles that took Telford's suspension bridge across the water to Llanfair, where a connecting train was waiting to complete the journey to Holyhead. Less than a year later the Britannia bridge was ready for traffic, and the " Irish Mail " was able to inaugurate its uninterrupted run between Euston and Holyhead on March 18th, 1850.

Nowadays, unfortunately, the train is a " mail " in name only. In 1852 Travelling Post Office vans (T.P.O.'s, for short) were introduced on the " Irish Mail " trains. These are the vehicles whose sides are fitted with a collapsible net of stout ropework, which Post Office men inside the coach extend at strategic points along the route to snatch up pouches of mail from lineside apparatus. Inside, one wall of the T.P.O. is covered with a honeycomb of pigeonholes. At a bench below the pigeonholes sorters are at work throughout the train's journey, sorting bags of mail taken on just before the train's departure, and also the bags caught up into the car at the lineside pick-up points. The latter are usually near large towns or railway junctions at which mail from a number of outlying areas can conveniently be gathered. Nuneaton, Llandudno Junction and Menai Bridge were the pick-up points of the down " Mail ", while the southbound " Mail " put off bags at speed that were caught in lineside nets at Bangor, Rhyl, Stafford, Tamworth, Nuneaton, Bletchley, Hemel Hempstead and Harrow.

For nearly 90 years these T.P.O.s justified the express's romantic title, but the air has conquered the more leisurely rail in this respect and aircraft now carry the mails in normal circumstances. The T.P.O. was withdrawn from the day " Irish Mail " at the outbreak of war, and the night train lost its vehicle in the following autumn. Another romantic feature of the train was terminated by the war as well—the picturesque nightly ceremony at Euston when an Admiralty messenger handed over to the " Irish Mail's "

A DOWN WESTERN DIVISION EXPRESS of the L.M R. emerges from Shugborough Tunnel behind "Royal Scot" 4-6-0 No. 46142 *The York & Lancaster Regiment.* [*P. B. Whitehouse*

guard a watch exactly timed to Greenwich, which the guard presented to the Holyhead port authorities as the warrant for the mailboat's exact departure time.

But loss of the cargo justifying, nominally, its existence, has not lightened the task of the " Irish Mail's " locomotive, which usually works unchanged throughout the 263¾ miles between Euston and Holyhead. With its sleeping cars the night train may load to over 500 tons, a serious proposition for a single locomotive over such a long journey, particularly when some quite severe gradients are encountered near the end of it, even if the stretches of uphill work are comparatively short. No restaurant car is carried on the " Mail ", but a refreshment service is carried on from a pantry in one of its coaches. In recent years summer business on the night " Mail " has been so brisk that it has been run in two parts every evening, the first non-stop from Euston at 8.45 p.m. to Holyhead in 5½ hours, and the second leaving seven minutes later and calling intermediately. With the cessation of mail traffic since the war, at least by rail, the day " Irish Mail " has operated in summer only, when it runs daily from Euston at about breakfast time.

The Route of the "Irish Mail"

THE first mile out of Euston is an unpleasant start to a long journey for the engine, as it consists of a stiff climb, some of it graded at 1 in 70-77, up to Camden, where there is a big engine-shed on the left. A maze of complex burrowing junctions marks the approach to the 1,182 yd. Primrose Hill Tunnel, through which the engine has a chance to gather speed on level track. Another 320 yd. tunnel at Kensal Green precedes Willesden Junction, where we are joined from the left by a useful route, much used by freight all the year round and holiday expresses in summer, which avoids the centre of London and provides direct connection with the Southern Region. Willesden engine shed is on the left near the station and on the right big marshalling yards extend all the way to Wembley; beyond them you will catch a glimpse of the most modern carriage servicing depot in the country, where the " Irish Mail " is serviced.

Famous Wembley Stadium, home of the F.A. Cup Final, is a landmark on the right as we approach Wembley Central, whence a long rise at 1 in 339 extends to Carpenders Park. Before Kenton there is a fine view of Harrow-on-the-Hill on the left, rising abruptly from the surrounding plain; the taller of the two spires is the parish church, the smaller the chapel of the famous public school, whose buildings cluster round it. The big Commercial Travellers' Schools adjoin the lineside on the right just before Hatch End station. Water troughs are laid in the cutting before Bushey.

NOTE: The figures in brackets after station names indicate mileage from Euston.

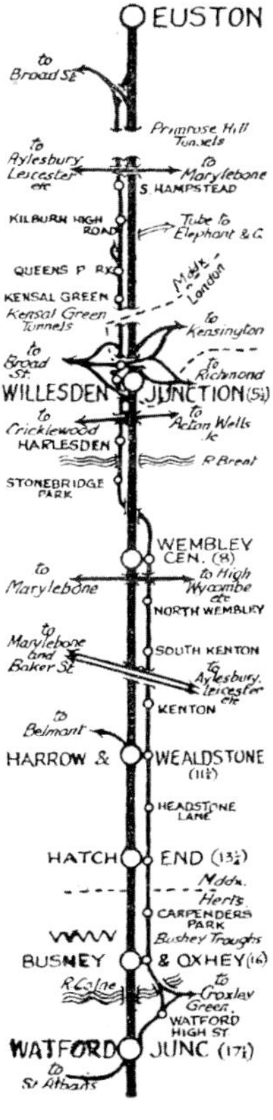

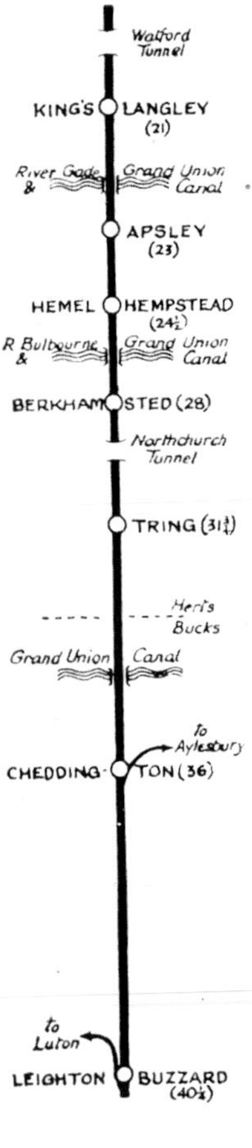

Watford Junction is the terminus of th L.M. electric trains from Euston and Broad Street and the L.T. Bakerloo tube trains. Just north of the station on the right, beyond the bridge, is the old Watford station, with a flight of steps built specially for the convenience of Queen Adelaide when she was travelling to and from nearby Cassiobury Park. To avoid desecrating this latter estate and Grove, onetime seats of the Earls of Essex and Clarendon, the old London & Birmingham railway was forced to construct the 1 mile 57 yd. Watford Tunnel. Beyond this tunnel, the Grand Union Canal joins us on the left as we climb the pleasant Gade valley, mainly at 1 in 335, to Tring, in the Chiltern Hills. Just before Berkhamsted, keep watch on the right-hand side for the few remaining traces of Berkhamsted Castle, where William the Conqueror was offered the crown of England and Geoffrey Chaucer once resided. The high ground on the right is mainly occupied by the historic Ashridge estate; the monument at its northernmost end was erected in honour of the third Duke of Bridgewater, great British advocate of canals in the late 18th Century.

Beyond Tring station the railway enters a deep cutting and begins an easy descent to Bletchley. Emerging from the cutting, the 762 ft. Ivinghoe Beacon, often the venue of gliding events, is conspicuous on the right; on the left, look out in clear weather for an obelisk crowning a hill-top, for it overlooks Chequers, the Prime Minister's country home. By the time we dive into the short Linslade Tunnel, beyond Leighton Buzzard, we shall probably have accelerated on the downgrade to

75 m.p.h. or more. If you want to check, keep a watch on the quarter mile posts as they speed past your window on the left. If you time the number of seconds the train takes between any two of these quarter-mile posts and divide the result into 900, you will have the speed in miles per hour; e.g., a quarter-mile covered in 12 seconds equals 75 m.p.h. By the way, the other little trackside posts on the left, with two arms inclined at varying angles like the hands of a clock, indicate a change of gradient; e.g., a post with the arms at " twenty to four ", with the minute hand marked " 400 " and the hour hand " 200 ", indicates a change of incline from a rise of 1 ft. up in every 400 ft. along to 1 ft. down in every 200 ft. along.

There is a glimpse of an allegedly haunted house on the left just before Wolverton, the small church-like building with a Gothic window adjoining a farm-house. Known as Bradwell Priory, it is all that remains of a 12th Century Benedictine priory once presented by Henry VIII to Cardinal Wolsey.

The big factory to the left of Wolverton station is the extensive carriage and wagon works of the L.M.R., where all manner of rolling stock from goods vans to the luxurious Royal Train have been manufactured; the latter is stored there when not in use. Originally the main line cut right through the middle of the factory.

Just before Castlethorpe, where the line begins a climb of 6 miles at 1 in 326-410, our engine takes its second " drink " since we left London. Its tender holds only 4,000 gallons (4,725 if it is a " Britannia " Pacific), whereas it will consume some 40-50 gallons per mile in the course of its 263¾ miles' run to Holyhead, so that it must take

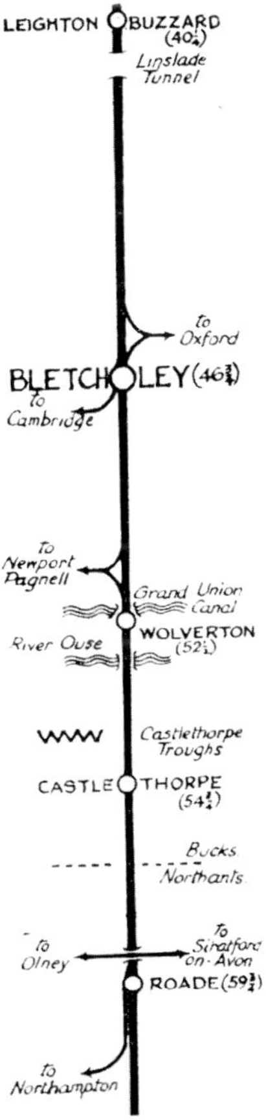

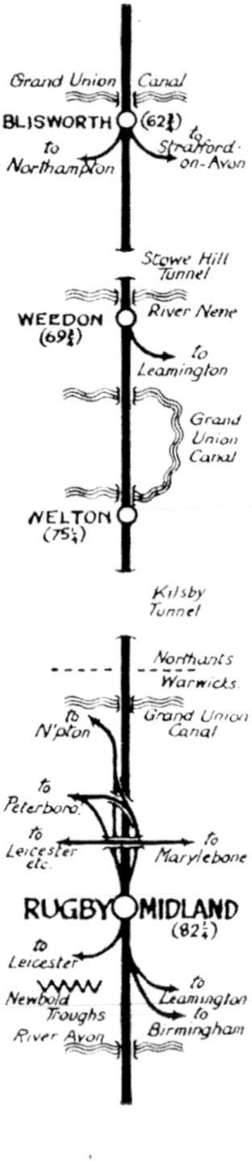

on fresh supplies en route. This is done at full speed. At suitably spaced intervals narrow troughs of water are laid between the running rails. As the engine approaches these troughs, the fireman lowers a sharp-bladed scoop beneath the tender which cuts into the water, forcing a stream of it up into the tank within the engine tender.

After we have threaded the 492 yd. Stowe Hill Tunnel, the Army's big Ordnance Depot is conspicuous on the left at the approach to Weedon, where roughly level track since Blisworth terminates before the 6-mile ascent to Kilsby Tunnel, mainly at 1 in 350. In the distance you will soon see on the left the tall masts of the B.B.C.'s short-wave transmitter for overseas broadcasts at Daventry. Then, beyond Welton, we dive into the 1 mile 666 yd. Kilsby Tunnel through a limestone mass which is an interesting watershed; from its southern flank flows water which, via the Nene river, runs into the North Sea, while streams from its other side join the Avon, which enters the Severn and thus the Bristol Channel. Kilsby Tunnel, built by George Stephenson, has had a chequered history; the workings were flooded during its construction, and ever since drainage of the tunnel has been a perpetual problem.

The twelve masts of the Hillmorton G.P.O. radio station on the right, one of the world's most powerful transmitters, herald the complicated junctions beyond the 3½-mile downhill approach to Rugby. On the other side of the long girder bridge carrying the former Great Central Marylebone-Leicester main line over us at right-angles, look out on the right for the big building labelled " British Railways Testing Station ". Inside it a big locomotive can be mounted on rollers and worked up to the highest speeds while it is still stationary; the engine is coupled to testing instruments, and, by varying the resistance the rollers offer to the engine's driving wheels, the engineers can simulate all types of load and gradient.

The celebrated Rugby School is invisible from the railway, except for the short spire of its octagonal chapel tower, which will be noticed above the town on the hill to the left as we leave the station. Soon we cross more water troughs and begin an undulating section of track to Bulkington, after which there is a noticeable descent through Nuneaton, the centre of a thriving colliery area. Incidentally, if the day is clear, there may be glimpses of the spires of Coventry beyond the second bridge over the line after Brinklow. From Atherstone, there is again a long and gradual descent through Tamworth, an interchange station of special importance to the G.P.O.; every night the special mail trains between Euston and Glasgow stop at Tamworth to exchange bags with trains running between York, Lincoln and Bristol on the former Midland Railway main line, which crosses over us here.

Some 3½ miles from Tamworth the engine has another chance to take water, at Hademore; then, on the left of the line, we shall be looking out for the three graceful spires of Lichfield Cathedral, severely damaged and desecrated in other ways by Cromwell's men in the Civil war, but since restored. Between Rugeley and Stafford the wooded ridge of Cannock Chase is visible to the left; despite its modern development as a coalfield, deer still roam its woodlands. Beyond Colwich one

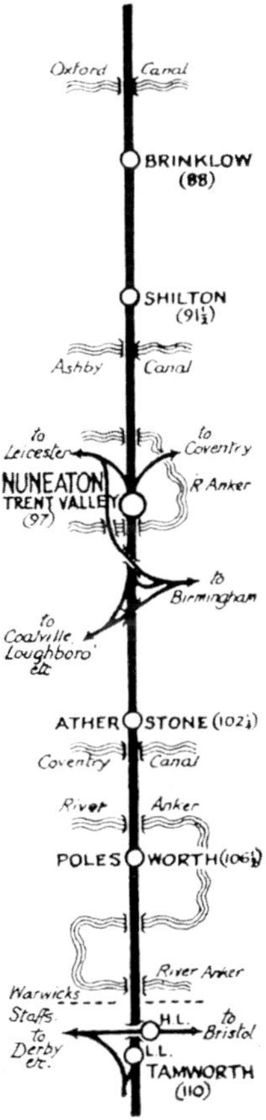

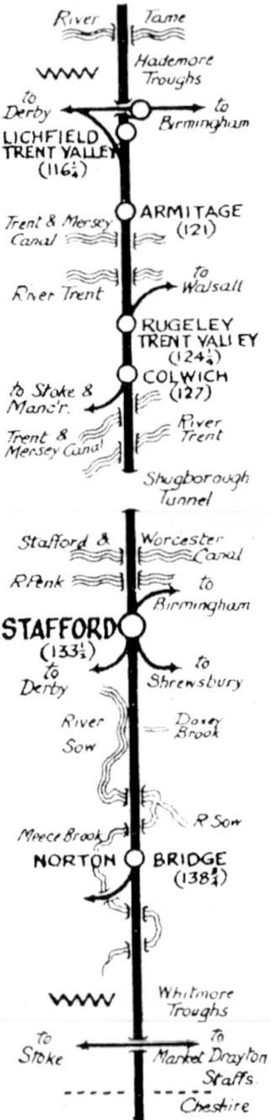

Right: The junctions north of Crewe—"Royal Scot" No. 46163 *Civil Service Rifleman* heads an express from North Wales off the Chester line.
[*S. D. Wainwright*

should keep a look-out for the richly decorated parapet, surmounted by heraldic beasts, of a bridge which carries the railway over the drive to Shugborough Hall, seat of the Earl of Lichfield; soon after we enter the 776 yd. Shugborough Tunnel.

Speed is slackened over the sweeping Queensville curve at the approach to Stafford, amongst other things the birthplace of Isaak Walton; the famous angler's timbered cottage, with one of his favourite streams running close by, adjoins the line on the right-hand side just beyond Great Bridgeford station. Here the railway begins a long climb of 12 miles at 1 in 400-600 to Whitmore troughs. From Whitmore there is a steeper descent, including 3 miles of 1 in 177, to Crewe.

At the height of the summer season, between 400 and 500 trains will be dealt with on a Saturday in Crewe's 16 platforms.

Of the two sheds, Crewe South is mainly for freight locomotives; the big express engines are allocated to Crewe North, on the left as we thread our way through the junctions north of Crewe.

The main line to Liverpool, Manchester and the north diverges to the right and in the " V " of the junction is the great Crewe locomotive works, with the carriage works on our left. The locomotive works was begun in 1843 to serve the Grand Junction Railway, by whom it was handed three years later to the L.N.W.R., and so to the L.M.S. in 1923. We pass first the joiners', then the millwrights' shops. Then we steam under a bridge embellished with three eagles mounted on shields displaying the letter " C "; actually this letter does not stand for Crewe, but for Conway, where the eagles used to decorate a bridge that was scrapped some years ago, whereupon the civil engineers decided to preserve the eagles on this new site. Beyond the bridge, on the left, is the superb new works apprentices' training school, and on the other side of the line, the extensive erecting shops of Crewe works. A conspicuous landmark on the left is now the clock tower in Crewe Park, donated to the town by the railway to commemorate the Diamond Jubilee of Queen Victoria. Crewe is also the home of the big Rolls-Royce car factory, to the right of the railway.

11

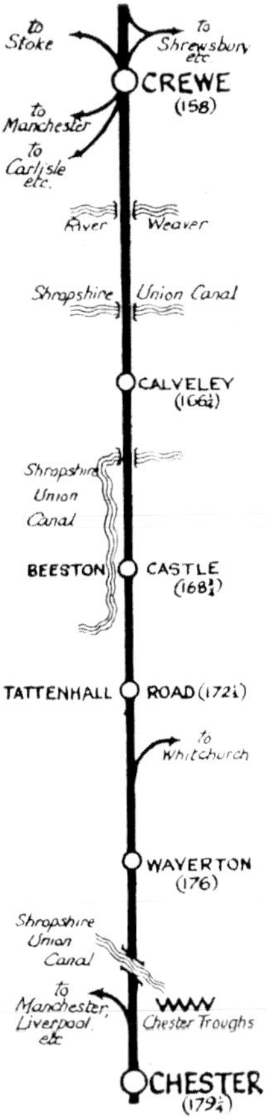

From Crewe to Chester the railway passes through some pleasant agricultural country, but with few lineside features to remark. From Calveley to Chester the gradients are for the most part gently downhill. The outstanding sight on this section is Beeston Castle, perched on a rocky eminence that rears startlingly from the surrounding plain on the left of the station, to which the castle gives a name; it was erected in the early 13th Century by Ranulph Bleundeville, seventh Earl of Chester. Hard by it is a more modern fortress, Peckforton Castle. The best view of both these castles is to be obtained by looking back after the station.

Marl pits are noticeable on the right beyond Tattenhall Road, and then there is a distant view of Delamere Forest, the remains of one of the great forests that covered much of Britain in primaeval days; this wooded upland was replanted in the early 19th Century to provide material for naval men of war to combat Napoleon. If it is a clear day the square tower of Chester cathedral will be visible on the left after Waverton and beyond, the distant hills of Wales. On the right, beyond the first bridge after Waverton station, is the site of the Battle of Rowton Moor in 1645, one of the decisive defeats of the Royalist forces in the Civil War; the unhappy Charles I watched the debacle from the walls of his besieged stronghold at Chester. Beyond the short Christleton Tunnel (160 yds. long) there are water troughs and then the junction with the route to Warrington and the north at the approaches to Chester station. Conspicuous is the conical 150 ft. high shot tower of a lead works, in which bullets are manufactured.

CROSSING THE DEE AT CHESTER—Class "5" 4-6-0 No. 45410 heading a North Wales train, on the left, runs neck-and-neck with W.R 4-6-0 No. 6831 *Bearley Grange* on a freight. [*P. M. Alexander*

13

The ancient city of Chester is the only one in Britain that can still exhibit a completely encircling city wall, in this case one 2 miles long, through which the " Irish Mail " tunnels soon after leaving the station. First comes the divergence of the line to Birkenhead on the right, then a series of tunnels. After the second of these watch on the left for a glimpse of an unusual triple lock which drops the Shropshire Union Canal 32 ft. very quickly to pass it through the walls. Then the railway cuts through a corner of the massive city walls, and one sees two towers to the right of the line. The nearest is Bonwaldestorhne's Tower and the other the Water Tower, so called because in olden days, when the Dee was navigable and Chester was an important port for Ireland, ships used to be moored to it. At the base of the Water Tower there have been erected a number of Roman columns and pillars excavated in Chester.

As the railway bears left a panorama of the city opens up. The 127 ft. high central tower of the red sandstone cathedral stands out from the buildings behind the city wall; near it are the Town Hall and the two surviving towers of the castle. Between the city wall and the river is Chester racecourse, occupying a stretch of land known as the Roodee (or Cross Island), because it was once completely surrounded by the water of the river and surmounted by a stone cross. Notice also on the left the superb 200 ft. long single stone span of the Grosvenor Bridge, carrying the main road to Wales across the river, it was opened in 1832 by Queen (then Princess) Victoria.

The " Irish Mail " is now launched on one of the railways engineered by the great Robert Stephenson, the Chester & Holyhead, which was completed in 1850. In fact, the Chester & Holyhead owes something to both the Stephensons, for it was George's verdict in favour of Holyhead as a port of embarkation for Ireland, and against Porth Dynllaen, between Caernarvon and Afonwen, after he had been appointed by businessmen of Chester to enquire into the relative merits of these two points as packet ports, that led the House of Commons to approve the Chester & Holyhead scheme; had it been otherwise, the " Irish Mail " might have travelled out of London via Oxford, Worcester, Ludlow, Craven Arms, Montgomery and Dolgelly—for this was the route proposed by the supporters of the Porth Dynllaen scheme.

The " Irish Mail " now takes a practically dead level and straight course down the estuary of the Dee to Point of Air. Soon after leaving Chester, we cross the border into Wales at a point now marked with an attractive lineside sign. At first the landscape is rather drearily industrial, though the cemetery-like slate quays on the right just beyond Saltney Ferry are a curiosity worth watching for; these quays are really a slate merchants' depot. The first range of the Welsh mountains, the Clwydian Hills, are coming into view on the left, and the tower of the old Hawarden Castle can be seen peeping over the trees on the first ridge; hidden from view is the newer Hawarden Castle, which was for many years the home of Mr. Gladstone. Now we approach an area of heavy industry. Alongside Chester's power station on the right near Sandycroft are an ordnance factory and an iron foundry, and then from Queens Ferry the view on this side of the track is dominated by the vast John Summers steelworks at Shotton, whose furnaces are a landmark as far as the mouth of the estuary; the plant now covers more than 250 acres and its strip mills are among the most modern in Europe. Beyond Connah's Quay, the short Rockcliffe Tunnel (98 yds.) precedes more water troughs, and then the traveller should look to the right for a glimpse of Flint Castle, just before Flint station; in this castle Shakespeare sets the capture of Richard II by Henry of Lancaster in *Richard the Second*, but although the former was imprisoned here he was actually taken captive at another point on the coast.

More heavy industry is encountered at Bagillt, with a lead works on the left

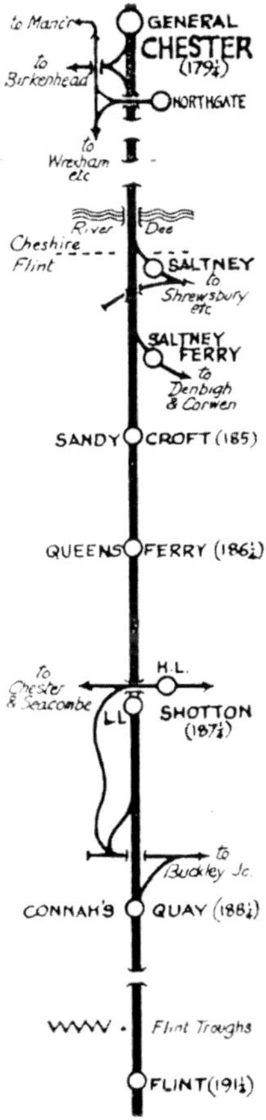

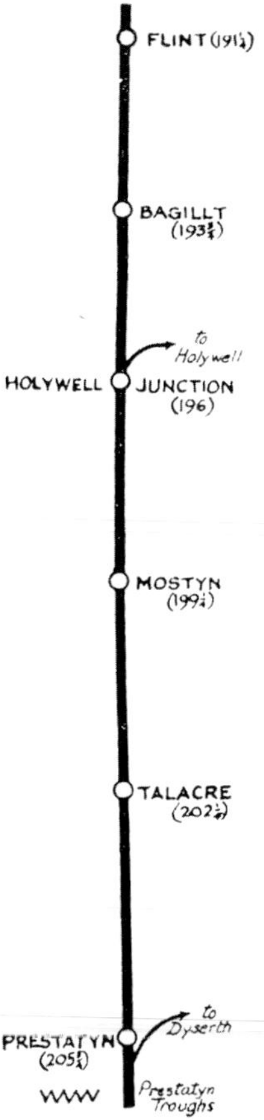

(served until a few years back by the lead mines in Halkin Hill behind, which were worked as long ago as Roman times) and Bettisfield colliery on the right; the workings of this pit extend right under the Dee almost to the Cheshire coast, where the town of Heswall, with its white watertower, is now conspicuous on a hill overlooking the Dee. Legend credits the spring of St. Winifred's well at Holywell with healing powers (despite the fact that the original spring has been diverted by draining works in the Halkin Hill leadmines, and the well is now supplied by a mechanical pump in an old mine shaft!); a more substantial religious relic is the ruins of the Norman Basingwerke Abbey on the left at the approach to Holywell station. The last of industrial Deeside is now coming into view —first Greenfield Colliery and the ruins of an old leadworks beyond Holywell; then the blast furnaces of Mostyn Iron Works on the right; and finally Point of Air colliery on the right, most of whose workings are beneath the Dee. We have now reached the mouth of the estuary, and are looking across to Hilbre Island and beyond to West Kirby, six miles away on the north-west tip of the Wirral peninsula. The " Irish Mail " makes a sweeping turn from north-westward to slightly south-westward, and the scenery changes (so, often, does the weather from bad to good at this point) from the untidily industrial to the pleasantly relaxing.

Beyond Prestatyn are more watertroughs and then, as we approach Rhyl, there is a beautiful prospect of the Clwydian Hills; the ruined tower-like structure which crowns the highest hill of the range, Moel Famma, is all that remains of a monument erected to celebrate the Jubilee of King George III. When Rhyl is past the Vale of Clwyd opens up to the view on the left, and there is a sight of the ivied towers of Rhuddlan Castle, an ancient stronghold established in 1277 by King Edward I, who set up his court here for three years after his great campaign against the Welsh prince Llewelyn ap Griffith, and here summoned Parliament to pass the division of Llewelyn's principality into shires on the English model—Caernarvon, Anglesey, Merioneth, Flint, Cardigan and Carmarthen. Further down the Clwyd valley can be glimpsed the distant square tower of St. Asaph cathedral, wherein stands the chair of the Archbishop of Wales. Abergele brings the railway close to the sea and there is a fine view along the coastline to the Little Orme headland, near Llandudno. Now, for the first time since we left Chester, the railway must face a serious climb, for the hills are closing in to fall into the sea as cliffs. At Llandulas a short stretch of 1 in 100 uphill begins and we lose two of the four tracks that have been continuous since Chester, except for $4\frac{3}{4}$ miles west of Connah's Quay, a section including Rockcliffe Tunnel. As the railway mounts up to the 485 yds. long Penmaenrhos Tunnel it is bridged by tramways carrying loads from the limestone quarries in the rocky cliffs to quays on the shore, where the stone is loaded into coasting vessels. At the tunnelmouth the lines turn downhill again at 1 in 100 to Old Colwyn.

The closed station of Mochdre and Pabo, beyond Colwyn Bay, is a spot of importance in railway history, for it was here that the first water troughs were laid down in 1857. They were a device of Ramsbottom, loco-

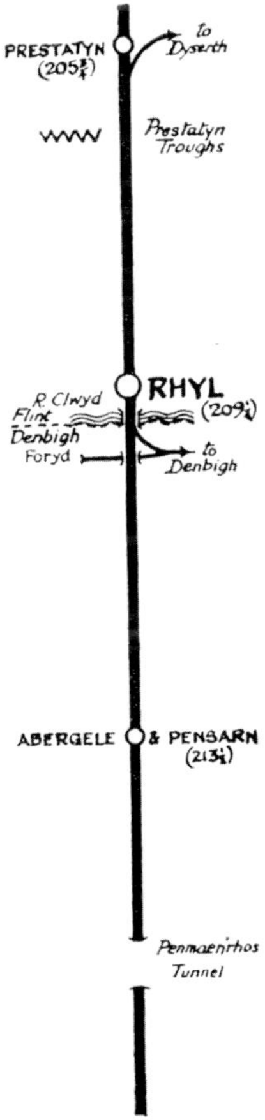

THE ANCIENT WALLS OF CONWAY CASTLE keep watch over a Bangor-Llandudno Junction stopping train as it approaches the tubular bridge. [R. E. Vincent

motive engineer of the L.N.W.R., to enable his company, by cutting out train stops for water, to secure a contract with the Post Office that required the " Irish Mail " of those days to maintain an average of 42 m.p.h. In later years the troughs were moved further westward, to Aber, but even so the Chester-Holyhead line has the luxury of four sets of troughs in only 60 miles—Christleton (near Chester), Flint, Prestatyn and Aber. The Welsh mountains proper are now upon us on the left on the other side of the Conway, sweeping up to the impressive summit of Carnedd Llewelyn, 3,483 ft. high and only 74 ft. below the height of Snowdon itself. Now, too, we get our first glimpse of Conway Castle as we approach Llandudno Junction, where there is a motive power depot, and many expresses on this route stop to attach or detach portions for or from the resorts along the coast. From Llandudno Junction the railway strikes out across the Conway waters alongside the main Holyhead road on the causeway engineered by Telford at the beginning of the last century. The causeway reaches out to an island in the Conway. From this island the road takes off on a graceful suspension bridge, but the railway is plunged into the massive tubes which Robert Stephenson used to bridge the last water gap. Each of them is 425 ft. long and weighs nearly 1,200 tons. The " Irish Mail " emerges from the tubular bridge right under the battlements of historic Conway Castle, which Edward I put up in 1284 to seal his Welsh conquests. The railway curves sharply round its imposing towers, then cuts through a corner of the Conway walls on each side of Conway station.

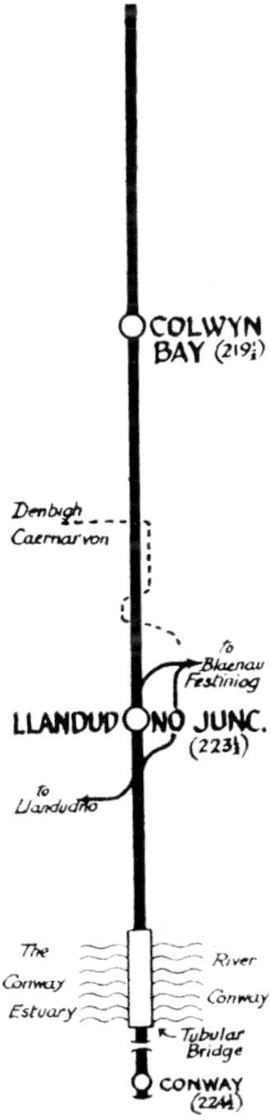

THE WALLS OF CONWAY bridge the railway outside Conway station Class "2" 2-6-0 No. 46424 is passing on a North Wales Land Cruise train. [*I. S. Pearsall*

Beyond Conway we look right across Conway Bay to the 679 ft. Great Orme's Head jutting into the sea, a height of special interest in that it is scaled by one of Britain's few funicular railways; this is a cable-worked system opened in 1902, which climbs steeply away from the streets of Llandudno to a marvellous viewpoint on the summit of the headland. The gradients of our route are practically level again from Conway to Aber, since Robert Stephenson laid his railway on the narrow strip of land between the great mountains on the left and the sea, but in so doing he incurred some substantial engineering works and exposed the railway to the attentions of the sea, which has more than once damaged the line during fierce winter storms. Along this section the railway has had to be built up in places on a stout sea wall, and several tunnels and a viaduct were necessary. First comes the 700 yds.-long tunnel through the Penmaenbach promontory, beyond which we get our first good view of Anglesey, and then the interesting 452 yds.-long Penmaenmawr tunnel, which has avalanche shelter extensions at each end to protect the railway from rocks and scree tumbling down from the mountains above in wet weather, which is apt to dislodge minor avalanches. The mountains and cliffs here are sadly scarred by extensive quarrying for granite. Beyond the tunnel is the sea viaduct already mentioned. After Aber water troughs a glance to the right will descry the lighthouse on Penmon Point and the distinctive shape of Puffin Island, off the easternmost point of Anglesey. On the other side of Aber we can see the capital of Anglesey, Beaumaris, across the water, and on the hill above it a conspicuous

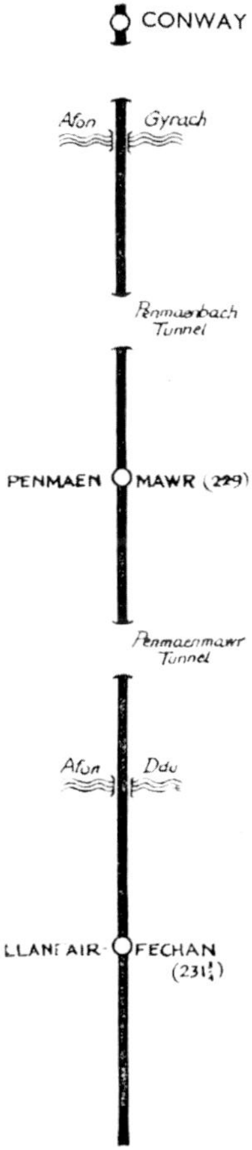

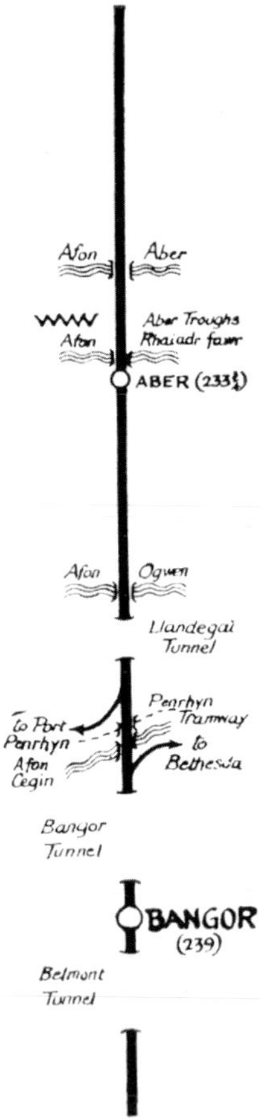

obelisk commemorating the Battle of Waterloo.

Meanwhile, if the clouds are not low, we should be getting some fine views of the Welsh mountains on the left. At Aber we have a prospect up a pretty valley to the Falls of Aber and Llwyd Mor mountains, nearly 3,000 ft. high. Then, emerging from a cutting further on as we climb up to Bangor, a whole range is lined up, split in two by the Pass of Nant Francon; to the left of this cleft are, in order, Carnedd Llewelyn, the 3,483 ft. Cairn of Llewelyn, Carnedd Dafydd and the 3,262 ft. Cairn of David; then comes the craggy Glyder Fach, 3,262 ft. high, at the head of the pass; and, on the other side of the defile, Carnedd y Filiast, the 2,694 ft. Cairn of the Greyhound Bitch, on which traces of the extensive Penrhyn slate quarry workings are visible, and finally the 3,029 ft. Elidyr Fawr, which hides the queen of them all, Snowdon, from our view. Railway enthusiasts will now be watching for the narrow gauge railway from the Penrhyn slate quarries to Port Penrhyn, which we cross between the 505 yds. Llandegai Tunnel and the 905 yds. tunnel at the approach to Bangor. On a non-stopping train there is little time to take in Bangor before one is plunged into the 613 yds.-long Belmont Tunnel on the other side of the station. The cathedral here, which suffered severely in the border conflicts, is not nearly so conspicuous as the cathedral-like building topping a hill on the right, for which it is often mistaken; the other is, however, the University College. For railway enthusiasts, the locomotive depot is on the left. As we leave the second of the Bangor tunnels, keep watch on the right for a view

Right: The sea wall at Penmaenmawr with compound 4-4-0 No. 41115 at the head of a local train from Llandudno Junction to Holyhead.
[*R. E. Vincent*

Left: Class "2" 2-6-2T No 41238 leaves Colwyn Bay with the North Wales Land Cruise train.
[*R. E. Vincent*

THE BRITANNIA TUBULAR BRIDGE over the Menai Strait. [Mark Pedley & Co.

of Telford's superb suspension bridge carrying the Holyhead road over the Menai Strait. This magnificent structure was completed in January, 1826; the principal span is 579 ft. long and 100 ft. above the water.

We are now approaching our own and even more remarkable bridge over the Menai Strait, Robert Stephenson's Britannia Tubular Bridge. Unfortunately, the rail traveller does not get the best impression of the structure, for, as at Conway, he is enclosed in one of the giant twin tubes of iron, totalling 1,380 ft. in length and weighing nearly 4,700 tons, which carry the metals 100 ft. above the water. The tubes are supported by massive stone towers, the centre one of which is higher than its neighbours and towers another 100 ft. above the tubes; it stands on Britannia rock in the strait—hence the bridge's name. Not the least impressive feature of this monumental piece of engineering, which was completed in June, 1849, are the great stone lions, a pair at each end, which guard the approaches to the bridge. Emerging from the Tubular bridge it is difficult to know whether to look left for another glimpse of its strange outline, the monument to Nelson and, beyond, the Marquis of Anglesey's seat, Plas Newydd, or right for the brief but wonderful prospect of the mountains rolling down to the water's edge on the mainland side of the strait and throwing off Telford's graceful suspension bridge to the Anglesey shore. Llanfair, the station which follows, is that remarkable place whose true Welsh name is alleged to run to a total of 54 letters, though purists maintain that its true title is not more frightening than Llanfairpwllgwngll—a

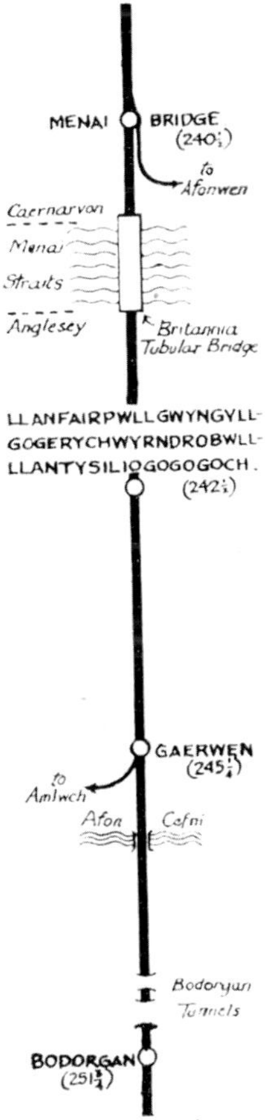

"Royal Scot" 4-6-0 No. 46125 *3rd Carabinier* heads the London-bound "Irish Mail" out of Holyhead. [G. Clarke.

modest 19. Now at last we have a view of the great Snowdon herself. Looking back on the left the whole range of the Welsh mountains fills the horizon, with Snowdon clearly recognisable by its triple peak. Our route now strikes the first substantial gradients since we left Chester. From a summit between Llanfair and Gaerwen it turns downhill to the Cefni river on a bank which culminates in gradients of 1 in 97 and 102.

At the foot of the bank we are among the marshlands of Malltraeth, once an active coalfield, and within sight on the left of St. George's Channel. Now comes a really stiff climb. For over a mile the gradient is 1 in 50 up, the summit being just beyond the two Bodorgan tunnels, 413 and 115 yds. long respectively. Bodorgan station is on a short stretch of downhill, but then comes a half-mile at 1 in 99 up before the descent at 1 in 107 and 136 through Ty Croes. Beyond Valley station is the embankment carrying the road and railway across the water to Holy Island. A well-preserved prehistoric relic is soon visible on the left; after the second bridge beyond the shore of Holy Island we can see on the horizon some 300 yards away the stone cromlechs of Trefignath, which date back to prehistoric times. Our destination is now coming into sight, and Holyhead breakwater stretches out into the bay on the right. The conspicuous obelisk on a height to the right honours an Irish mailboat captain who was drowned in 1832, and who was a great friend of the poor people of the port. Soon we are passing Holyhead motive power depot on the right and descending the steep bank to our journey's end.

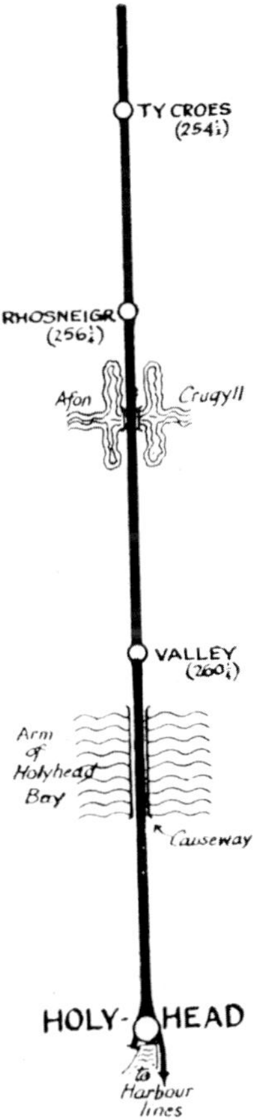

27

Close up of a " Royal Scot " 4-6-0—No. 46167 *The Hertfordshire Regiment* [Donald Kelk

Motive Power of the " Irish Mail "

THE locomotive of the " Irish Mail " will normally be a " Royal Scot " 4-6-0 or a " Britannia " 4-6-2. The former are the rebuilds since 1943 of a type designed by Sir Henry Fowler for the L.M.S. in 1927; in the latter part of the last war a start was made, under Sir William Stanier's direction, on modification of the whole class with new taper boilers, new cylinders and double chimneys and blastpipes, and all the " Royal Scots " have now been converted in this way. The " Britannia " is the standard Class " 7 " mixed traffic 4-6-2 of the post-nationalisation British Railways range, introduced in 1951; in recent years five of these engines, so far unnamed, have been allocated to Holyhead motive power depot for duty on the " Irish Mail " trains.

LOCOMOTIVE DIMENSIONS

	" Royal Scot " 4-6-0	**" Britannia " 4-6-2**
Locomotive Weight:	83 tons	94 tons
Boiler Pressure:	250 lb.	250 lb.
Cylinders (diam. × stroke):	(3) 18 in. × 26 in.	(2) 20 in. × 28 in.
Driving Wheel diameter.	6 ft. 9 in.	6 ft 2 in.
Tractive Effort:	33 150 lb.	32,150 lb.

"ROYAL SCOT" CLASS—NUMBERS AND NAMES

46100 Royal Scot
46101 Royal Scots Grey
46102 Black Watch
46103 Royal Scots Fusilier
46104 Scottish Borderer
46105 Cameron Highlander
46106 Gordon Highlander
46107 Argyll and Sutherland Highlander
46108 Seaforth Highlander
46109 Royal Engineer
46110 Grenadier Guardsman
46111 Royal Fusilier
46112 Sherwood Forester
46113 Cameronian
46114 Coldstream Guardsman
46115 Scots Guardsman
46116 Irish Guardsman
46117 Welsh Guardsman
46118 Royal Welch Fusilier
46119 Lancashire Fusilier
46120 Royal Inniskilling Fusilier
46121 Highland Light Infantry, City of Glasgow Regiment
46122 Royal Ulster Rifleman
46123 Royal Irish Fusilier
46124 London Scottish
46125 3rd Carabinier
46126 Royal Army Service Corps
46127 Old Contemptibles
46128 The Lovat Scouts
46129 The Scottish Horse
46130 The West Yorkshire Regiment
46131 The Royal Warwickshire Regt.
46132 The King's Regiment Liverpool
46133 The Green Howards
46134 The Cheshire Regiment
46135 The East Lancashire Regiment
46136 The Border Regiment
46137 The Prince of Wales's Volunteers (South Lancashire)
46138 The London Irish Rifleman
46139 The Welch Regiment
46140 The King's Royal Rifle Corps
46141 The North Staffordshire Regt.
46142 The York & Lancaster Regiment
46143 The South Staffordshire Regiment
46144 Honourable Artillery Company
46145 The Duke of Wellington's Regt. (West Riding)
46146 The Rifle Brigade
46147 The Northamptonshire Regiment
46148 The Manchester Regiment
46149 The Middlesex Regiment
46150 The Life Guardsman
46151 The Royal Horse Guardsman
46152 The King's Dragoon Guardsman
46153 The Royal Dragoon
46154 The Hussar
46155 The Lancer
46156 The South Wales Borderer
46157 The Royal Artilleryman
46158 The Loyal Regiment
46159 The Royal Air Force
46160 Queen Victoria's Rifleman
46161 King's Own
46162 Queen's Westminster Rifleman
46163 Civil Service Rifleman
46164 The Artists' Rifleman
46165 The Ranger (12th London Regt.)
46166 London Rifle Brigade
46167 The Hertfordshire Regiment
46168 The Girl Guide
46169 The Boy Scout
46170 British Legion